A Front Row Seat

NANCY OLSON LIVINGSTON

A FRONT ROW SEAT

An Intimate Look at Broadway,
Hollywood, and the Age of Glamour

Published by The University Press of Kentucky

Scholarly publisher for the Commonwealth,
serving Bellarmine University, Berea College, Centre
College of Kentucky, Eastern Kentucky University,
The Filson Historical Society, Georgetown College,
Kentucky Historical Society, Kentucky State University,
Morehead State University, Murray State University,
Northern Kentucky University, Spalding University,
Transylvania University, University of Kentucky,
University of Louisville, University of Pikeville, and
Western Kentucky University.

Editorial and Sales Offices: The University Press of Kentucky
663 South Limestone Street, Lexington, Kentucky 40508-4008
www.kentuckypress.com

Cover Photo: © Disney

I'VE GROWN ACCUSTOMED TO HER FACE (from "My Fair Lady")
Words by ALAN JAY LERNER. Music by FREDERICK LOEWE
Copyright © 1956 (Renewed) ALAN JAY LERNER and FREDERICK LOEWE
Publication and Allied Rights Assigned to CHAPPELL & CO., INC.
All Rights Reserved
Used By Permission of ALFRED MUSIC

Cataloging-in-Publication data is available from the Library
of Congress.

ISBN 978-0-8131-9619-0 (hardcover)
ISBN 978-1-9859-0038-7 (paperback)
ISBN 978-0-8131-9620-6 (pdf)
ISBN 978-0-8131-9621-3 (epub)

This book is printed on acid-free paper meeting
the requirements of the American National Standard
for Permanence in Paper for Printed Library Materials.

Manufactured in the United States of America.

Member of the Association
of University Presses

To Liza, Jenny, and Christopher
and
My special thanks to Christopher,
whose assistance made this book possible

Write your name with kindness,
love and mercy on the hearts
of all you meet and know
and you will never be forgotten.
—From the autograph book of my paternal
grandmother, Nancy Anne Johnson, 1880

Contents

Contents

Book 2

Contents

Contents

Photographs follow page 184.

Book 1

Introduction

On the morning of June 14, 1986, I received a call from my daughters, Liza and Jenny Lerner, telling me that their father, Alan Jay Lerner, had just passed away. This is the letter I wrote that morning to both of them. I have saved it all these years.

June 14, 1986

Dear Liza and Jenny,

When you called me last night to tell me it was a matter of hours before your father would die, I was filled with a helpless sadness, reminded of life's errors, human mistakes and those irrevocable choices we made so long ago that changed all of our lives forever.

I awakened at dawn with the feeling that someone or something had tapped me on the shoulder and knew in an instant that Alan was gone. He was already . . . everywhere.

It was already on the news, Alan Jay Lerner was dead. It seemed ludicrous that my first phone call came from the White House. Was *My Fair Lady* his first success, they asked. President and Mrs. Reagan wanted to make a condolence statement and could I review his work in the correct sequence? Yes of course I could. *Brigadoon* was the first. It opened in 1947 . . . three years before we met. The motion picture, *An American in Paris,* 1950 . . . It was then that we met and married. After that *Paint Your Wagon.* The year was 1951 . . . the year you were born Liza. Another motion picture, *Royal Wedding* followed that same year . . . two years later, you were born Jenny. 1956 *My Fair Lady.* . . "To Nancy With Love." And in 1958 *Gigi* . . . we were divorced shortly after.

Camelot was written in 1959 and *On a Clear Day* in 1960. Nothing of any real significance was ever written again. The White House representative thanked me for this information and hung up, leaving me with a cyclone of images twirling in my head.

I remembered a dream, a recurring dream I had while I was married to your father.

He and I were on a large ocean liner in the middle of a ferocious storm. The sky and sea were dark and threatening and the boat was obviously sinking. There was a small life raft standing by. It was already filled with people; however, there was a space for one more person. As the dream ended, I knew that I would have to give Alan the remaining seat. His terror seemed to me so towering and pervasive that I could not bear to leave him alone to die . . . I would have to be the one to stay behind and . . . drown.

I remembered standing in the bedroom of my parents' home, putting on my wedding dress, taffy colored silk, with ecru lace circling the hem and framing my shoulders—my father bursting through the door, sobbing, holding me and telling me he didn't want to lose me—my mother's face chalky with mourning, tears poised and ready behind her lids—the sound of Lohengrin's March on the family piano. Fritz played for us that day and Alan and I could not wait to leave the small, awkward reception. We were determined to get back to his house in time to hear our favorite radio show. Lovemaking would have to wait for Jack Benny.

I remembered Edie, Alan's mother, victim and executioner, and his tortured father, Joe. His brothers, Robert and Richard, his first wife, Ruthie, and their beautiful child, Susan.

I remembered being the best roller skater on Woodlawn Court in Milwaukee, Wisconsin, and I remembered the exact moment I decided to be an actress—a decision that would bring me to Hollywood to make motion pictures and to meet the most powerful, fabled, and extraordinary people in the world, which inevitably led me to your father and your both being born.

I remembered labor pains, two beautiful children, little girls, hair the color of clover honey, viking blue eyes, sweet, sweet children, climbing on our laps, hugging and kissing mommy and daddy.

I remembered the fascinating and revealing stories my mother and father told me about growing up in the beginning of this century. The heartbreaking stories of your father's childhood.

I received a phone call this morning from my friend, Shirley. She had just finished the *New York Times* story about Alan's death. She took my breath away when she said that it was inherent in the story that Alan had an abused childhood. Is that really revealed or is Shirley a witch? I must re-read it someday, but not now.

I know that you have always thought of your father and me as being separate. But the truth is that many years ago we met, fell in love, married, and had both of you and were a family. I would like to tell you the story of our lives—about your parents and grandparents and a time that you barely remember. Someday you and your children will be curious to know these things and they will matter to you.

I want to tell you about the years that followed this marriage— about the torture of being left and being forced to find my way alone in the world while taking care of both of you at the same time. I want to share with you the hard lessons I had to learn—and how only then was I able to find the perfect partner to spend the rest of my life with and to bring us all together. Bringing a step-sister and step-brother into our lives was a challenge, however, having a new baby brother was a joy. We were a complete family at last.

I'm sure you think of me not only with love but with a degree of skepticism. How in the world did I ever put all the pieces together? Part of my journey has been filled with dreams that seemed to have pointed the way. Perhaps they will help put the tiny fragments of the mosaic of our lives in place.

I will set this all down for you as faithfully as I can.

Love,
Mother

1

Rockland County, September 1950

I had just turned twenty-two and had recently married the renowned young librettist Alan Jay Lerner. Alan and Frederick Loewe, two of the most promising writers for the musical theater, were creating a new musical titled *Paint Your Wagon*. They were working in Alan's studio at our home at Camphill Farm in Rockland County, New York—waiting to be called for the lunch that our domestic couple, Anna and Otto, were preparing in the kitchen beneath me.

Before this day, it seemed to me that my life was on a trajectory of an exciting relationship, with the promise of a fantastic adventure in the world of theater arts, friendships with the most gifted people of the twentieth century, beautiful children, and a secure and rewarding life ahead of me. I had started with dreams of becoming an acknowledged and successful actress but was thrilled to put them aside in exchange for this new life.

That morning I spread out on my desk all the reviews of a movie I had performed in more than a year earlier. There was a kaleidoscope of descriptions, each demanding attention—each filling the air with ego-fulfilling excitement . . . and danger. Paramount Pictures had already asked me to reconsider my leave of absence, and my agent, whom I had not spoken to in months, was now leaving endless messages.

I was paralyzed by what lay in front of me. The *Los Angeles Times*: "One of the most remarkable pictures ever produced." The *New York Times*: "A powerful story . . . a great motion picture." *Herald Tribune:* "One of the greatest films ever to come out of Hollywood." The film was titled *Sunset Boulevard,* and it was an overnight cultural phenomenon.

It starred Gloria Swanson as Norma Desmond, William Holden as Joe Gillis, Eric von Stroheim as Max the butler, and a new young actress, Nancy Olson, in the part of Betty Schaefer.

More phrases leaped off the pages: "The hope that propels young people to try their luck in Hollywood is exemplified by Betty Schaefer, a studio reader with writing ambitions who is beautifully portrayed by Nancy Olson." "Nancy Olson . . . comes over with a wallop." "Nancy Olson is perfect in the part." Every major newspaper and all the trade papers were filled with glowing praise.

The night before, Alan and I had gone to the Lafayette Theatre in the nearby town of Suffern to see *Sunset Boulevard* with a small group of friends. Halfway through the film, the screen went dark, and the lights came on. Everyone thought there might be an emergency, and we would have to leave immediately. In a few seconds, a voice came over the loudspeaker. "Ladies and gentlemen, we would like to announce that one of the stars of this motion picture is in our audience tonight. Will Nancy Olson please stand and take a bow?" I was flabbergasted and wondered if this had ever happened to anyone else!

Every emotion was in disarray. There were tantalizing possibilities to pursue. My little-girl dreams of being married to the perfect man in the most luxuriously secure surroundings were being threatened by this sudden new recognition of my own talents.

What was the path I had taken that led me to this moment? It's a mystery I can only unravel by starting at the beginning.

2

The Beginning

On July 14, 1928, Evelyn Olson was lying on a bed in Deaconess Hospital on Wisconsin Avenue in Milwaukee, Wisconsin. Her narrow frame trembled with pain, and after many hours of prolonged suffering, it was clear that the child who was trying to be born would have to be taken from her by surgery with a Caesarean section. And because the child never experienced the trauma of traveling through the birth canal, she arrived with all of her small features delicately and perfectly in place. I found a letter my father sent to my aunt Ethel describing me at my birth. He wrote, "It's a girl—only one, and the sweetest little thing you ever did see. She has light blue eyes, but it is beyond me to say who she looks like."

Dreams have visited and haunted my sleep all my life. Some have frightened me—some have made me laugh—and many have informed me about where I am in this life—in this universe. Many I have forgotten; others have remained as vivid as the night they appeared. Some might question a dream I had many, many years after I was born, but it remains in my memory because it was so powerful.

I dreamed that I was floating upward, and I distinctly heard the clinking sound of metal colliding with metal. I was increasingly in pain from a bright light shining in my eyes. I tried to close them, but the light was piercing through my lids. At the same time I heard sounds of oohing *and* aahing; *it was a chorus of human voices making these sounds.*

The dream startled me so much that I sat up in bed wondering what it could have been about. Suddenly it occurred to me that it was a memory of being born. The sharp sounds were the instruments thrown into a metal dish; the bright light was the operating-room light over my mother's body. As I was being lifted up, the intensity of the light was painful, and the human voices were expressing their delight in witnessing the miracle of birth. I know that bright lights bothered me for many years as a child; I needed to look away. And yet I pursued the bright lights in front of the camera and on stage and waited for the *oohs* and *aahs* of the audience.

Isn't it amazing how our very first experience can take us on a journey that already knows its destination? It also must be remembered that our ancestors dating back to more than a million years ago . . . their DNA is still within us. Our parents, grandparents, and great-grandparents have left an indelible imprint on who we are. . . . This is *my* story. . . .

3

My Ancestors

I am sorry I never knew my two grandmothers, but I have photographs of them. I know stories about them, and I remember tears in my father's eyes when he spoke of his mother. I heard regret and incompletion in my mother's voice when she told me about hers.

I look at the picture of Mathilda Nybald Bergstrom, my maternal grandmother, and she reminds me of someone I know. Pale skin and hair, fine bones, with long Mongolian eyes. Her eyes are exactly like my daughter Jenny's, and there is something courageous and brave about her steady gaze—qualities that my daughter Liza has always possessed.

Mathilda Nybald left Sweden when she was still in her teens and came to America in the early 1890s. Speaking only her native language, she lived in New York City for about two years, working as an upstairs maid until she saved enough money to join her cousins in Grand Rapids, Michigan. There she met Victor Bergstrom, who had left Sweden when he was twenty and had come to America with valuable skills: he was an excellent machinist and a tool-and-die maker. He could make anything with his hands, and he came with convictions. He was a socialist and a strong union man.

Victor and Mathilda married and in 1898 had their first child, Edith. In 1900, they had another little girl, Evelyn, my mother. The four of them moved to Milwaukee, Wisconsin, to take advantage of a work opportunity for Victor, and, soon after, three more children were born, Ethel, Carl, and William.

My mother, Evelyn, was a high-spirited, little tomboy beauty. She was bright, ambitious, and extremely independent. Being one of five children, she learned how to aggressively look out for herself. The entire family spoke only Swedish until Evelyn went to school when she was about five years old. After that, she insisted that only English would be spoken in their home by everyone, including her parents and the babies. The last thing she wanted to be called was a "dumb immigrant," a derogatory expression used frequently at that time.

I never heard her speak anything but English, and we all assumed that she had lost her original language. But to everyone's surprise, especially hers, when she attended Ingmar Bergman's film *Wild Strawberries,* she found herself not having to read the English subtitles because she understood every Swedish word they were saying.

Education was the obvious key to unlock the door of acceptance in the New World. When Victor noticed little Evelyn was constantly singing and on perfect pitch, he designed and forged an iron gate to trade for a toy piano. It was my mother's Christmas gift when she was six years old, a memory that stayed with her forever. She quickly taught herself how to play every song she knew and somehow managed to persuade the family to purchase a second-hand upright piano when she was about eight. She gave piano lessons to the neighborhood children and charged a dime, which was quite a bit of money when you consider what it could buy.

In the summers, Evelyn's father would give her a nickel and an empty bucket to take to the local saloon and have it filled with beer. She loved this assignment because there was a free lunch counter. With the purchase of beer for five cents, you could also have all you could eat from the buffet. She was a skinny little girl who remembered always having food on the family table, but it never seemed to be enough. She would place her bare feet on the cool brass footrail and reach up high on the counter to platters of homemade sausage, freshly baked bread, potato salad, chopped liver, and an array of the richest and most delectable Wisconsin cheeses.

Evelyn must have been an effective salesperson, for she persuaded a surprising number of families to allow her to teach their children how to play the piano. She regarded her accumulation of dimes from this endeavor as her personal fortune and guarded them with secrecy and emotional zeal. Her hiding place was under the stairway runner, a strip of carpeting tacked to each step that led up to the second floor of the house.

One day she was about to add to her hidden treasure when she noticed the carpeting had been firmly retacked to the stair. In a panic, she pulled the tacks from the floor and searched frantically for her dimes. They were gone! She ran to her mother with hot tears of indignation, accusing her brothers and sisters of stealing her very own hard-earned money. Her mother put her on her lap and confessed that she was the thief who had taken the dimes. She had been worrying about how to pay an overdue bill and while cleaning the stairs had discovered them. She did not know they belonged to Evelyn; all she knew was they were a heavenly gift that was desperately needed. My mother told me this story many times, the stinging hurt still visible in her eyes and voice.

Can you imagine how determined and resourceful Evelyn must have been? Somehow, she managed to work and scrimp and save enough to get the necessary lessons to become an excellent pianist and accomplished musician.

When she was thirteen years old, she entered a piano contest given by a musical society in Milwaukee. On a bitterly cold January night, she took a streetcar and traveled by herself across the wintry city to a hall filled with the families and friends of the other contestants. She won first place and came home alone with a gold medal safely tucked under her mitten, pressing into the palm of her hand. She held it tightly as she ran up the stairs to her sleeping parents to excitedly tell them of her triumph. When she told me this story, she made absolutely sure that I understood how hard her parents worked every day of their lives and that the reason she couldn't awaken them that night was that they were so utterly exhausted.

The Bergstrom children were extremely bright and always at the top of their class. Every one of them graduated from college: my mother with a bachelor of arts degree from the University of Wisconsin, Edith with a master's degree from Columbia University, Carl with a master's from MIT, Bill with a master's in business administration from Harvard University, and Ethel with a PhD in education from the University of Wisconsin. All of them became teachers except Carl, who was an engineer. None of this was accomplished without enormous effort, struggle, and sacrifice, which produced an anxiety within my mother that would stay with her for the rest of her life.

I remember Grandpa Bergstrom as a very handsome man. He had thick, wavy, untypically Scandinavian dark hair streaked with gray, as well as high, smooth cheekbones, a small straight nose, deep cornflower-blue eyes, and a shy, uneven smile. He never attempted to play with me or cuddle me. The only emotion I felt for him was on Christmas Eve when he dressed up as St. Nicholas and scared me to death.

However, I do have one sweet, mysterious memory of him that has remained with me all these years. When I was about seven years old, he was spending the summer with our family at our cottage on Enterprise Lake in northern Wisconsin. One night I awakened from a bad dream and called out. He came and sat on the edge of my bed, stroked my hair, and sang me a song. The words were in Swedish, which I didn't understand, but I did realize that this lullaby was very familiar and meaningful to him, and he was sharing with me an intimate part of himself.

My grandmother, Mathilda, died before I was born. When I think of her, I wonder what kind of courage and initiative it must have taken to leave her family when she was still in her teens, knowing she would probably never see her mother and father again, and travel alone to America. My mother said she saw her mother cry only once. She came home from school one day and found her mother sitting with a letter in her lap, quietly weeping. The letter was from Sweden and said that Mathilda's mother had died.

In 1900, the year Evelyn was born, Henry Olson was six years old. Henry was my father, and when I tell you about his childhood and parents, you will have a greater understanding of why he was so different from my mother.

John Olson, Henry's father, was born in America in 1871. John's parents had been born in Norway and had come to America as bride and groom to settle in Wisconsin, where they had six children. All of John's brothers and sisters became farmers who acquired and made prosperous some of the richest and most beautiful farmland in central Wisconsin. Their children's children still own and run those farms today. However, my grandfather, John Olson, chose instead to own and run the general store in the community. The small twin towns Gratiot and Wiota were the center of this rural area, where mail, supplies, and services were sought. Most of the farmers were Norwegian, but there was a small group of Irish settlers as well, so it isn't surprising that John had a partner whose name was O'Malley.

I don't know why John's education stopped after the eighth grade, but I do know that he was shrewd and sly, had a ready wit, could recite the classics in Norwegian and English, add and subtract faster than any human I have ever met, and, more than anything else, relished and succeeded in making people laugh. These were not the attributes needed for farming, but they were absolutely perfect for running a general store.

Nancy Anne Johnson, Henry's mother and my namesake, was a patrician woman whose family had been born in America for many generations. In fact, I have a trunk that some members of her family used to store their belongings when they crossed the Atlantic from Norway to America. The date painted on it is 1786. Nancy's father, Lars Johnson, and her brothers were lawyers. Her mother, Amanda Campbell (the only non-Scandinavian that I can find in my background), had brothers who were Union officers in the Civil War. Nancy Anne was born and raised in Minneapolis, but she must have had relatives and spent time in Gratiot and Wiota, Wisconsin.

13

I have a little autograph book of Nancy Anne's written in her own fine, exquisite hand: "Gratiot and Wiota, 1880." She was fourteen then and used this book to record her friends' messages of friendship and love and to write her own philosophy of life and desire for purity and perfection. Here is a sample of her wisdom:

Envy shooteth at others, but woundeth herself.
Denying a fault doubles it.
Foolish fear doubles danger.
Speak well of all, or not at all.
Zeal without knowledge is fire without light.

(My father learned the following lesson very well.)

Duty is one of the first principles of mankind.
Boasters are cousins to liars.
Richest is he who wants least.
Study your own nature well.
A sneak is like a snake to be shunned.
Heed not what flatterers say unless their price you wish to pay.
Remember the worst of people have good qualities.
Never betray a friend and much less yourself.
To err is nature, to rectify error is glory.
Of all the things I despise, it is deceitfulness.
Be master of yourself before controlling others.

And I found her attitudes toward being female extremely interesting:

Modesty is a guard to virtue.
A pretty face will sometimes make a fool of a young girl.
Proud looks make foul work in fair faces.
I have always tried to make people respect me, especially young men!

I am not sure if I agree with this:

Household work should be a woman's first schooling.

14

I don't think I agree at all with this one:

Men generally are better than women.

But I am sure I agree with this:

Never marry if you don't love.
Never give up the ones you love if they are worthy to be loved, come
what will.

I find the next lines when she thinks about her mother particularly touching:

Mother, home and heaven.
Momma always wanted to do some good in the world. Oh if I only
could be as good as she was.
I have often wished I could be as pure as Momma was.

And her last entry in the book I found the most touching:

Write your name with kindness, love and mercy on the hearts of all
you meet and know, and you will never be forgotten.

Anne's purity and search for perfection may well have kept her what was considered a spinster in those days, for she did not marry John until she was twenty-seven years old, a rather mature age for a bride in the 1890s. John was only twenty-two, and I am sure was an irresistible, handsome, fun-loving rogue who swept Anne off her high horse, undaunted by the disapproval of her family. My father, Henry, was born a year after their marriage, and a little girl followed two years after that. Both deliveries were excruciatingly difficult for Anne, the second being a breech birth in which Anne barely survived and the child did not. After that, Anne became terrified of ever having any more children and vowed she never would. This must have placed a great strain on the marriage and was replaced, for Anne, with an emotional dependency between mother and son.

Henry's family lived in the center of town next to his father's store. His cousins lived on the surrounding farms. His mother expected him to excel in school, which he did, but his father also gave him his own horse so that he could escape and race bareback across the fields, joining the life and work on the farms.

Perhaps the single most vivid experience that changed Henry's destiny and brought him eventually to Milwaukee to meet my mother and produce my brother and me was his relationship with the local doctor.

Remember, at the beginning of the twentieth century only a few people had radios and cars, and there were no airplanes, television, computers, Facebook, or Instagram. You created your own fun and interests without any of the electronic invasions of today's world. Henry became fascinated with the local doctor's life and in particular with the respect and gratitude that the people felt for him. He would travel from farm to farm in the doctor's horse and buggy, help him boil water for his tools, watch him lance a boil, bandage a wound, and deliver whatever medication was available at that time to help people who were ill.

I remember him telling me that in the middle of the night he would go with the doctor to a farm where someone was extremely ill. He described the farmer at the entrance of his road frantically swinging a lantern to signal that it was his farm that needed help. The minute the doctor's buggy appeared, the expression on the farmer's face changed to one of hope. Of course, the doctor could do very little to help people who were seriously ill, but he did bring morphine for pain; at least that was some relief. I also remember my father telling me about an epidemic of typhoid fever and visiting the living rooms of many farms with the entire family in coffins, from the largest of fathers to the smallest of children. My father was determined to become a doctor, not just any doctor, but a doctor with the best skills he could bring to help and heal people.

When Henry was a teenager, his mother insisted that they move to a larger community so that Henry could receive the education she wanted him to have. So his father sold his interest in the general store, and they moved to Beloit, Wisconsin.

After graduating from high school, Henry became a premed student at the University of Wisconsin. He was then accepted in the Columbia University Vagelos College of Physicians and Surgeons in New York. After graduating at the top of his class, he interned at Presbyterian Hospital with a specialty in surgery. He became so adept with his hands that he could tie a knot in a piece of string buried in his pocket. It was only after becoming a truly skilled surgeon that he realized that surgery was not what he had envisioned it to be.

It did not give him the satisfaction that he was seeking. It didn't matter how expertly you removed a tumor and sewed the patient back up; the patient would die six months later anyway because there was no treatment for containing cancer cells. It was during his internship, however, that Henry delivered his first baby, and the experience helped him realize that the gift he was looking to give was the kind that involved handing a child to its mother.

He left Presbyterian Hospital and interned at Lying-In Hospital to specialize in obstetrics and gynecology. The people who worked with him realized he was a star, and he soon received many offers to partner with some of the leading doctors in New York City. However, his beloved mother was dying of diabetes, and that bond could not be denied.

He returned to Wisconsin and started to practice in Milwaukee, a completely unknown young doctor arriving with superior knowledge and expertise. He was diligent and worked extremely hard, and although he was unusually shy and modest, it was evident that he was special. He eventually became the head of the Gynecology and Obstetrics Departments at St. Joseph's Hospital, Deaconess Hospital, and Columbia Hospital. His mother died six months before insulin became available.

When Henry met my mother, a vivacious Swedish beauty, he fell in love and swept her off her feet. They were married on Christmas Eve in 1925. She gave up her teaching career and became the wife of a doctor and, eventually, a mother of two children.

I was born on July 14, 1928, and my brother, David, was born five years later, on September 19, 1933.

4

Growing Up in Milwaukee

In 1927, Charles Lindbergh flew over the Atlantic; in 1929, the stock market crashed; and in 1930 the Great Depression began. My mother's childhood had prepared her for this period. It was comparatively easy for her to be thrifty, and, of course, my father was able to provide a modest yet decent income, more than most fathers. They bought a house on Woodlawn Court on the west side of Milwaukee. The neighborhood consisted of the families of other doctors, some lawyers, a judge, and a few struggling businessmen. My mother always had household help, and she had great fun in creating quite a wonderful home in this rather middle-class house. There were four bedrooms upstairs, and a maid's room downstairs. My room was next to my parents', and I remember every corner of it. In fact, my twin beds, bureau, bedside table, mirror, and desk chair are now comfortably placed in one of my guest rooms on Alpine Drive in Beverly Hills.

Certain events of my childhood remain in my mind. I had two best friends, little girls my age who also lived on Woodlawn Court—Carol Habeck and Harriet Verden. There was a distance between us, however, that I always felt but never understood. I would like to be truly nonjudgmental and finally face what our differences were. And I want to make clear that I remember them with great affection and am still grateful for their friendship and the fun we had. But what was this gulf between us that was always there?

I think it started with my parents. They were extremely different from our neighbors. They were more educated and certainly much more sophisticated and in touch with what was going on in the world. I believe we were the only family who had a live-in housekeeper and had two cars, one for my father and one for my mother. My father was a prominent member of the medical community, and because Milwaukee was a comparatively small city (about three hundred thousand people at that time), he was a well-known and well-respected citizen. They belonged to the Milwaukee Athletic Club, one of the status institutions in town. In fact, I spent almost every Saturday winter morning at the club's giant pool, where I learned how to swim and dive. I especially looked forward to having lunch in the grand dining room and being served a delicious salad followed by the most fabulous chocolate éclair. (I don't care much for chocolate, but this éclair was something special.)

I also remember being very conscious of how I spoke the English language. I don't particularly recall my mother making it an issue, but I do remember being constantly corrected. My brother, David, says that she was somewhat obsessed with speaking properly. To this day, it is important for me to speak well; I don't think it's an affectation, just something ingrained in my young mind. Perhaps that contributed to Carol and Harriet thinking I was different, not like them. I do know they seemed to take particular delight in probing for my weaknesses. There is one incident that stays in my mind to this day as one of the more traumatic moments I have ever experienced.

Carol had a playroom on the second floor that was attached to an attic closet. In the closet was the most enchanting, large music box I have ever seen. It was about four feet long, a foot and a half high, with a glass top that revealed a large brass cylinder when you looked inside. Why it was hidden in the closet is beyond me; I would have put it in my living room, where I could look at it and play it every day. When you wound it up and pressed a button, the cylinder would start to turn, and it played the most heavenly music. Whenever I went to Carol's house, I always headed for the closet.

Carol decided that she finally had me where she wanted me. On my fifth or sixth visit to the music box, she casually stood by the door and watched my ecstasy with a certain amount of contempt, and before I knew it, she turned off the closet light, slammed the door, and locked it from the other side! I was terrified, particularly because I did not trust Carol to ever let me out. She listened to me cry, plead, and scream and finally decided to open the door. You would think that I would have learned my lesson, but no. On many more visits, she very convincingly promised me that this would never happen again, and she would be delighted to let me in the closet to listen to the music. Of course, in only a matter of minutes the light would go out, and the door would be slammed shut, and I would be locked in again. I wish I could remember some of my more joyful moments as well as I remember this experience. So much for Carol.

Harriet was another story. She had lots of brothers and sisters and came from a different culture entirely. If my memory is correct, her slightly older

19

sisters wore nail polish and were experimenting with lipstick at a very young age. My mother was very contemptuous of children growing up too fast. I thought it was fascinating, but this behavior nevertheless put a breach between me and Harriet.

My childhood education is a collage of scattered memories, some happy and some truly upsetting. I remember being in kindergarten; my teacher's name was Miss Burnshine. Her family were undertakers, which may explain her dour expression and severe personality. I had three terrible encounters with Miss Burnshine. The first was when she asked me how to spell "Olson," with an "on" or an "en." I said I would ask my father and report back to her. When I asked my father what the proper way to spell "Olson" was, he said either way is correct. I couldn't wait to report this news to Miss Burnshine, who immediately attacked me and said that I didn't know what I was talking about and that I was a very stupid little girl. I obviously forgot to ask my father how *we* spelled "Olson."

The second encounter was when Miss Burnshine and her assistant could not control the class. Her solution was to go to the closet, put on her hat and coat, and announce that she and her assistant were leaving and would not be back until the next day. They then closed the door and locked it from the other side. I panicked. I truly believed that Miss Burnshine would not come back, and I would have to spend the night with these unruly children. I started to cry uncontrollably until she opened the door and said she hoped we had all learned our lesson. She also snapped, "Nancy, stop crying like a baby!"

My third memory of Miss Burnshine makes me cringe when I think of it, even today. It was the Wednesday before Thanksgiving, and we were invited to share with the class how we celebrated the holiday in our homes. I enthusiastically raised my hand and described an enchanted weekend with my parents and baby brother at my grandparents' home in Beloit, a small town in Wisconsin about seventy miles away. I'm sure I got carried away, as only I can, and talked about my father driving through the rolling hills of the Wisconsin countryside, with red barns tucked into the landscape and the tepees of dried corn husks dotting the horizon, and I shared how we counted the cows and sheep and horses in the fields. My grandmother would have ready the most delicious roast turkey and stuffing, served with mashed potatoes, and followed by apple pie or minced pie, whichever you preferred. After dinner, my grandpa would put me on his lap and tell me stories in Norwegian and then tell me in English what the story was about. My mother and father would sleep in the large brass bed in one guest room, and David and I would share the other. We would spend the night and wake up to pancakes and bacon and slowly drive home at the end of the day.

In those days, schools celebrated the Thursday of Thanksgiving but resumed school on Friday. To my horror, we did not spend the night in Beloit but returned to Milwaukee, and I was expected to go to school the next day. But how could I? I had already told everyone that I wasn't going to be there. I wish I had had a bit more guile and lied about a stomachache or a sore throat or something that would keep me home, but I didn't. I slipped into the classroom hoping that no one would see me, but of course Miss Burnshine seemed absolutely thrilled that she could criticize me in front of the class— something like, "Well, little Nancy Olson, it seems your story was nothing but a lie." I tried to explain that I did go to Beloit and that in the past we had stayed overnight, but not this time. She responded that I was nothing but a liar, and she didn't ever want to speak to me again. What made her single me out so viciously? What was there about me that ticked her off? I wonder to this day.

I had the most trouble with a group of boys when I was in the third grade. They wanted to chase me home, corner me, and kiss me. This was not necessarily because I was so irresistible but more because I was such a perfect petrified target. They were bullies, and it made them feel powerful to see me so frightened of them. I became so desperate that I went to the teacher, Miss Meets, and told her that I didn't feel well just so that I could leave school early and get a head start. I definitely didn't know how to handle this harassment, and I don't remember other girls dealing with the same problem. Again, what made me the most desirable victim?

Finally, I must have confessed all of this to my mother, and she took action. One boy named Otto Angerstein was particularly mean to me. He would wait in the bushes ready to spring on me as I walked by. My mother said she would walk behind me, leaving enough distance between us so that it was not evident she was there to interfere. Poor Otto! I don't think he ever experienced anything like the wrath of my mother, who told him that he was a bully and a nasty little boy and that she was going to see to it that his parents and the school knew about his behavior. My mother began to have the repu- tation of someone to be wary of, and her nickname became the "Big Bad Wolf of Woodlawn Court!"

One clue partially explained why I was always singled out, and it sur- prised me. There was a boy who lived on Woodlawn Court named Jim Sav- age. He seemed particularly resentful of me, and I couldn't figure out why until one day when he was with a group of kids teasing me, he suddenly blurted out with great drama and feeling, "I bet your father has a five-dollar bill in every sock!" Was that it? Did his parents discuss our family? Were we resented because we seemed to be better off? Maybe.

A nice thing happened when a new family moved next door. They were Irish Catholics, and their name was Dooley. They had five children, all with Irish names. The two girls, Shannon and Patricia, were well behaved and great fun to play with. Patricia was exactly my age, and we became best friends. Her bedroom was directly across the driveway and hedge from my bedroom, and on warm spring nights, when the screens were put on our windows to replace the storm windows, we would talk endlessly into the darkening night. They were a nice family and didn't seem to resent us at all. What a relief!

The winters in Milwaukee were brutal. After the first snowfall sometime in late November, you rarely saw the ground again until the beginning of April. I remember the icy winds coming off Lake Michigan and chilling not only my flesh but my innermost bones.

My mother and our housekeeper used a washing machine in the basement with a wringer attached to a large sink. When as much of the moisture as possible was removed from the clothes, they would put the damp wash in a basket, go up the stairs, out the kitchen door, and to the backyard, where thick ropey lines and wooden pins were waiting. They had to plan their wash with the weather, hoping for a day that was sunny even though it was ten degrees. I remember going out to test the wash and report to my mother whether it was dry enough to bring in. Some of the clothes were frozen stiff. It is only now when I look back that I realize how challenging it was to keep house at that time.

But it was the spring that was so seductive and exciting. I loved to roller skate and ride my bike and became extremely expert in executing both. When the nights were warm enough, I would race through my dinner and run outside to play hide-and-seek and a game called "Run, My Good Sheep, Run!" I have never known anyone other than the kids on Woodlawn Court who had ever even heard of it. As darkness fell, my mother would come out of the front door to tell us that it was time to go home and go to bed. Patricia and I would look at each other, knowing that the evening was still young. I would run upstairs, get ready for bed, turn off my lights, and kneel down in front of the open window, my elbows on the windowsill and my nose pressing against the screen, waiting for my friend. The only things that came between us were the fireflies that for a brief moment lit up the night.

5

The Lake

When I was about six years old, my mother went to northern Wisconsin with my uncle Dutch Keithley, who was married to her sister, Ethel. The Keithleys and my parents bought properties next door to each other on a beautiful lake named Enterprise and hired two Norwegian carpenters to build homes for both families. As usual, our home was much bigger and more elaborate, but we shared the pier and several boats. There was a common pump to supply water to both houses but no electricity. Spending summers on Enterprise Lake was a magical time for David and me. In fact, we spent all winter long dreaming about it.

A thousand acres of land to our right were owned by the Chicago Kraft Cheese family and were preserved in their natural state. David and I became acquainted with deer, raccoons, chipmunks, skunks, snakes (not poisonous), turtles, porcupines, and the hundreds of birds that arrived from the South to build their nests at about the same time we moved into our summer home.

I remember taking the canoe through a small canal, watching the beavers build their dams, and picking the most luscious wild raspberries to bring home. My mother had an old-fashioned ice cream maker, and she used the raspberries to make homemade ice cream, the most divine culinary creation that I have ever tasted. We had Coleman lamps and kerosene lanterns brightly lit at night so we could read and play endless card games.

Our living room was projected over the hillside. It was two stories high with a peaked roof and lined in knotty pine beams. On the wall facing the lake was a huge domed window. My mother had ordered the glass from the Pittsburgh Glass Company, and to this day the company still talks about trying to deliver it in one piece on the winding gravel road to our house. The two carpenters could not possibly install this window without help, so my resourceful mother went to the local Civilian Conservation Corps camp (created by President Franklin Roosevelt to provide jobs for the unemployed) and hired a group of young boys to help. The closest town was a small community called Elcho. It had a general store, a post office, a doctor's office, and a train station; no more than a few hundred people lived there.

My mother's father, Grandpa Bergstrom, lived with Aunt Ethel and Uncle Dutch and spent several summers with us at the lake before he died. He was an expert fisherman and cleaned and prepared the freshest and most delicious pike, which he cooked in an iron skillet in fresh butter purchased from the local farms. We also had freshly picked lettuce, tomatoes, string beans, corn, scallions, zucchini, and broccoli as well as homemade bread. Since we were a doctor's family, there was an emphasis on eating healthy foods and preparing them carefully. Of course, there was always every kind of cheese that Wisconsin produced. The taste of fresh cottage cheese is still in my memory, and since that time I have never been able to find anything resembling it.

What a charmed life we had at the lake. How many children have seen a snake jump on a frog and swallow it whole as the frog croaked frantically? Who ever saw a turtle about ten inches long digging a hole with its back feet and, once the hole was the right size, start to drop its eggs? After each of the ten eggs dropped, the mother turtle would take one of her back legs and carefully cover it with dirt. When this task was completed, she slowly disappeared under the ferns and the brush.

How many children remember canoeing at midnight over a lake without a ripple in the still night air? It was so quiet the only sound was when we gently put the oars in the calm water. The lake was as smooth as a mirror as we followed the silvery path of light reflected from the moon and its beams. And how many children remember lying down on a pier over the water as the night descended, revealing the universe and its trillion stars? One forgets what the night sky is like far from city lights.

And the storms! Could we ever forget their violent and ferocious attacks, whipping the water into turbulent waves, the black clouds blazing with lightning that destroyed everything it touched? Watching these storms come across the sky from the giant window in our cottage was like watching a thrilling and terrifying movie in a huge theater. These memories will never leave me, and as I write about them, I regret that I never thanked my parents for giving me this wonderful gift while I was growing up.

6

World War II

While David and I were spending falls and winters at school and summers at the lake, our parents were planning a huge change in their lives and ours. They bought five acres of land in Fox Point, a choice suburb of Milwaukee. This magnificent property overlooked all of Lake Michigan, and they were very excited about building their dream house. The Depression was ending, and my father was becoming more and more successful and prosperous. It was time to leave Woodlawn Court and live in a different environment. It was also a time when I was maturing and developing in many ways.

I had inherited my mother's musical gifts and passions as well as her strong interest in the arts, and I gained a new awareness and curiosity about the world around me. I'm not sure how many other children and their parents listened to the New York Philharmonic Symphony every Sunday afternoon following their traditional Sunday midday meal. Every Saturday afternoon I listened to a live performance of the Metropolitan Opera Company on the radio. I still remember Milton Cross's voice describing the sets and the costumes, telling the story, and interviewing a very sophisticated group of commentators on opera. I was excelling in my piano lessons and looked forward to the classical music class that I attended with my mother every Monday night. We also attended performances by the visiting opera and theater companies that came to town. As I write this, I realize how special my parents were and how fortunate I was to be with them.

But there were also serious challenges, not only with my peers but also with my mother. She was loving and doting until I began to approach adolescence. I don't know why she felt so bothered by my maturing, but somewhere it triggered a strange competitiveness in her. My father absolutely adored me, so perhaps that had something to do with it. My mother had two Caesarians, and I know my father did not want her to become pregnant again. I'm sure that his control of this issue was in conflict with her needs for intimacy. Birth control was in a primitive state at that time and lacked certainty, whatever the method. His freedom to love me so much had to be controlled so that it wouldn't fuel the fire of her jealousy. It was only years later that I began to put all the pieces together.

When I was thirteen, the world as we knew it stopped. We all found ourselves facing a critical period for our country, not to mention a critical time for every individual on the planet. It was the beginning of World War II, and Europe was being slowly destroyed. Hitler was a psychotic dictator who had visions of ruling all of us. My parents were aware of his demonic behavior toward his neighbors and especially toward the Jewish community long before most of their friends even thought about it, much less discussed it. My mother was a flaming liberal, my father more moderately conservative. Politics was a volatile subject within our family and also among our closest friends. My family's alarm about what was happening so many miles away was in such contrast to my peers and their parents, who only seemed to want to remain uninvolved. As I was growing up, which was preoccupying enough on its own, my life was becoming more and more defined by the advancing German army and the devastation of Europe.

There was one night that stays alive in my memory even today. It was June 14, 1940. I was eleven years old, and my mother took me to the Milwaukee Auditorium to see a visiting company's performance of the opera *Rigoletto*. We were seated on wooden folding chairs, and it was difficult for me to see over the heads of the audience in front of me. But I heard the music, which was magic to my ears, and I remember smiling at my mother when I heard the tenor sing one of his beautiful arias. But it was the intermission that changed this festive event. People applauded and started to leave their seats when suddenly a loud voice came over the speaker system. It said, "Ladies and gentlemen, please remain seated; we have an announcement to make. The BBC has just announced that Paris has fallen to the Germans." The entire auditorium sat down and was silent. I looked at my mother and saw tears in her eyes.

But it was Sunday night, December 7, 1941, that truly changed everything for all Americans. I was upstairs in the small, paneled library doing my homework. Aunt Ethel and Uncle Dutch were downstairs with my parents listening to the news. I heard my mother exclaim, "Oh, no! Oh, please! Oh, no!" My father said something like, "Oh, my God!," and I heard my gentle aunt Ethel start to sob. I slowly descended the stairs, not wanting to know what happened but needing to know. When I walked in the room, my mother said, "The Japanese have bombed Pearl Harbor. Our country is going to war."

My father was too old to be drafted and, as a doctor, was especially needed to stay home and help take care of the community. My brother was seven years old, much too young to even think about being a soldier. But the country was at war. My parents' trip to Cuba was canceled. Some friends watched their young sons go to war, never to see them again. The country had no tanks, fighter airplanes, or weapons and was barely recovering from the Depression. Because we were in the Midwest, we did not fear air raids or any kind of attacks, but there were no more automobiles to buy, widespread shortages of certain foods and supplies, rationing of oil and gas, and the greatest disappointment of all for my family, there was not going to be a house built in Fox Point. Every piece of scrap iron, copper, cement, and brick was reserved for the war. I think that in addition to how depressing the war was to my mother and father, their personal disappointment about having to shelve their dreams was also deeply profound.

7

Theatrical Dreams

Perhaps you have wondered how I became an actress. The beginning was a decision I made a long time ago, putting me on a path that would lead me to Hollywood, my first marriage, two beautiful daughters, and an extraordinary life. It happened at a Penny Dance in a combined junior and senior high school in Milwaukee. The gymnasium was open to everyone at the lunch hour for dancing to records played over a loudspeaker. You paid a penny to get in. The older boys seldom asked a seventh- or eighth-grade girl to dance, so for a year and a half I paid my penny just to watch.

But an unexpected thing happened. The ninth-grade class put on a Thanksgiving play in the auditorium for the entire school. I played the part of the ingénue and wore pumps with a small heel and a fairly grown-up dress and for the first time was allowed to wear makeup. I was nervous when I made my entrance but felt surprisingly comfortable as the play progressed. The audience seemed to stop fidgeting, too.

When the play was over, I gathered up my books and went to the cafeteria for lunch. It was different. Strangers stopped to talk to me. Someone asked me to join them at the head of the line, and the teachers whispered and smiled at me. After lunch, my friends and I headed for the gym. As I dropped my penny in the box, I felt a tap on my shoulder. There stood the Number 1 boy in my romantic fantasies, Donald. This gorgeous senior took me in his arms, and the two of us glided to the middle of the dance floor. It was hard to breathe or swallow. "You are a wonderful actress," he murmured, sending a signal to the hair on the back of my neck to stand straight up and the space between my shoulder blades to tingle. I tried to say "thank you," but it sounded more like "ack voo." "What did you say?" he whispered in my ear, the delicate drums swelling and pounding to the rhythm of the music and repeating one word over and over—*actress, actress, actress!*

I told my parents how exciting this experience was, and I think that triggered their decision to take me out of the neighborhood school and transfer me to Wauwatosa High School, which was in an adjoining suburb. My parents had the power to make this happen, and I am forever grateful. I was with kids from families more comparable to mine and with much more sophistication than my present peers. I was also in one of the most superb high schools in the Midwest.

I was like a hungry young tigress signing up for everything—the choir, the forensic team, the drama programs, everything that I always longed for. In the Gilbert and Sullivan operetta *H.M.S. Pinafore,* I played the part of Buttercup; in *Pride and Prejudice* I played the leading lady, Elizabeth; and in *The Importance of Being Earnest* I played the nurse. I loved being in the company of Jane Austen and Oscar Wilde as well as my talented new friends. I also decided to try speechmaking and entered the state contest. I wrote a speech entitled "The Teenage Bill of Rights" and won the city, the county, and finally the state contest.

When I finished my junior year, I was accepted at Northwestern University's program in performing arts for high school students who completed their third year. This was possibly the most rewarding experience I ever had during that period. Two students, a boy and a girl, were chosen from each state, and I found myself in the company of very talented and interesting young people. We were called "Cherubs" on the campus because we were obviously so much younger. I have never met a "cherub" who does not remember this summer in their life as possibly the most special; the program is still offered every summer, and the high school students are still referred to as "Cherubs."

All of these experiences were set in front of a backdrop of a ferocious world war. We were untouched in some ways but always with an underlying sense of anxiety about what to expect in our new world. Perhaps the most vivid memory for me during this time was sitting on a park bench on the Northwestern campus overlooking Lake Michigan. It was August 6, 1945, and Hiroshima had just been bombed into oblivion. I knew that the world would never be the same, and it was essential that I adjust to that reality. I wondered how my dreams of being a grown-up with an exciting career, a happy, loving marriage, and beautiful children living in a safe world would ever be possible.

Of course, I fell in love, too. Pete Stevens, wherever you are, I want to say thank you for finding me so beguiling. Your passionate fantasies were quite obvious, and when you kissed me after the senior prom, you scared me to death with the depth of your feeling. When we went to the University of Wisconsin together, you had a lot of competition, and I was flattered by all the older young men pursuing me. I simply didn't have time for my high school sweetheart, and I'm sure I was not very sensitive to your feelings. Please forgive me and know that I hope you are living a wonderful life.

I think it's important for me to tell you that my mother had a strict attitude about values and principles. She also was very sensitive about her own disadvantages growing up in a struggling immigrant family. I will never forget standing in the upstairs hallway listening to her talk on the phone to someone who wanted to invite me to become a member of the Junior League. I heard her say, "Absolutely not! I was never invited, and I will not have my daughter be a part of your decadent organization." I was disappointed and felt denied another kind of experience, so when I went to the University of Wisconsin as a freshman, I was determined to rush for the sororities on campus. I very carefully researched what was considered the hardest group to get into and the most respected and desirable sorority house to be a member of. I didn't dare go to my mother for her approval or disapproval but went to my father instead. I told him what I wanted to do and asked if he would please see that the necessary letters of recommendation were written. He had been a member of a well-known fraternity when he was at the University of Wisconsin and was eager for me to have a taste of that experience. I decided that I wanted to be a Kappa Kappa Gamma.

When it came time for the invitations to be issued, I was given a card to list my first three choices. Instead of putting down three, I put down one and thought, "If I don't get to be a Kappa, I'm not interested in joining any of the others." As luck would have it, I was invited and pledged to be a Kappa Kappa Gamma. I loved it but also felt somewhat removed from the sorority experience. It truly wasn't me, as hard as I tried. My mother had done her work well; her Democratic principles were deeply engrained, and I will never be free of them. I hope that's part of my charm!

I also experienced a little bit of success in my pursuit of being an actress. Although I was a freshman and not allowed to try out for the Wisconsin Players, I auditioned anyway and won the coveted role of Lady Wishfort in Congreve's play *The Way of the World*. Destiny was like a magnet facing the North Pole, pulling me in only one direction.

My aunt Ethel and uncle Dutch were moving to Los Angeles, California, each with a new job opportunity. Uncle Dutch was invited to be a dean in the business school of the University of California at Los Angeles (UCLA), and my parents thought that it would be wonderful to drive across the country and visit them. In fact, they thought, wouldn't it be wonderful if I could attend the summer-school semester at UCLA, particularly because of its outstanding theater arts program? I lived in the Kappa house and attended the most exciting classes I had ever experienced up to that point. In fact, I felt so happy and fulfilled there that I decided to transfer from the University of Wisconsin to UCLA.

I have always known how important it is for a budding performer to go to college. You have the opportunity not only to play many parts but also to become acquainted with the great writers and gain some understanding and exposure to history, literature, science, and how the world came to be as well as how it works today. This experience is invaluable. Where else do you have a chance to get acquainted with William Shakespeare, Tennessee Williams, Maxwell Anderson, George Bernard Shaw, Samuel Beckett, Molière, and so many of the great classic playwrights?

It was the part of the leading lady in Ferenc Molnar's *The Play's the Thing* that changed the direction of my entire life. As I was taking off my makeup in my dressing room, someone knocked on my door, and I opened it to see a small, courtly gentleman, who asked if he could talk to me. He explained that he was the head of Paramount Pictures' talent division, Milton Lewis, and would like me to visit him at Paramount. I cannot deny that I was quite thrilled and couldn't wait for our appointment. A screen test was arranged with one of their contract players, George Reeves (TV's Superman in the 1950s). Apparently, the test was a success, and I was signed to a standard seven-year contract, which at the time was about $300 a week. Because I was not yet twenty-one, the law put my parents in charge of my income, and instead I received my usual allowance for much less.

I have never worried about money, and to this day it truly doesn't matter to me to be super rich. As long as I have the things I need for my security and aesthetics, I am very happy, and I am also smart enough to know how truly fortunate I am to have them all.

8

My First New York Adventure

Spending time at UCLA with a group of wonderful young people just as passionate about the performing arts as I certainly was exhilarating; we knew every play on Broadway and every song in every musical by heart. At the same time, my personal life was also becoming highly intriguing. I was dating George Englund, a very attractive, seductive, talented, and troubled young man from New York—the first of many "troubled" men in my life—and I had just been signed by a major Hollywood studio!

George had moved to New York City to be with another actress he was pursuing, Cloris Leachman, who would ultimately become his wife. At this time, I had no knowledge of their relationship. All I knew were his sweet letters and phone calls from the East Coast telling me that he missed me. I went to Paramount Pictures and said I wanted to visit New York for a week and needed two tickets to attend six plays and musicals. The studio arranged the flight, reserved a small single room for me at the Plaza Hotel, and purchased two house seats for everything I wanted to see.

I arrived on a Saturday night in late August 1949. Sunday evening George and I attended the Actors Benefit performance of *South Pacific* with Mary Martin and Ezio Pinza—I was enchanted.

Monday night we saw *Death of a Salesman* with Lee J. Cobb, Mildred Dunnock, and Arthur Kennedy. I was stunned.

Tuesday night we went to a small theater on Forty-Fourth Street and saw *Where's Charley?*, Ray Bolger delighting everyone as he sang "Once in Love with Amy."

Wednesday night we saw *Detective Story* with Ralph Bellamy and the fresh young talent Lee Grant, revealing the genius of the Actors Studio training.

Thursday night we saw *A Streetcar Named Desire* with Marlon Brando and Kim Hunter. I still hear Marlon's plaintive wail: "Stelllllllaaaaaaaaa!"

32

Friday night we saw *Mister Roberts* with Henry Fonda and David Wayne. I had no idea that someday I would know both of them and actually do a play with David.

Saturday night was our last night to attend the theater. It was Cole Porter's legendary *Kiss Me, Kate,* the perfect note on which to end my thrilling first visit to New York.

After every performance, George and I went to Sardi's for a glass of wine and a light supper. He then took me home and kissed me at the front door of the Plaza; his kisses were possibly the most exquisite I have ever experienced.

The New York theater was at its most glorious moment in history, and I do believe this trip influenced the rest of my life.

9

Paramount Pictures—the Beginning of a Career

Can you imagine a UCLA student, a doctor's daughter from Milwaukee, Wisconsin, walking through the gates of Paramount Studios with a seven-year contract in her pocket, knowing that she was possibly being groomed to be a "movie star"? It was 1948, and on my way to the talent department I would detour to the center of the lot. It resembled a small town square, with the large executive offices to the south, and on the west side there was a long sidewalk in front of all the stars' dressing rooms, their names prominently printed on the doors. I might bump into Bing Crosby on his bicycle followed by his cronies—Bob Hope with his joke writers—Jerry Lewis clowning for anyone who came by—and Dean Martin following slowly behind Jerry, looking only slightly amused. Bill Holden and Alan Ladd usually walked alone, and the women under contract seemed to stay in their dressing rooms or the makeup department. In the Paramount commissary, I watched the great filmmakers enter, Billy Wilder, William Wyler, Hal Wallis, Cecil B. DeMille, George Stevens, as well as the Oscar-winning songwriters Jay Livingston and Ray Evans ("Mona Lisa," "Que Sera, Sera"). I sat as close as I could to the writers' table. I loved hearing them erupt in raucous, self-appreciating laughter.

I always knew that I wanted to be an actress, probably a stage actress, but the possibility of being a "movie star" seemed like a distant dream. After the studio signed me, I continued to go to school, but in my free time I was drawn to explore Paramount, absolutely fascinated with the life and the people and the possibility of joining them in making films.

My first assignment came quickly. The studio was going to lend me to 20th Century-Fox to star opposite Randolph Scott in *Canadian Pacific*. The fact that I was to play the role of Cecille, described as a multiracial character of Canadian Indian background, seemed ludicrous as I was such an obvious fair-skinned, blue-eyed Scandinavian. And Randolph Scott? He was two years younger than my father! What were they thinking! I explained my reservations to Milt Lewis, who calmly looked at me and said, "Nancy, they want you to play the part, and that's what you're going to do." "But, Milt," I said, "the film is in color! Do I really look like an Indian?" Milt answered, "They are going to rinse your hair every morning with a dark dye, and, after all, you're playing the part of a 'half-breed,' which explains your blue eyes."

My mother was thrilled and said she would accompany me to Canada for the duration of the shoot. She had heard about these junkets and the behavior toward young girls, and she was coming to protect my virginity. She'd bring a gun if necessary! I explained that Mr. Scott was older than she was and not to worry, but actually I was relieved. I needed moral support to see me through this challenging event. I had never made a movie before, and it was going to say on the screen, "Introducing Nancy Olson." Where did my courage come from, or was I just too young to understand what a daunting assignment I had just been handed?

My mother and I arrived in Calgary, Canada, and drove through the mountains to the Banff Lodge. Although I had visited Yellowstone Park and Glacier Park, I was not prepared for the majesty and beauty of the mountains of Banff and Lake Louise. The lodge was elegantly comfortable with a breathtaking view from every window, including my mother's and my suite. Randolph Scott was extremely courteous, almost to the point of being courtly. His wife was at his side every moment and seemed to make a great effort to behave absolutely correctly. They were not the typical "showbiz" couple; in fact, I think Randy was one of the very few performers allowed to join the Los Angeles Country Club. But the real patrician of our group was Jane Wyatt, who played the part of the woman Randolph's character was involved with. Jane came from an eastern private-school background and was married to a very prominent investment banker. She was darling with me and remained a good friend through the years. The fact that the script had Randolph leave her and fall in love with me was more than ridiculous, and anyone who believed it had to be crazy. However, I pushed my character forward with as much strength as I could muster (I even horse-whipped Victor Jory) and hoped for the best. Believe it or not, most of the public accepted my performance (with grace, I hope).

Everything seemed to be falling in place. They were shooting the film during the summer, so I did not have to cancel my plans to attend school in the fall. When I returned to campus, though, everything seemed a little unreal.

It is hard for me to explain going to my classes at UCLA on a Monday and then visiting a set at Paramount Studios on Tuesday. There was great curiosity and interest in this new "UCLA student starlet," particularly from the older executives, producers, and men in general. I became increasingly aware of how vulnerable I was and what an interesting target I might be.

When *Canadian Pacific* was released, the interest tripled. In fact, there is one incident I will never forget. I was walking down one of the alleys on the lot when the senior publicity executive approached me and said, "Nancy, Mr. Howard Hughes wants an appointment with you in his office tomorrow afternoon. I have promised that I will personally bring you to the Goldwyn studios at three o'clock. Please meet me in my office at 2:30, and I will drive you over."

I said, "I can drive myself. I will follow you, and you can arrange for my parking and getting inside the gate." I was not going to have him drop me off and leave me without a means of escape.

The next afternoon the publicist escorted me to the second floor of a building on the Goldwyn lot, introduced me to the secretary, and left. I waited about ten minutes, and she said, "Mr. Hughes will see you now." Please understand, I knew a fair amount about Mr. Hughes and even in my virginal innocence was determined that I would not be one of his trophies.

I walked in the room and found Mr. Hughes sitting behind his desk. He had a mustache, a visible hearing aid in his left ear, and was wearing an open shirt in a pale yellow—he could have been somewhere about my father's age. He told me to sit down and said how much he enjoyed *Canadian Pacific*.

I knew I was in an impossible situation. I certainly did not want to offend Mr. Hughes, but it was important to make it clear to him that out of all the people in the world, if there was one person he should not be interested in, it was me! Thank God, he gave me the opening to do just that. He said, "Miss Olson, tell me about yourself."

I immediately asked if he had ever been to Wisconsin. I think he nodded, murmuring something like, "Once or twice." "Well," I began, "it is the most interesting place in the world to grow up." I told him everything I could about Milwaukee and its culture, its people, its schools, its museums—but I didn't stop there. I then told him about my summers on a lake in northern Wisconsin, describing the fishing, the sailing, the canoeing, the mosquitoes, . . . and much more.

There was a moment of silence. He cocked his head to the right, looked at me, got up from his chair, and said, "I think I will now walk you to the gate and your car." I immediately stood up and said, "How nice of you. Thank you."

We left the office together and walked down the stairs to the street level and through the various alleys to the front gate. On the way, an elderly gentleman came out of one of the buildings and seemed shocked to see Mr. Hughes walking on the lot. Apparently, he never did. The gentleman was Sam Goldwyn Sr., who with a startled expression on his face said, "Howard, why are you out walking?" Mr. Hughes said, "Sam, this is Nancy Olson; she was born in Wisconsin and lived on a lake when she was growing up." Mr. Goldwyn looked perplexed and said to me, "Hello, it's nice to meet you." Mr. Hughes then pressed the button to open the gate, motioned to the parking lot across the street, and said, "Goodbye, have a safe trip home." I heard the gate close behind me, and when I turned back, I saw him walking as fast as he could back to his office. It was evident that he wanted to personally see that I left the lot and that the gates were locked behind me.

I went back to school and tried my best to complete the semester. I had certainly intended to graduate, but it was harder than ever to concentrate on school. My attendance and grades suffered, but I was saved by my next assignment at Paramount Pictures. Much to my parents' regret, I dropped out of school and started preparations for shooting *Sunset Boulevard*.

10

Sunset Boulevard

Where do I begin?

How many young actresses ever have the opportunity to play a wonderful part in one of the greatest films ever made? Is it a part of one's destiny? That opportunity certainly didn't come to me because I deserved it or because it was obvious that I was so brilliant and talented. I think Billy Wilder had a vision of the character Betty Schaefer. I remember him casually starting a conversation with me when the two of us bumped into each other walking to the cafeteria on the Paramount lot. He asked me about UCLA, about where I came from—he asked me what it was like to grow up in the Middle West. These were rather mundane subjects, but he seemed interested and persistent. When I read the script, I found that my character was described as an aspiring writer, and I think Billy thought of me as a somewhat articulate and educated young woman. I also have always been somewhat outspoken, and he wanted the girl to be strong. I'm only guessing, but that's what occurs to me today. Again, I was young and stupid enough not to be intimidated. When I look back, I think to myself, "What was wrong with you? Were you so naive not to be just a little bit nervous?"

I had no idea who Gloria Swanson was. It was my mother who filled me in about her great stardom in the 1920s and 1930s. Mae West had apparently been the first choice to play Norma Desmond; thank God, she refused. This film was dangerously on the cliff of sliding into high camp. If anybody, particularly in the Norma Desmond role, had gone overboard, the film could easily have been destroyed. Gloria was the inspired choice, and so was William Holden. They originally wanted Montgomery Clift to play the role of Joe Gillis, but he also refused. The film would never have been what it is if Gloria and Bill had not played these two parts.

Bill Holden grew up in Pasadena, California, with an austere mother and distant father. He attended Pasadena Junior College and started working in radio, where he was discovered by a Paramount talent scout. His first two movies are legendary classics, *Golden Boy* (1939) and *Our Town* (1940). This success was interrupted by the war. When he returned from the military, his career was increasingly fragmented with undistinguished pictures and roles. He married Brenda Marshall (Ardis Ankerson Gaines) and adopted her infant daughter. They had two sons.

At this point in Bill Holden's life, he was beginning to lose his career. He was already drinking too much, he was in a marriage that wasn't really working, . . . he was beginning to feel desperate. I think he brought all of that, all that was going on in his life, into the role of Joe Gillis—a man who was also desperate. You didn't really believe Joe Gillis would get involved in this kind of situation unless he were. To me, it was extraordinarily gifted casting.

Over the years, people have asked me, "What was William Holden really like?" It's become a cliché in my life. I can see it coming, and I always begin by saying, "I know, you want to know what William Holden was *really* like." I was too young to remember him in his breakthrough performances in *Golden Boy* and *Our Town*. I thought of him as an actor in somewhat minor, light-comedy roles and therefore had never been captivated by him on-screen.

The first day I visited the set and met him, I was greeted by a tall, slender, very handsome thirty-year-old man. The day he shot the pool scene with Gloria Swanson, I saw his beautiful architecture as well. He had a long, toned torso with wonderfully shaped legs, and I loved his hands, which were very elegant and beautifully shaped. But I think it was his voice that attracted me the most. It was a seductive baritone that anyone who ever heard it never forgot.

At first, he treated me with polite and mild interest mixed with a certain amount of skepticism—I was completely unknown. His real focus was creating a relationship with Billy Wilder because he knew this role was an opportunity that could change his career and his life—and it did.

He seemed a little shaky at times, which I slowly realized was from excessive drinking the night before. As we started to work together, he was becoming much more interested, warm, and even sometimes endearing. I also realized that he was a very talented actor, and given this role he finally revealed his consummate "movie star image" on the magical silver screen.

In *Sunset Boulevard*, who can ever forget the entrance that he makes wearing his white tie and tails with his luxurious Vicuna coat thrown over his shoulders as he arrives at the party scene at Artie Green's (Jack Webb) apartment. The close-up of his beautiful profile remains in my memory to this day.

Please understand that I did not have a crush on Bill. He was married and had children, and it wouldn't have occurred to me to be even mildly flirtatious—just midwestern friendly and appreciative of his patience and kindness in the scenes we did together. But I think it was standard procedure for the leading man to make a play for his leading lady off-screen as well as on.

One night after shooting one of the office scenes, Bill asked me to drop by his dressing room before I left the studio. He ostensibly wanted to go over the next day's shoot. I arrived, and it was obvious he had been waiting for me in the small living room, along with a bucket of ice, vodka, scotch, and an open bottle of very cold, ready white wine. I have already explained how naive I was at this time in my life, but I did realize that I had not been invited to discuss our work but to join him for a drink in a more intimate atmosphere. Perhaps our relationship could take a turn—even if it were just for one evening. I can't remember exactly how I excused myself, but I did it quickly and I hope kindly, but certainly emphatically. He never crossed the line again, and I think we retained a deep affection and regard for each other that lasted through the years.

Male movie stars are a different breed of humans. Very few are graduates from Ivy League universities (Jack Lemmon was an exception, having graduated from Harvard). I don't mean to imply that they are ignorant, but generally they are not interested in academia or science or engineering. But they have an inner incandescence that the camera understands and knows how to exploit. It can never be learned; it is simply there, and it is extremely powerful. I am so grateful to Billy Wilder for casting Bill Holden in *Sunset Boulevard* so that the light inside of Bill would finally be captured on film for the world to see.

Billy Wilder and Charles Brackett were the cowriters and producers of *Sunset Boulevard.* Both men were witty and smart but otherwise complete opposites. Billy was a German Jew and a survivor of World War II in Europe (his mother and grandmother were killed in the Nazi concentration camp Auschwitz), and as a result he had a very special point of view about the world and the people in it that was quite different from that of Charlie, who came from a privileged life and background. I remember that Mr. Brackett (I called Billy "Billy" and Charlie "Mr. Brackett") had graduated from Williams College and Harvard Law School. His father was a New York state senator, banker, and lawyer who traced his American roots back to the Massachusetts Bay Colony in 1629. The best words I would use to describe him are *patrician* and *urbane*. I always enjoyed hearing how he used the language, and I loved his stories about his family. Both producers were very talented, but I think it was their differences that ultimately made them such a good team, as diversity in a partnership can be valuable.

I'm sorry to say that as much as I liked Edith Head, who was head of the wardrobe department, she simply could not dress me for this role. Billy and I agreed that everything she chose was wrong. Billy's solution was for me to wear my own clothes. I didn't have a great wardrobe at the time and did not know where to shop, so I put together what I had as best I could. Billy seemed to like what I wore when I visited the set before my first scene was shot. In the famous party scene where Bill is in white tie looking gorgeous, I am sitting on the edge of the bathtub in one of my better dresses. It was a dark-green, off-the-shoulder wool gown with a large oval gold and ivory cameo pin that my father had given me for my birthday several years earlier. My daughter Jenny still has that pin somewhere in her jewelry drawer.

I was very nervous the first day I shot the scene in the office with Bill and Fred Clark (as Sheldrake, the film producer). Billy seemed to be pleased; however, I wish I could go back and do it again. By the time we shot the scene on the back lot, I was much more comfortable and more innovative. I picked up an apple on the set and used it as a prop as Bill and I walked along and talked. It seemed like such a natural thing to do, and Billy liked it, too.

That scene is beautifully written and well remembered. In part of the dialogue, Joe Gillis (Bill) asks Betty Schaeffer about her background and personal life. She explains that she came from a motion-picture family; her father was a grip, and her mother a seamstress, both working on the lot. This was actually a description of the life and family of Billy's wife, Audrey Wilder. When as Betty I confess that I wanted to be an actress and had my nose fixed to accommodate the camera, Bill looks at my profile and says, "Nice job." I cannot tell you how many letters I received asking me, "Who fixed your nose? What is the doctor's name?" Was it really that believable? I also received a letter from a friend only a few years ago that said, "You still smell like freshly laundered linen handkerchiefs." This line, which Bill said so tenderly, is quite wonderful and again describes the character that Billy had in mind. (My nickname at the University of Wisconsin was "Wholesome Olson.")

I never had a scene with Gloria Swanson, but we had a telephone conversation, and she came to the set to read the off-stage lines, as I did for her. The thing I remember so vividly about Gloria was not only her friendliness and welcoming attitude but also her excitement and belief in this film. Of all the people involved in *Sunset Boulevard*, Gloria knew that this film could be a great one, and it was an opportunity for her never to be forgotten again. Most people don't realize that at this time she was only in her early fifties and still very beautiful. But she was more than willing to be photographed harshly, knowing that it was important for Norma Desmond to be "over the hill."

Erich von Stroheim came with a history of being one of the great film-makers of the past. He was very polite but somewhat distant. He would arrive on the set dressed in his butler's costume and white gloves. His greeting was always the same: he would nod and in a most formal way look at me and say, "Good morning, Miss Olson." I would answer, "Good morning, Mr. von Stroheim." He positioned his chair with his name on the back as close to the camera as he could get. He watched Billy's direction with such focus and attention that I wondered if it made Billy uncomfortable.

Many people talk about the love scene on the balcony on the Paramount lot. In fact, it won a contest as one of the greatest love scenes ever filmed. This is the moment that Joe and Betty recognize their passionate interest in each other and embrace. I must confess, I was scared to death. The scene was actually played on a balcony, with the camera on a dolly two stories high, and we shot the entire scene at night.

When I arrived at the studio and walked to the balcony, I realized there was a party going on! Tables had been set up on the street directly below the balcony for the cast and the crew and various guests. Audrey Wilder was there; Bill Holden's wife, Ardis, was there; Charlie Brackett with his entourage; and God knows how many others. And they were there to watch our love scene!

We started to rehearse and were very constrained as to how we moved toward each other for the benefit of the camera. The entire scene was to be filmed in one shot. During the rehearsal, Billy would get to the point of the embrace and just say, "And at this point, Bill, just take Nancy in your arms and kiss her." He also made it clear that he was going to fade out this scene with the embrace and was unsure as to how he would cut the film, so it was particularly important for us not to break from each other until he said, "Cut!" He said it might seem too long, but it was very important not to stop kissing! Good God, I thought!

Billy said, "Action!" and we started the scene. There was absolute silence from our audience. The moment came when Bill speaks the line, "What happened?," and I answer, "You did." And he takes me in his arms, and we kiss and we kiss and we kiss and we kiss until . . . finally a female voice from the entourage below screamed, "Cut, God damn it, cut!" It was Mrs. Holden.

About a quarter of the way through shooting, our film created a buzz on the lot. Every day at six o'clock, the entire studio—executives, directors, technical people—attended the dailies in a small theater. There could be as many as fifteen movies being filmed at the same time, and every bit of film shot one day was shown on the following evening. The people involved in their respective projects would show up to see how their work looked and leave immediately after their dailies were shown. But once *Sunset Boulevard* began to evolve on the screen, everyone stayed to watch its dailies, apparently totally mesmerized—in fact, they had to bring in extra seats!

The strong feelings this film evoked from people in the industry demonstrates how powerful it was. It is so rare when a story hits exactly the right notes and touches on all the right nerve centers. There was a famous moment after a small private screening that Louis B. Mayer attended. Mayer stood up and walked over to Billy and shouted, "How could you do this to us?!" Billy turned to him and said, "Go fuck yourself!," and walked out.

This film tells the brutal truth about a part of the motion-picture business and how it can ruin one's life. To be exploited for other people's profit can be both painful and humiliating. Even though one is paid, sometimes a great deal, and receives tremendous ego-fulfilling rewards, to be portrayed as larger than life is distorting and destroys the delicate balance between reality and fantasy.

Creating stars sold tickets. The studios were constantly hyping the qualities that created an irresistible commodity. This was particularly possible when someone had not only all the tangible and obvious assets (beauty, personality, etc.) but also the most important quality of all, vulnerability. A perfect example was Marilyn Monroe. We have to acknowledge that people who are willing and cooperative about making themselves accessible to exploitation are both accessories to the crime as well as victims. There are no easy answers except in perhaps those rare especially talented artists like Meryl Streep, who offers her extraordinary range of talents but does not sell them with all the hype. She is not a "movie star" but a brilliant character actress.

Empowering vulnerable people in the movie industry is as irresponsible and contemptuous as our current political parties empowering ignorant and angry citizens.

Sunset Boulevard had a strong impact on me, and perhaps that is why I still have the script, the only one I have ever kept. When you read it today, you realize the particular art form that making motion pictures is. It's not just the dialogue of *Sunset Boulevard*, which is brilliant enough, but it's the way Billy used images to tell the story. Everything you see on the screen is described in the script. The rats feeding on some garbage at the bottom of the empty pool; the light coming from the movie from her past that Norma and Joe watch as she holds her cigarette in a unique apparatus—all of that is described in detail in the script, including the smoke from the cigarette getting into Bill's eyes.

My first husband, Alan Jay Lerner, said to me once that no one goes to a bookstore to buy a motion-picture script, but they do buy the great plays, which are considered part of literature. That is because you are viewing a play through the proscenium arch, and the dialogue propels the story. In a movie, however, a close-up of an actor with one tear rolling down his cheek tells it all. When *Sunset Boulevard* was made into a musical by Andrew Lloyd Webber in 1993, Billy Wilder made a famous comment, "It's like my movie in a permanent long shot."

A few years before Billy died, he was honored by the Directors Guild of America, and after the ceremony they were going to show a fresh print of *Sunset Boulevard*, so the organizers asked me to speak as I was the only member of the cast still alive. I thought a lot about what I was going to say. I started to think about what establishes a work to be considered a "work of art." It occurred to me that one of the ingredients is when the language becomes part of the culture. How many times have you heard "I'm ready for my close-up, Mr. DeMille" or "I am big; it's the pictures that got small"? Even the lines from the balcony scene between Bill and me are still quoted. I will say to someone telling me a story, "What happened?," and they will slyly answer, "You did."

I also realized that the story of the characters in *Sunset Boulevard* and the tragedy for them all was that they were opportunists—even Betty Schaeffer, who wanted to be a writer and used Joe Gillis to help her, but then found herself in love with a broken and desperate man who had sold his soul for his survival, and Norma Desmond, who wanted to be "the greatest star of them all" and allowed herself to be exploited by an industry that casually threw her away when it was done with her.

I have often wondered if I was not deeply affected by the truth of this story. I knew even then that I did not want to be a movie star who would someday be thrown away.

For a film to be categorized as one of the greatest films ever made is so extraordinary and demands some kind of an explanation. Why does this film appear regularly on Turner Classic Movies or return to the big screen for special viewing every decade or so? Why has the gay community identified with it so passionately? Why does everyone, every generation, both men and women, respond to it so intensely even in the twenty-first century?

What distinguishes an attempt to create a work of art from the actual creation of a true work of art that everyone understands? Everything that has been written, painted, or composed was to share an understanding of a unique view of life, to interpret and explore it—to expose it, to force us to face it—and perhaps ultimately to embrace it. In other words, a great work of art reveals the truth.

Motion pictures are a unique form of art. They tell a story with the camera. The director guides the actors, the set designers, the costume designers, the music composer, and the editor. The director is at the center, keeping all the pieces together. Above all, the motion pictures that survive through time are those that tell a compelling truth. *Sunset Boulevard* is one of those films, and it is particularly relevant to today's culture. We are living and breathing in an environment where the bottom-line goal is the pursuit of profit—creating commodities to sell. In today's culture, Donald Trump, Republicans, Fox News distort and hide the truth in their pursuit of power, profit, and gain, yet, despite their attempts, the truth is never destroyed. It is like a piece of gold in the sun.

When *Sunset Boulevard* was completed, it took everyone's breath away. It was deemed a masterpiece even then; we all were nominated for Academy Awards, and even though none of us won, we knew we were going to be part of history. Bill and I became the new "couple" on-screen. We were immediately cast in three more pictures—*Union Station, Submarine Command,* and *Force of Arms.*

An interesting footnote regarding *Sunset Boulevard* and how it tied together many parts of my life: I didn't know it at the time, of course, but my future brother-in-law, Jay Livingston, and his songwriting partner, Ray Evans, appeared in the film. They are seen seated at the piano at Artie Green's New Year's Eve party, performing and singing one of their Academy Award–winning songs, "Buttons and Bows."

II

Hollywood

My adolescent dreams seemed to be coming true. But, after a while, as the gates closed behind me at seven o'clock each morning, I began to feel a creeping dissatisfaction. My twelve-hour days consisted of getting my hair and makeup done, getting fitted for wardrobe, rehearsing, shooting, and endless waiting. I became alarmed at the quality or the lack of it in my life. I had no time to meet young men, nor did I know anyone I wished to spend time with. My movie career had created an awkward distance between my college friends and me, and soon I found the only fun I had was that of a voyeur at Charlie and Jean Feldman's extraordinary and legendary Hollywood parties.

Charlie Feldman was a brilliant and enigmatic man. An agent (his clients at Famous Artists included Gary Cooper, Marlene Dietrich, Preston Sturges, Lauren Bacall, and Howard Hawks) as well as a producer (*To Have and Have Not, Red River*), he was the first in the industry to "package" films, bringing the property, writer, producer, stars, and director in one unit to sell to the studios. That process took individual decision-making and leverage away from the movie moguls and perhaps erased the creative, thoughtful process of putting various talents together. He also arranged for the biggest stars, who were at that time paid only weekly salaries, to own their own films, shielding them from the whims and dictatorship of the studio executives. Other agents such as Jules Stein and Lew Wasserman followed in Charlie's footsteps, creating a different Hollywood and losing something valuable as a result.

My first invitation to the Feldman home came one afternoon in the form of a phone call from Charlie's secretary for a very small dinner on the coming Saturday night. Because I had never even met Mr. Feldman, I hesitated. But, after all, I was a client of Famous Artists, and he was head of the agency, so it was appropriate, wasn't it? I explained all of this to a very impatient secretary, who only wanted to be sure I would be there at 7:00 p.m.

My first evening at 2000 Coldwater Canyon may not have been the most enjoyable I ever had there, but I only wish I could remember what happened to me last week as well as I remember every moment of that night.

I arrived at seven o'clock in a black, fitted suit with a burgundy-velvet, ruffled collar (with perfectly matching lipstick), white kid gloves, and single-pearl earrings. The house was surprisingly small and set quite close to the street. There were no endless acres of lawn or a tennis court or a guest cottage or even a pool house. I saw a simple, rambling, one-story building covered with ivy and vines and surrounded by flower-filled terra cotta pots. One would never guess that behind those walls was a treasure trove of famous secrets and a meeting place of the most powerful, glamorous, talented, and beautiful people in the world.

I was met at the front door by a maid, who ushered me through the foyer, my high-heeled pumps clicking behind her on the shiny red-tile floor. I noticed paintings on the walls, with elaborate frames and little lights hanging over them. They reminded me of paintings I had seen in museums and art books.

The maid left me at the entrance of a sitting room. There was a grand piano on the right displaying an array of framed pictures, their faces turned away from me. The tile floor continued into the room and was covered with muted, softly colored oriental rugs. One wall had a row of wood-encased windows and French doors that opened onto a brick-paved, plant-filled courtyard. There were more of those wonderful paintings with the little lights hanging over them.

Dazzled, I stood there like a person blinking under bright lights after a long time in the dark. I had only a few seconds to gain my equilibrium before I quickly realized I was not alone. There was a woman sitting on the far sofa, with two tiny white poodles beside her. I couldn't see her face; she was looking down at a needlepoint canvas, her fingers intensely jabbing a needle in and out. The dogs saw me first and started to bark. She commanded them to stop and me to come in and sit down. She said she was expecting me and was about to introduce herself when I interrupted and said that wasn't necessary. I knew who she was. She was Joan Crawford.

Mr. Feldman mercifully appeared in the doorway. As a child, I had been encouraged to stand when an adult entered the room. Thank God I wasn't taught to curtsy as well because I found myself leaping to my feet and shyly extending my hand. He smiled warmly, helping me relax a bit, and appraised me with a quick professional glance. I felt like I was being auditioned for a play, and I wondered if he thought I was right for the part. Behind him was another man. He was much younger than Mr. Feldman, taller and extremely thin. He walked in with a slight shuffle and an amused, somewhat detached air. His name was Jack, and he sat beside me. There was something elusively interesting and different about him. I didn't find him particularly handsome or charming but again sensed that I was being auditioned by him. I decided to make the best of a rather awkward situation.

I asked Jack where he came from. It had to be somewhere in the East because he had a distinct accent. He said that he was from Massachusetts, and I explained that I was from Wisconsin and was longing to visit Massachusetts someday. When it was revealed that he was a congressman, I became very excited. Could he be a Democrat by any chance? What a coincidence! He was, and so was I! The maid came to say there was a phone call from England for Mr. Kennedy and that dinner was served. Jack said that he would be brief and would join us in the dining room.

Miss Crawford dominated the dinner conversation with bitter tales of romance and broken love affairs. She ended her tirade with a warning to me to never trust men. As I pleaded with her not to feel that way, I caught the two men smiling at each other and raising their eyebrows to the ceiling.

The plan was that after dinner we would drive to the Beverly Wilshire Hotel to see Kay Thompson and the William Brothers. I wanted to use the powder room before we left and was directed down the bedroom corridor to a bath connected to a guest room. On the way back, I started to put on my white kid gloves when an arm reached out from one of the bedroom doors, seized me, and pulled me into the dark and a suffocating embrace. Panic, confusion, humiliation, and a sickening nausea swept over me. Who was doing this to me? Good God! It was Mr. Kennedy. Fear and anger filled me with the needed strength to free myself, retrieve my lost glove, and remind him that we had barely met.

With my heart pounding, I went back to the foyer and frantically wondered what to do. Should I leave, or should I stay and take Mr. Kennedy to the Beverly Wilshire as planned, while Mr. Feldman and Miss Crawford went in Mr. Feldman's car? I decided to see the evening through and drive the congressman to the hotel . . . in silence.

You would think that this incredible evening would have ended after Kay Thompson's performance. But no. Miss Crawford insisted that we all stop at her house for a drink. She lived in Brentwood, which was on the way home for me as I was living with my aunt and uncle in the Pacific Palisades, so Jack climbed into my car again, and we followed Mr. Feldman and Miss Crawford to Bristol Road . . . in silence.

Joan Crawford had a kind of furious energy that assaulted the air around her as she moved through it. Her house was still and sad and seemed to wince as she turned on the lights. Perhaps the most traumatic moment of the entire evening was when she shoved us up the stairs and into the bedrooms of her four children. They must have been very young because I remember they all were sleeping in cribs, although one girl seemed curiously too big for hers. Bright lights, their mother's voice, strangers moving about their beds—all startled and frightened them. They whimpered through her insistence that they tell "Uncle Charles" that they loved him. Jack and I looked at each other helplessly and begged her to let the children go back to sleep.

I said goodnight to all of them, ran down the gravel driveway to my car, and drove home as fast as I could.

I think it cost fifteen cents to call the Palisades from the airport. I was surprised the first time Jack called, but the next time I heard the clicking of nickels, I knew that it was probably him. Both times he said that he had just arrived in Los Angeles and asked if I would like to go to the movies. It didn't matter how bored I was or how eager I was to get out of my aunt and uncle's house, the thought of the physical ingenuity and brute force it would take to defend myself wasn't worth it. Virgins have amazing strength, but Jack was obviously an experienced and formidable opponent.

I did, however, accept the next invitation to attend a party at Charlie Feldman's, but only after I was reassured that it was a large black-tie dinner for at least seventy people. I would be Jack's date for the evening, but I would meet him there and leave him there. I wasn't thrilled at the thought of being seated with him, but I wanted to attend the party and thought I could handle things surrounded by so many people.

When I arrived, I asked the butler if there was a more central powder room. I didn't want to be trapped again while walking down the bedroom halls. "Yes, it is off the foyer," he said. I felt much safer and joined the guests around the pool for cocktails.

It was late summer, twilight, and people were silhouetted against the darkening sky and green garden, their profiles highlighted by flickering candles in crystal vases—beautiful, chiseled, elegant profiles. Gary Cooper standing tall and straight, so handsome, so beguiling with his sweet friendly smile. Cary Grant a little vague, remote, but utterly charming. Humphrey Bogart, a mischievous, up-to-no-good grin on his face, looking for the joke, fun, and laughter. I remember a deep, rough, coughing kind of laughter: Kirk Douglas, sharp-featured, exuding stud energy, intelligence, and determination. James Stewart, the opposite of Kirk, somewhat homespun, simple, nice.

The women glowed in their chiffon, silk, and organdy dresses—spectacular beauties, lit up and carefully accented with pearls, diamonds, and brilliantly colored precious gems. Rocky Cooper and Gloria Stewart were obviously products of eastern boarding schools, with incredible style, and both were great hostesses. Betty Bogart (Lauren Bacall) was so incredibly chic and smart, and Anne Douglas was the only woman in the entire world who could possibly be married to Kirk. But the most beautiful woman I ever saw, other than a young Elizabeth Taylor, was Gene Tierney, so impeccably dressed by her husband, Oleg Cassini.

Years later Sam Goldwyn Jr. still blushed when we reminisced about that evening. As he stood on the opposite side of the pool from me, engaged in an animated conversation, holding his drink in his right hand, gesturing with his left, he took one tiny fatal step backward and pirouetted himself into the deep end of the pool. He came to the surface, clutching his glass, sputtering chlorinated apologies, and swam with great dignity—in his tuxedo—to the steps of the shallow end. Leaving a trail of wet, soggy footsteps, he went home to change.

Jack Kennedy was the quintessence of cool. I enjoyed talking to him that night; I loved speculating about politics. Although I persisted, he barely tolerated our conversations. Who was I to have an interesting or worthwhile opinion? I was, after all, some little doctor's daughter from the Midwest, an actress under contract to a studio, a . . . "female." I don't mean that he wasn't interested in us (women), but it was rather like the overwhelming craving for chocolate and just as emotionless. Once he had that rich piece of chocolate fudge, he could then go on with the real craving in his life, which was an incredible ambition deftly pursued and attained by a unique and visceral intelligence. That combination, along with a sense of this country and where we should be in the world, was what I always thought was his core and understanding of his destiny.

Perhaps because he was so outrageously rude at our first meeting, I challenged him with the kind of conversation that was not completely acceptable between a young man and a young woman at that time. It was barely polite, but I couldn't help myself. I told him that I knew what he was thinking and where he wanted to land. I said quite fearlessly, "I know what you're after! You, Jack Kennedy—you want to be president someday!" He was not happy with this conversation, but I felt he was fair game. I can only assume that several years later when our mutual friend Chuck Spalding mentioned my name to Jack, Jack's response was, "You always did like strange girls!"

Charlie and Jean Feldman were divorced but remained bonded all their life; their friendship was deep and involved. They shared the house, six months a year for each, and both were incredible hosts. I was fortunate to be friends with both. Charlie was generous and kind to me always, and I will never forget how impressed I was with Jean's style, intelligence, independence, and toughness. The photographs on the piano were of Greta Garbo, Darryl Zanuck, Carole Lombard, and the classically beautiful Jean with one of her best friends, Cole Porter. Many of these photos were taken by Jean.

I would like to tell one more story, a chilling one, before I close the door of 2000 Coldwater Canyon. Charlie was an orphan and lived in an orphanage for the first six years of his life. One day a wealthy man named Feldman came to the home to adopt a son. He picked five boys and lined them up against the wall. He then walked to the opposite side of the room, opened his arms, and announced that the first boy to reach him would be his son. I was never able to look at Charlie without seeing a little boy race across the room, knowing that his survival depended on getting there first.

12

Marilyn Monroe

Perhaps this is the place for me to describe Marilyn Monroe, which is a daunting challenge almost impossible to execute.

One evening I was invited to a small cocktail gathering at 20th Century-Fox with some producers and a group of young up-and-coming actors being groomed for screen stardom. I was there for about twenty minutes when I noticed everyone turning and watching a young woman making a somewhat awkward and yet utterly fascinating entrance. She was blond and fair and had a distinctively pretty face as well as a body that highlighted a more-than-ample bosom and an extremely provocative round bottom. Who was she? What was she? What was there about her that was so riveting? It seemed clear to me that she was terrified, even knowing that she was making an incredible, if somewhat bizarre, impact. But her voice and what she said made the greatest impression on me. She talked like a little baby—cooing, beguiling, pleading, flirting, hanging onto the arm of the person she was talking to (always male, of course). If I had closed my eyes, I would have assumed that this was a child of maybe six or seven years old talking to her beloved uncle.

I was always intrigued with her as her career developed and blossomed into superstardom. I never forgot her vulnerability and wondered what would become of her.

The next time I saw her was years later at a large party at the home of Paula and Lee Strasberg on the Santa Monica beach. Marilyn wanted to become a more serious actress and had been working with Lee Strasberg, who was the leading drama coach of that time. She was now married to Arthur Miller, the renowned American playwright, a union I could never quite understand. When she saw me, she recognized me and, holding onto her husband's arm, cooed, "Daddy, it's Nancy Olson! You remember her from *Sunset Boulevard.*" If I had closed my eyes and only listened to her voice, I would have said that a young girl of about eleven or twelve was trying to please her father with a wonderful discovery for him. Miller was not impressed or interested.

Marilyn was the quintessential result of a thousand pieces pasted together to create a super "movie star." Each piece was put in place by the magicians of the industry: the publicity manipulators feeding the hungry press; the producers offering opportunities to appear on-screen after sexual favors were delivered; the makeup artists; the light and camera crews, lighting and filming her at just the right angle; the directors who understood how to use her; the professional actors giving her the space to deliver what she uniquely could; and, most of all, the history of poverty, abuse, lack of love and trust and family and education, all of which created a vulnerability and an insatiable need for the spotlight at any cost.

I think of Marilyn with great sadness—a tragic figure who haunts us all.

13

Courtship

Although my career was continuing to be more than I could have dreamed possible, my personal life was suffering. Little did I know that it was about to take a turn and put me on a trajectory of joy, adventure, romance, and unimaginable suffering; in other words, I was going to start living my true life.

In 1949, Alan Jay Lerner was at the Hotel Bel-Air writing the screenplay for *An American in Paris* to be filmed at MGM, produced by the legendary Arthur Freed and directed by the equally legendary Vincente Minnelli.

One morning the *Los Angeles Times* Hollywood columnist Hedda Hopper wrote an article about me, including a picture. She wrote about how excited Paramount was about their new up-and-coming young actress—a UCLA undergraduate and the daughter of a prominent doctor from the Midwest. She claimed that I was not the typical starlet on the lot. Alan read this and called a mutual friend of ours, Alain Bernheim, a successful literary agent at Famous Artists, and asked him if it was possible to introduce us.

I couldn't imagine why Alain Bernheim, whom I did not know that well, insisted that I have a home-cooked dinner at his mother's apartment, but it was evident when I arrived that I had been invited to meet a somewhat delicate-looking man, not quite as tall as I was in my high-heeled shoes. He greeted me rather formally, observing everything carefully from behind oval glasses with a slightly self-conscious gaze. I was fascinated with the twirling of his cigarette inward between his thumb and forefinger, which he managed to do without burning the palm of his hand. I liked his face. Although it was not conventionally handsome, it had a kind of sensitive attractiveness, acute vulnerability, and enormous seductiveness. But who was he?

He said he was a writer, and someone mentioned *Brigadoon*. My mother had written to me from Milwaukee that a production of a recent musical had played there and that it was truly the work of a poet and a genius—Could this man be that person?

Courtship is an art, and Alan was its master. Indeed, nothing in this entire world delighted him more or filled him with such exquisite pleasure as wooing. It was a game, a dance, a sport, a vocation, an avocation—every nuance of it thrilled him. It invaded and shaped his work. It disrupted and destroyed much of his life, but nothing stopped him. The winning in this pursuit took precedence over everything else. He was compelled to recapture the good feeling it generated, and it was usually not complete until there was a wedding.

Alan's choreography for our courtship was perfection. After Alain Bernheim's little dinner, three or four days elapsed before he called. I had been waiting long enough to wonder if he ever would. His voice was low and warm. He said he was working very hard in his suite at the Hotel Bel-Air. Facing a blank piece of paper every day was difficult, and being alone and away from home was depressing. Could I possibly rescue him and have dinner one night that week?

I was still living with my aunt Ethel and uncle Dutch in the Pacific Palisades and casually mentioned to them that I would not be home for dinner on Tuesday. The only unusual thing they noticed was the time it took me to get dressed that evening. The doorbell rang—I heard voices and with my cheeks faintly flushed made my entrance (I was very good at that).

Alan stood up as I entered the room. I had forgotten just how short he really was, but I was prepared. I had purchased a new pair of shoes with a very little heel for just this moment. He stood as tall and straight as he could, pushing his ribcage up and out. Our eyes met at exactly the same latitude. He was wearing a fitted, navy-blue pin-striped suit with a pale-gray silk tie; it had a faintly European flavor, which vaguely disappointed me. I would have preferred him in more understated Ivy League attire, but at least he wasn't wearing elevator shoes. That pleased me. It somehow made him more trustworthy.

We said our goodbyes and went out the door to his car. I was not prepared for the long limousine with a chauffer holding open the door. Alan explained that he had never learned how to drive, and there was no other way to pick me up.

We had a quiet dinner in a little Italian restaurant somewhere on Melrose Avenue. I was starving, but I didn't eat very much. I was too fascinated with this intriguing man who knew so much more about the world than I did. And just imagine—I could even hum the songs that he had written lyrics for. Beautiful words. Poetry. That was it! He was a poet. The expression in his eyes behind those glasses—tender and crushed by life—the sweetness in his voice—the delicacy in his choice of words—oh, God, so charming.

I kept asking questions.

"Why don't you drive?"

"I have lived in New York City all my life and have always had a car and driver."

"Where did you go to school?"

"I went to school in England as a boy, then to Choate and Harvard."

"When did you start to write?"

"I have written all my life, but it became serious at the Hasty Pudding Club at Harvard."

"How did you meet Frederick Loewe and Kurt Weill?"

"I met Fritz at the Lambs Club, and Maxwell Anderson introduced me to Kurt and Lania. We all live in Rockland County, very near each other."

I swallowed. Should I mention how much I admired Maxwell Anderson's work and the scenes from his plays that I had done at UCLA? I decided against it.

"What are you writing now?"

"A film called *An American in Paris*. The Gershwin family has given me the catalog of Ira and George's songs to choose from, and I am writing an original motion-picture script for them."

I swallowed again. Should I tell him that I was in love with everything that the Gershwins had written and that I played all of their songs on the piano? I decided he wouldn't be interested.

"Tell me about your family—your parents."

"They were originally from Germany, of course. My father and my uncles founded the Lerner Shops."

"Have you ever wanted to get married?"

"No. But I have been married twice to the wrong people for the wrong reasons, and I have a child, Susan."

For me, everything stopped at that moment. There was danger in the air. "Twice?" I said weakly, reminding myself not to mention this part to my mother.

I was subdued. I looked down and noticed his hands. They were small and well formed. He wore a gold ring on the little finger of his right hand, the round, flat top engraved with his initials. But his nails—they were almost nonexistent. He reached for my hands and said that he had been admiring them all evening. He loved long, slender fingers with well-groomed nails. He,

56

sadly, had a terrible affliction—he bit his own unmercifully, especially when he was working so hard and when his life was in such an unhappy turmoil.

I had an early appointment the next morning—wardrobe fittings for the film I was about to make with Bing Crosby. I hated to leave, but it was getting late.

He sat in the corner of the long back seat of the limousine, leaving a space between us. He asked about my family, career, dreams—he listened, laughed, frowned, twirling his cigarette between his fingers. He said he wanted to see me again. I told him I would be happy to teach him how to drive. He walked me to the door, smiled, and left. The dance had begun.

14

The Dance

Edith Head was the most famous clothes designer in Hollywood. She was small and trim, impeccably groomed, and well mannered. She never changed her own style, keeping her dark, straight hair short with bangs, and was never seen without her round, tinted glasses. Edith dressed with taste, understatement, and an understanding of her own chic. She was a nice woman, too, and treated me with courtesy and kindness.

Her office and fitting room were filled with framed sketches of the clothes she had made for the stars—Barbara Stanwyck, Betty Hutton, Hedy Lamarr, Marlene Dietrich, Elizabeth Taylor, and Audrey Hepburn. As I walked in that morning, I saw several drawings of me on her desk. Examining them, I did not feel they reflected me or the character I was playing in my film with Bing, *Mr. Music,* but since I didn't have a clear image of who I was in the first place, and since the girl in the script eluded me as well, how could I expect Edith to capture and create the perfect wardrobe?

Much too uncertain to express my views to her and too polite to be critical, I would just have to accept her not-quite-right designs. I might have been more upset, but I had a secret. I was about to have a personal adventure and perhaps might even get to find out who I was through someone else's eyes— someone so sensitive, so smart, so special. I called my aunt to ask if I had received any phone calls.

I returned Alan's call immediately. He was excited. He had solved a problem with the script, and the writing was going well. Could we have dinner tomorrow night to celebrate? After I said yes, there was a pause before he murmured, "Nancy, you obviously are very good for me."

I had now been under contract to Paramount for about a year, had completed the filming of *Sunset Boulevard,* and for the first time began to feel part of the studio life. Although Bing Crosby and I had not been introduced, I observed him many times on the lot—walking along dressing-room row, entering the commissary, visiting the sets he worked on. My impression was always the same. He was crystal cool, surrounded by an entourage of undistinguished cronies who laughed too quickly at his quips, opened doors for him, moved his chair, and walked a pace and a half behind him. Bing kept the distance between them with just a glance from his icy blue eyes.

Making *Mr. Music* was a blend of getting to know a talented and extremely complex man, Bing Crosby, working in an atmosphere of fun and warmth, and starting an exciting new romance in my life. Unfortunately, I was much too young to play opposite Bing, which contributed negatively to the end result. In fact, everyone treated me as if I were a charming child whom they were fascinated with as well as very protective of. Bing surprised me with real warmth—never flirting, only appreciating and teaching. He was an utter pro. I attended some of the recording sessions for the songs in the movie, and he seemed to be so at ease and knew exactly how he wanted each song to be. However, I was not impressed with the songs, but who was I to have such an opinion? But I think I was right. After many years of being exposed to the greatest songs ever written in the twentieth century, my opinion remains the same.

My second date with Alan was at the Hotel Bel-Air. He had a large suite, and we dined in his sitting room. It never occurred to me that he might try to seduce me, and I was right. He was far too clever for that. Of course, he offered to send a car for me, but that made me feel uncomfortable. My parents had ordered a new Ford for me, but the Cadillac they had ordered for themselves came through first, and as they planned to drive my car across country, they decided to drive the Cadillac instead. Can you imagine a very young girl driving around Los Angeles in a brand-new, shiny maroon Cadillac! I definitely looked like a kept woman.

As I was starring in *Mr. Music,* I worked almost every day of a six-day week. Alan and I had an early dinner in his suite several times a week and went to restaurants on Saturday and Sunday, transported in the limousine. There were several days at a time that he completely disappeared. Finally, I had the courage to ask him where he went. He answered me very seriously that he was spending his time in Las Vegas getting a divorce from Marion Bell, his second wife. Apparently, to get a Nevada divorce, he had to be in the state at least one or two days a week of a six-week sequence. This news was depressing, but I pushed it out of my mind and was determined to continue my fairy-tale romance.

People have asked me over the years, "How could you possibly have been so swept away by a man with such an obviously troubled past?" He was certainly gifted but clearly destructive to himself and others. I have asked myself the same question and have learned to forgive both of us. You have to realize that I was twenty-one, with stars in my eyes, and a door was being opened for me to be a part of a world I had always worshipped. My mother's incredible musical talent was handed down to me, and if I do say so myself, I was a very accomplished pianist. I also had an ear. Any song I heard was embedded in my mind to the point where I could go to the piano and play it perfectly, including all the key changes.

15

Lee and Ira Gershwin

As I was growing up, I had an unusual exposure to music—symphonies, opera, musical theater—but nothing prepared me for the introduction to the extraordinary Saturday nights at Ira and Lee Gershwin's home.

The Gershwins lived in the 900 block of Roxbury Drive in Beverly Hills, and when you stepped through the front door, the first thing you saw was a large Modigliani painting of a young girl that took everyone's breath away the first time they saw it. The large living room was superbly decorated, with comfortable sofas and chairs conveniently positioned to face the piano—a Steinway Grand, of course.

Saturday night at the Gershwins' was a ritual meeting place for all the out-of-town writers and composers as well as the regulars. Oscar and Betty Levant were always there, Oscar seated at the piano playing everyone's hits as they entered the room.

When Arthur Schwartz walked in, he shoved Oscar to the end of the bench and began to play his own songs as beautifully as I have ever heard them.

Arthur's songs still haunt me; Howard Dietz wrote the lyrics, some of the most urbane, witty, and special. Sweeping melodies with incredible lyrical visions: "Dancing in the Dark," "I See Your Face before Me," "If There Is Someone Lovelier Than You." Arthur was a very charismatic and sexy man; tall, good-looking, and charming. He was famous for his pursuit of women, which I'm sure was always successful. His wife was charming, but she was an invalid with severe heart disease, which provided him with the excuse to take his sexual pursuits elsewhere. I did not realize at the time that he would be part of Alan's and my life in the future.

Burton Lane was another Saturday-night regular. He and Yip Harburg had a hit on Broadway, *Finian's Rainbow*, which played at the same time as *Brigadoon*; however, it was *Brigadoon* that won the New York Critics Award.

Burton also played the piano superbly—haunting melodies with an under-current of emotional sadness. I admired his talent very much, but I never understood his inner rage, which interfered with his life and work. Burton also came into Alan's and my life at a later time.

Harold Arlen always arrived late but headed for the piano as soon as he did. When I think of composer Harold Arlen, the wizard of *The Wizard of Oz*, I am reminded of the word *melancholy*. There was a sweet sadness, a sense of a great loss, about him. You have never heard "Somewhere over the Rainbow" played as simply and beautifully as when Harold sat at the piano, sometimes with Judy Garland sitting beside him, a drink in her hand, softly singing the lyrics as if they were coming from a far, far away place. Judy was often at the Gershwins' and regularly sat with Oscar singing all the show tunes. Harold also came into our life in a strange and dramatic way, but I'll get to that.

And there was Ira . . . Ira Gershwin, the king of the American song, along with his brother, the genius George. Ira was one of the sweetest, nicest men I have ever known. He was unassuming, extremely cordial, and self-effacing in the most easy, natural way. I remember there was always a cigar between his fingers and real delight in welcoming his guests and listening to their work.

His wife, Lee, on the other hand, was possibly the only truly wicked woman I have ever met. She was the chicest female, with extraordinary taste in clothes and jewelry. Her sophisticated hostessing was impeccable, and her careful assessment of every person in the room was recorded for possible future manipulation. Her fingers were like razor blades, ready to cut and hurt whenever there was an opening. I always wondered where this unyielding sharpness came from.

The story of Lee slowly began to unfold for me as the years that I knew her went by. Apparently, she was in love with George, who couldn't return her feelings, never married, and never had a serious romance. So she married his brother, Ira, the sweet, accommodating man who I am sure never pursued a woman on his own.

One night, years after I knew her, they were showing old family movies at their home. There were scenes of George and Ira and Lee. Lee was quite animated, laughing and warmly interacting with the two brothers, but there was something wrong. She looked different, not just younger, but she had a different face. It was her nose, a larger, prominent nose, which was now tiny and bluntly unreal. Had she done this for George?

If Ira married her, I am sure he loved her just the way she was. This rela-tionship always made me sad. I'm sure that Ira and Lee had separate bedrooms at opposite ends of the house. She was always respectful and loyal and wore the mantle of being Mrs. Ira Gershwin importantly and I think gratefully. It was her only redeeming quality.

These Saturday nights in this magical place, filled with some of the most interesting, talented, complex, and unforgettable people, were for me like an opium den for an addict. It is now somewhat understandable, at least to me, how Alan Lerner created a desire within me to be with him for the rest of my life.

16

The Dance Continues

The space between us in the backseat of the limousine became smaller and smaller, eventually collapsing into a blissful embrace. There was much ecstatic making out, but with the understanding that I was a virgin and would remain that way until the day I was married. Please remember this was 1950. I don't expect this attitude to be accepted by my daughters, son, and grandchildren. One night Alan whispered, "Marry me. Please marry me." I was thrilled to answer, "Yes," and was convinced that I alone could make this man happy, standing by his side as he wrote his masterpieces and being a loving partner in a new, fascinating life. Oh, God! What a fool I was . . .

What I didn't realize was that this man came from an extremely complicated and destructive background and that I was about to be drawn into a relationship that could easily have destroyed me. I was twenty-one, Alan was thirty-one and already married twice. He came from a culture that I was totally unequipped and unprepared for. My parents were not anti-Semitic; however, I came from a very WASPy world and did not really know any Jewish families. The Holocaust was a horror to me but in my mind was only created by the terrible German Nazis. I did not fully realize that the Jewish families that came to America from the worst kind of oppression in Europe were the victims of the cruelest kind of bigotry in this country as well. I had so much more to learn, and as painful as this new marriage turned out to be, I am a far wiser and more educated person than I ever would have been had I not whispered "Yes" to Alan.

After Alan presented me with a beautiful diamond ring, he invited me to join him in New York to meet his mother and visit his home in Rockland County. His mother was long divorced from his father and was remarried to a very sweet, timid man, Alan Lloyd. Her name was Edith, but everyone called her Edie.

Edie Lloyd was barely five feet tall and perhaps close to two hundred pounds (her actual weight was kept a secret). She was obviously well corseted and wore high-heeled, sling-back shoes and dresses that were custom made by a very expert seamstress. Her hair was pale blond, framing a beautiful peachy complexion and soft blue eyes. Her fingers were adorned with extraordinary diamond rings, one of them with a large marquise-shaped stone that was her pride and joy. The brooches and earrings she wore were equally large and spectacular and faintly vintage in design. I think it was her voice that startled me the most: deep and strong, as if coming from a place of certitude that warned the listener not to trespass too closely.

They lived at 480 Park Avenue and were obviously products of what we used to call the "nouveau riche." I remember thinking there was something too calculated about the decor; it was overdone. I was also surprised at how much she wanted to impress me and to make it clear that she was a very important person and prominent member of society. I remember her saying to me, "I know only the best people in New York." I was somewhat shocked at this childish statement, which was antithetical to what I had been taught growing up. There is an old midwestern saying: "Don't toot your own horn!" Edie became part of the mosaic of my new life, and as critical as my first impression of her was, learning the story of her life changed that. As her life began to unfold for me, I became increasingly sympathetic.

My visit to Rockland County and Alan's house on Camphill Road was the beginning of an extraordinary new life. The house was one of the earliest homes built after the Revolutionary War—General "Mad Anthony" Wayne's residence; a letter from General Wayne to General Washington inviting him to visit was framed and prominently displayed over the mantle in the pine-paneled study. The rooms were small and simply decorated; upstairs there was a master bedroom with a working fireplace and slanted roof over the master bed that created a great feeling of intimacy. There were also two small bedrooms with a bath of their own. In addition to the study downstairs, there was a living room with a large Steinway Grand, a dining room that continued the pine paneling from the study, and a large screened-in porch surrounding the back and side of the house. There was also a big kitchen with an adjoining bedroom and bath for the help.

The orchard behind the house had rows of apple trees and a small cottage for a gardener and caretaker. The front of the house had a long sloping lawn with beautiful hundred-year-old trees that led to a swimming pool surrounded by tiles hand-painted by Alan's neighbor, Henry Varnem Poor. Below that there was a tennis court.

Across the road was a newly built structure that had two guestrooms, a connecting bath, and a large studio workroom for Alan. It contained a small Steinway upright piano, a desk with a typewriter, and large comfortable sofas and chairs. Underneath this building was a three-car garage.

I was introduced to Otto and Anna, the couple who cooked, cleaned, and served dinner in a formal European style. Otto also put on his chauffeur's hat and drove Alan everywhere. Although I had grown up in a household that always had a live-in maid and had never made my own bed, I had never lived like this in Milwaukee, Wisconsin.

One of the most interesting events of this visit was the luncheon given by Alan to introduce me to his friends Lania and Kurt Weill. Mr. Weill seemed extremely curious and slightly amused at Alan's new love. Lania, who eventually became one of my best friends, was more honestly interested.

Alan and Kurt had written the musical *Love Life* together, which had the makings of a really important work. Elia Kazan directed the play, Alan wrote the book and lyrics, and Kurt, of course, composed the music. It was a wonderful score, but the book was the problem, as it always was for Alan. One of the particularly lovely songs was a favorite of mine, "Here I'll Stay." After lunch, I asked Kurt if he would play it for me. To my surprise, he said he really didn't enjoy playing the piano. This shocked me! How could he compose such extraordinarily sophisticated and beautiful music if he didn't enjoy playing the piano? Alan said, "Nancy, why don't you play it?" and I, of course, with my youthful exuberance and naïveté said, "I'd love to."

We walked into the living room, where I sat at the piano, my heart beating wildly, and started to play. Alan sat beside me and sang the lyrics. I have joked through the years that I believed he sang those words to tell me he would stay with me . . . forever.

17

Marriage

My parents were moving from Milwaukee to Los Angeles. My father retired from his medical practice at a very early age to please my mother, who wanted to come to this new fascinating place to be with her daughter who was making movies. My father had a national reputation and was immediately asked by the new medical school at UCLA to become a clinical professor there. They bought an acre with a lovely house on it in Brentwood Park, which was eventually inherited by my brother and his family, who continue to live there.

Can you imagine telling my parents when they arrived that I was going to get married and move to New York to live with my new husband? My mother, for all her admiration for Alan Lerner's work, was beside herself with grief at losing me (as well as her fantasies). My parents were not anti-Semitic, although many of their friends were horrified that I was marrying a Jewish man. This was not my parents' major concern; they were more worried about the fact that he had already been married twice and that I was just twenty-one years old. Looking back, I can sympathize with their panic.

We were married one Sunday afternoon in my parents' new house, with my brother, David, my aunt Ethel and uncle Dutch, Alan's mother, Edith, and his stepfather, Alan Lloyd, attending. Fritz Loewe played the Wedding March from *Lohengrin* on our family piano, and the ceremony was conducted by the minister of the Unitarian church that my parents belonged to.

Edith Head had designed my dress, a simple and lovely taffy-colored, knee-length taffeta gown with ecru lace framing my shoulders and appliquéd on the hem. There was a wedding cake, tears from my father, and an expression of grief on my mother's face that I will never forget. We left in time to return to the house that Alan was now renting to listen to our favorite radio program, *Jack Benny*—a prelude to his taking my virginity away forever.

I don't think I could have asked for a more magical destination for our honeymoon. In 1950, Honolulu, Hawaii, was the most exotic place; the scars of World War II were still fresh, but the healing had begun. There was a mixture of handsome naval officers in their crisp, white uniforms, many well-dressed Asian businessmen, the gentle Polynesian population, and just a smattering of tourists from America and the Western world. The stately, pink Royal Hawaiian Hotel dominated Waikiki Beach, with only the small and much older Outrigger some distance away. I was transported with aesthetic pleasure by its foreign elegance; everywhere I looked there was an even more breathtaking display of the most fantastic plants and masses of incredible orchids. Every time I turned a corner, there was something beautiful to behold. The air was soft, warm, caressing, and filled with a delicate perfume. The waves were pristine; the warm water softly washed over you. Every sense was in tune with seduction.

Perhaps it will be obvious to the reader, but it still eludes me why I brought John Hersey's book *The Wall*, the story of the last survivors of the Jewish population in Warsaw, Poland, to read on my honeymoon. Maybe someone simply said, "This is a great book; you must read it!," or maybe I needed to know more of the history and culture that I was being introduced to. I read it and wept.

On the plane to Honolulu, we were surprised to see the composer Harold Arlen and his wife, Anya, whom I had never met. They, too, stayed at the Royal Hawaiian and joined us on the beach for lunch or an occasional dinner in the most fabulous room next to the beach and close to the waves. The two-story glass doors were opened facing the sea—a sensual as well as a culinary delight.

Anya was very beautiful and extremely chic, but there was a deep sadness and despair within her. She seemed as fragile as the most delicate piece of Venetian glass that could shatter at any moment. Harold was so attentive and solicitous but also in his own deep despair. Alan told me that Harold's father was a cantor in a synagogue. When Harold met Anya, a beautiful chorus girl in one of his musicals, he fell deeply in love. However, his extremely Orthodox past became a giant obstacle as his family would never completely accept this gentile girl. Their long courtship and subsequent marriage were a secret for a long time, and he never dared to have children. Anya developed a deep depression and became suicidal many times. Apparently, she had been recently institutionalized and had come to Hawaii to start a new, happier chapter with Harold. I was saddened to learn that Anya was institutionalized again the following year. She never recovered.

The only upsetting incident of this idyllic honeymoon occurred one morning when the phone rang in our room. It was Western Union calling, and they asked Alan whether he was alone. This seemed an odd question, but apparently it was the policy of Western Union at that time to consider someone's privacy before delivering a message of someone's death. The message was from Lania Weill telling Alan that Kurt had suffered a major stroke and was not expected to recover. Alan went out on our balcony and, after carefully closing the louvered doors behind him, began to weep. I did not know what to do to ease his grief except to honor his wish to be alone. We had several somber days in which I encouraged him to tell me all that he valued and remembered about his friend and colleague. I think it helped.

There is one story about Kurt and Lania's life that I will never forget. Alan explained to me that in 1933 Hitler and the Nazis were already persecuting and isolating the Jewish community. Although they were allowed to leave the country, they could take nothing of any value with them; all of their possessions and wealth would automatically be confiscated by the German authorities.

The Weills' ingenuity and bravery amazed me. They carefully began to sell all of their art, jewelry, home furnishings, and real estate, which they sold in exchange for gold bricks. They took their car and their gold to a famous sculptor friend, who removed the car's fenders and melted the gold into exact copies. He attached the gold fenders and repainted the entire vehicle. Kurt and Lania started their journey to the border of Switzerland with nothing more than the clothes on their backs and two passports. The border checkpoint was on a small hill, which presented a challenge because their car was now so heavy. The German guard examined every corner of the car looking for anything of value and, finding nothing, allowed them to leave Germany forever. This story and so many others that Alan shared with me over the years were true gifts that gave me another view of the world.

We came home tanned and happy and looking forward to going to Camphill Farm for our new life—and what a life it was! Burgess Meredith lived next door with his new wife, Kaja (beautiful and at least three decades younger than Burgess). Maxwell Anderson and his wife, Mab, also several decades younger, and Lania Weill were among Alan's closest friends. They were all much older than I, but we became very close. Every Saturday night we played poker, which I became fairly adept at, but I was still no match for Mab and Lania.

The cartoonist Bill Mauldin also lived close by with his wife, Natalie, who was only seven or eight years older than I. We became good friends, both of us having babies at about the same time. Bill, of course, was one of the great poker players, as were the cartoon writer Milton Caniff and his wife, Bunny, also neighbors and friends.

Henry Poor and his wife never played poker but did join us for cocktails and dinner with their very talented daughter, Anne. Anne Poor became one of the leading artists in America and was particularly gifted at capturing children on canvas. When my two daughters were four and six, I asked Anne to paint them. It amazes me that her images reflect exactly who they were and still are to this day. The paintings, now hanging in my living room, are two of my great treasures and give everyone who sees them extraordinary pleasure.

Two of my best friends in the community lived right up the road, Don and Katrina Ettlinger. Katrina was about fifteen years older than I, but she came from the Midwest, which gave us a bond and a mutual understanding about life, values, and the world. Don was one of the most entertaining and delightful people I have ever known; no one could make me laugh as often as he did. I remember sitting on their patio having an early evening cocktail and having so much fun. Long after I left Rockland County, we remained friends, and they played a significant role when I faced the end of my marriage.

Edie and Alan Lloyd visited us often. I will never forget the first weekend they spent with us. I had carefully planned a small dinner with a few of the people they knew in the community and had purchased several new decks of cards to play Edie's favorite game, Canasta. The day before she arrived, she called and asked what I was planning to serve for her dinner party. I explained that we would begin with a jellied consommé, followed by a main course of roast beef and Anna's delicious homemade Yorkshire pudding. Our vegetable would be julienned string beans, followed by the salad course, and the meal would end with Anna's custard in glazed butterscotch sauce. When Edie said, "That's all?," I stammered, "Y-y-yes." "First of all," she said, "you must be sure that there is a dab of sour cream and a teaspoon of caviar on top of the jellied consommé, and it must be served with Anna's homemade cheese sticks—and you cannot have string beans without sautéed almonds, and how could you possibly consider your salad course without a cheese platter?! There must be three cheeses: one mild, one strong, and one soft, preferably goat cheese. And how could you have a custard dessert without the thin pecan cookies that are a specialty of Anna's?!"

I have never forgotten this lesson in menu planning and have felt deeply insecure all my life whenever I have to plan one. I came from a culture of "waste not, want not," but I soon learned that Alan felt that I had failed him as a head of household unless something fell out of the refrigerator door when he opened it. He didn't have an enormous appetite; he just wanted what he wanted when he wanted it, and it had to be there.

18

Frederick Loewe

I am surprised that I have only barely mentioned Frederick "Fritz" Loewe, who dominated so much of Alan's and my life. Alan introduced us shortly before we were married, just in time to ask him to play the piano at our wedding. Fritz was even smaller than Alan and only a year younger than my mother. He was seventeen years older than Alan and had such an amazing history and life story in the early part of the twentieth century coming from Germany to America.

If you look up his biography online, you will learn that he was born in Berlin of Austrian parents, went to a military school from the time he was five, and became an accomplished pianist, even winning the coveted Hollander Medal. His father was a famous singer of operettas, and Fritz played often for him. He came to America in 1925, struggled to survive, and did not meet Alan Lerner until he was well into his forties.

This is what I know about Fritz not only from Alan but from Fritz as well.

Fritz's mother was seventeen when she fell in love with a Jewish operetta star. The couple ran away when she became pregnant and was never truly accepted by her family again. This marriage was unhappy and filled with the turmoil of his father's transgressions. Fritz was put in a military academy at the age of five, where he was beaten and harassed by his classmates, who considered him a "little Jew." He never forgot an incident in which he was forced to drink his own urine. This humiliation created a rage within him that was made bearable only through his love and pursuit of music. Somehow, he managed to become a pianist of considerable accomplishment, and to this day I have never heard anyone who could play as beautifully or move me more than Fritz at the piano.

He talked of near starvation during World War I in Germany, but he was somehow able to make it to America in 1925. He married a woman I never met who was a seamstress making hats at Hattie Carnegie. They struggled through the Depression, with Fritz playing wherever he could. One of his assignments was playing the organ at Radio City Music Hall. He put his mother in a nursing home, and when they called him to say that she had passed away, he replied, "You're only telling me that to make me feel good." He was quite proud of this retort, also telling me how much he hated his mother and wife and how happy he was to be out of both relationships.

Fritz played often at the Lambs Club, which Alan visited frequently after graduating from Harvard. One day Alan asked Fritz if he would be interested in collaborating with him on a musical. Their first effort on Broadway was a review called *What's Up?* It played only about a week and a half, but Brooks Atkinson, critic of the *New York Times,* said in his review, "Although *What's Up?* does not really work, watch for the partnership of these two new writers—they have great promise."

This comment encouraged them to keep going, and they wrote a new musical, *The Day before Spring,* which did not get rave reviews but ran for about nine months and was bought by MGM. The night it opened, they read the reviews at Sardi's, walked over to the Algonquin Hotel, rented a small room with a piano, and began writing *Brigadoon,* which was a tremendous hit, winning the New York Critics Award and establishing Fritz and Alan as genuine Broadway talents.

I always wondered why Alan left Fritz to write a musical with Kurt Weill, but I understand it today. Kurt was a world-famous composer, and it was enormously flattering to Alan to have Kurt's interest in writing a musical together. This was Fritz's first taste of Alan's infidelity, something he vowed he would never forget, and he said he would never work with Alan again. The sad truth is that Fritz could never work with anyone else. He was trapped into waiting for Alan's next call. When Alan had the idea of writing a musical about the California Gold Rush, he called Fritz and suggested that they start creating a new work titled *Paint Your Wagon,* and Fritz, of course, said yes. It was a little easier for Fritz to say yes since *Love Life* had not gotten very good reviews. In fact, I'm sure the invitation thrilled him!

As I look back, it becomes increasingly clear that although Alan had great regard for Fritz's music, he never felt that Fritz was quite good enough. Fritz's first exposure to the theater and music was the operetta, and Alan felt there was something a little dated about his composing. He always thought that he should be writing with Richard Rodgers or a more current, "with it" composer. I don't think Alan ever acknowledged to himself that he was truly a terrible book writer. He would never be a good playwright; his gift was knowing how to highlight the drama with music and songs, and nobody wrote better lyrics.

19

Rockland County

In the spring of 1950, I moved into my new home and settled into my new life with new friends. The honeymoon was still in gear, which added romance and excitement and an incredible sense of adventure. Fritz spent the summer with us writing *Paint Your Wagon*. He was a croquet addict, and at about 5:30 in the afternoon the three of us would take a tall cool drink and play an intensely competitive game of hitting those wooden balls through those small hoops, laughing hysterically at Fritz's frustration at not being able to beat us. All of us had a very special sense of humor, and we all thought that each one of us was extremely amusing. Laughter has seen me through many difficult days, but I remember these days as being joyfully funny and loving. What I didn't realize was that it was about to change. Dark clouds were gathering, and a storm that I was totally unprepared and ill-equipped to deal with was about to descend.

I never wanted to make another movie. It seemed to me to be extremely boring compared to my exciting new life. However, I was not prepared for the reaction to *Sunset Boulevard* when it was released in the fall of 1950. There had not been a reaction like this to a film in a very long time, and I found myself being written about, talked about, and pursued. This attention was compounded by the release of *Mr. Music* with Bing and *Union Station* with Bill Holden. Alan had to go to California to write the movie script for *Brigadoon* and planned to be there for at least three or four months. We rented a house, and the pressure on me to make another film was enormous. Warner Bros. insisted that I make *Force of Arms* with Bill Holden, and I simply did not know how to get out of it. I also discovered that I was pregnant and showed up at the studio at 7:00 a.m. so nauseated that all I wanted to do was find a place to put my head down and go to sleep. I also sensed a diminished interest and attention from my husband, which I did not understand. My mother was thrilled to have me back on the scene and made incredible demands on my time and attention. Michael Curtiz was the director of the film, and all I remember was him screaming at me as I struggled to deliver some kind of a decent performance. In the midst of all this, I was nominated for an Academy Award for my role in *Sunset Boulevard.* Alan and I attended the ceremony knowing that I probably was not going to win, which was the least of my concerns at that time.

20

Plane Crash

I remember having to be in California for some studio publicity. Alan decided to stay in New York to continue working. I stayed with my parents in Los Angeles and returned to New York as quickly as I could. In those days, we flew to New York with a stop in Chicago to refuel.

My father always drove me to the airport, and on this particular morning we commented on the fog rolling in from the ocean. I was not a comfortable flier and felt somewhat anxious about the increasing loss of visibility. When we arrived at the airport, I asked various officials if it was safe to take off in this weather. I even asked the stewardess before I entered the plane. She explained that planes were not landing, but it was perfectly safe to take off as we would be out of the fog in a matter of minutes. I'm sure it was rude, but I couldn't resist asking, "What if something happens to our plane before we get out of the fog, and we suddenly have to land?!!" She rolled her eyes, gently pushed me into the plane, and said, "Please take your seat."

I sat in the window seat of the aisle two rows in front of the center door through which we had entered. I looked around and noticed that Elizabeth Taylor and her new husband, Nicky Hilton, were seated about four rows ahead of me on the other side of the plane. I also noted that the extremely famous director John Ford was seated with one of his favorite actors, Ward Bond, at the front of the plane.

The four engines on this TWA plane were turned on, and we slowly started to move away from the terminal, joining the other planes lined up to take off. I kept looking anxiously out the window to see if I could still see the terminal. It was a dim shadow in the distance.

Finally, it was our turn, and the engines roared as we raced down the runway and started to climb ever so slowly. I kept looking out the window for a patch of blue, which never appeared. As I became more anxious, I suddenly felt the plane shudder. I could barely see the tip of the wing, but it looked as if the outer engine had stopped. At that moment, I heard the voice of the captain telling us that we had just lost an engine. He reassured us that the plane could fly on three engines, but it was important to land as soon as possible. We were going to fly over the ocean to release our fuel and would be landing immediately after.

He had barely finished telling us this when the plane suddenly began to shake again. An engine on the other wing had also stopped. There was an immediate message from the captain stating that there was no time to dump our fuel; we would be making an emergency landing in Long Beach, and everyone should lean forward in their seats and remove all sharp objects from their clothing.

At that point, a third engine was lost. The plane started to shake violently and went into a stall. To prevent it from crashing, the pilot put the nose down to gather speed. I know it sounds ridiculous, but I sat there thinking the headlines were going to read, "Actress Elizabeth Taylor and Director John Ford in Major Plane Crash—with Ward Bond and Nancy Olson!"

Two seconds later we were flying over the airport's fence. It was the first thing I saw that indicated we might be near the ground. This airport did not have a long enough runway to handle our large plane, and the pilot had to fly in very fast so we would not plunge to Earth. We overshot the runway and landed at the far end of the tarmac, breaking through a fence so fast that we hardly felt it shatter apart. The right landing gear and one wing hit the ground and began to break up as we sped across the muddy field. I braced myself for what I thought was going to be the end, but the plane screeched to a halt, the nose barely touching a freeway with traffic stopped in both directions.

Fire trucks and ambulances came screaming through the broken fence on their way to save us; the pilot came out of the cockpit, and we broke into applause, not realizing that we still were in great danger of exploding.

I remember he had light hair and pale-blue eyes and was the color of a bleached sheet; his lips were purple. He shouted, "I need two volunteers at the main door. Everyone use your nearest exit and depart from this plane immediately!"

We were tipped on one wing, and the main door was at least nine or ten feet from the ground. The two volunteers held onto the bottom of the open door and dropped down to the grass. Two members of the crew took each of us, held us under our arms, and released us into the extended arms of the two men below.

It's amazing the courage you can have in an emergency. You could never persuade me to jump ten feet, even from a diving board. However, I didn't think twice and just took a leap into the air, trusting that the two men below me would catch me before I crashed to the ground. They caught me and shouted, "Run!" I started to run as fast as I could through the lumpy field until I realized, "Oh my God, I left my brand-new mink coat on the plane!"

When I turned around, I realized that I had run past everyone; in fact, I was almost close to the broken fence, but the mink coat was my number one concern at this point. The fire engines were spraying the plane, and I raced back to them and pleaded with them not to spray through the door.

I did get my fur coat and my luggage back, and my father returned to the airport to pick me up. Believe it or not, the next morning on the front page of the *Los Angeles Times* was a story about the plane crash and all the celebrities who almost lost their lives. There was a picture of me wearing my fur coat, and my father carrying my bag as we left the airport.

The next evening I got on the train for a three-day trip to New York. It took me several more trips on the train before I realized that I could not waste that much time, and I would have to start flying again.

21

Liza and Me

We returned to Camphill Farm, and in the spring of 1951 Fritz and Alan completed *Paint Your Wagon*. I remember it was my suggestion to cast Olga San Juan in the role of Elisa, the young Hispanic girl. Olga came to Rockland County that summer to hear some of the score, and I sensed a great interest in her from Alan. I truly did not understand any of this. I was getting ready to have my first child, fixing a room for the baby and another for the nurse. We traveled back and forth to New York City as the production came closer. It was hot and humid, and I was getting bigger and bigger. In fact, I was enormous!

The baby was expected to arrive the second week in October, and I was in no condition to join Alan on the out-of-town tryouts that were taking place in Philadelphia. There were problems with the production and mainly with the book, which was no surprise since Alan was the author. The score was lovely, which again was no surprise with Alan and Fritz's magic.

Alan was not focused during our phone calls and not overly interested in how I was doing, which made me extremely anxious and persistent yet determined to avoid facing what could possibly be wrong. My parents were coming to be with me for the birth. This seemed like a good idea, especially since Alan was in Philly dealing with his own challenges. He came back home a few days before the birth but seemed so preoccupied and distant that I had an anxiety attack severe enough to make him run over to the guesthouse to get my father the doctor to come and help me.

It was clear that Alan could not wait to get back to Philadelphia. He pretended to be concerned about me, but something else was driving him in another direction. I understood his concern for the problems that the new musical was facing, but there was something more that I could not identify. He left the next day.

Two days later my father drove me to the Presbyterian Hospital in New York City to have my beautiful daughter, Liza. It was a very difficult birth, and I'm not sure I had the best obstetrician. However, Liza and I survived, and Alan arrived two days later to see us. Again, he seemed strangely removed, but I was determined not to panic.

I took the baby home, and after my parents felt that I was securely settled and had a very good professional nurse helping me, they went back to California.

Alan did not return home until the company came back to New York for the opening of *Paint Your Wagon*. Although we talked on the phone every day, it was a very anxious time for me. Partly because of my youth, my figure returned to its normal slender self in about two weeks, and my energy returned as well. I was ready to renew a happy family schedule, but when I look back, I realize how truly naive and stupid I was. I knew that something was different about my husband. His lack of attention and interest in the baby alarmed me, but I refused to acknowledge that anything was irreparably wrong.

We arranged to stay in a suite at the Plaza Hotel during the week of the opening, with parties and a hopeful celebration to look forward to. After the opening-night performance, we stopped in Sardi's long enough to read the not-very-good reviews, and I remember Olga's husband, the actor Edmond O'Brien, grabbed me and said, "You and I are in trouble." I didn't stop to continue the conversation but left with a sinking feeling. I was confused and extremely frightened. I remember returning to the country and taking Liza in my arms, weeping, and whispering, "Liza, darling, we are in trouble."

It is hard for me to write about this period in my life. There are things that I still do not totally understand. Alan suggested that I go to a psychiatrist and had his psychologist recommend someone. Dr. Frank was a very compassionate man, and although I didn't make any progress in solving my inner problems, he saw me through that difficult period. What remains mysterious to me to this day is why Alan was determined to continue our marriage.

In fact, after our separation and divorce, I was told the entire story of Olga and Alan's romance, and yet Alan came back to me with a renewed commitment to our relationship. I asked Dr. Frank if he knew the history of Alan's affair with Olga, and he replied that he did. I was amazed and demanded to know why he hadn't shared this with me. He very quietly and with a great deal of certainty said that Alan's doctor had told him that Alan wanted the marriage to continue. I am sorry that I did not challenge him as to why three men decided what my life should be without consulting me.

It was not easy for me to pick up the pieces of my shattered marriage, but I somehow prevailed, and Alan seemed determined to make it work. At this time, he was contracted by MGM to write a screenplay for *Green Mansions,* so we again rented a house in California.

22

John Wayne

One morning I received a phone call from my agent, who said that John Wayne was making an independent film for his new company and was interested in my being his leading lady. He also mentioned that they were planning to shoot the film in Hawaii. I was intrigued. I had never met John Wayne, and although I understood he was an icon in the industry and had a presence on the screen that was much larger than life, there was something a little mysterious about him. I remember dressing very carefully for my interview with Mr. Wayne. I wore a pale-gray linen suit with pearls around my neck and a red, wide-brimmed hat set at a very provocative angle. John was extremely gracious and focused and seemed amused and fascinated with me as well as my hat! He ended the interview almost beseeching me to "please, please" make this film with him.

I did not read the script that carefully but ascertained enough to know that I should never do this film. It was extremely political, with John Wayne's character pursuing the evil communists in the Polynesian world. However, it was John Wayne, Hawaii, and a welcome break from spending every day with Alan, and I was certain that no one would ever see the movie or take it seriously anyway. It would open somewhere in the suburbs and be gone in a matter of weeks, and I, in the meantime, would have a most interesting experience.

It was a fabulous experience! And the film did indeed open in the suburbs with no one paying any attention. What I didn't realize was that this film would be played over and over and over again on the television late shows. All my life someone will remind me that they saw me in *Big Jim McLain*.

Hawaii was still an intoxicating place but beginning to change dramatically. The Royal Hawaiian no longer dominated Waikiki Beach. In fact, the producers arranged for me to stay at one of the brand-new hotels, the Surfer. The beach was now crowded with tourists, and the magic that I had felt just three years earlier was not the same. But I came to this place with an entirely different agenda; it was work, and I wanted to discover who this towering movie star really was. My dreams were not as pristine as they used to be, but my curiosity and hunger to understand what the world and people and life were all about remained alive as ever.

John Wayne was a large man, with broad shoulders, slender hips, and long legs; his head was a sculptor's dream. He took being a movie star and actor very seriously. He was completely professional and knew what he was doing in front of that camera at every moment. He was a hard worker and cheerleader for the cast and crew. The moment he walked into the makeup trailer in the morning, everything became more intense and heightened. The force of his personality and presence was amazing. He knew how to charm and make you laugh even through his hangovers. Everyone called him "Duke," except me. It seemed almost like an affectation, which made me somewhat uncomfortable. I called him "John" and noticed he never corrected me.

One morning John came into the makeup trailer and announced that we were all having dinner together with the screenwriter and his wife. He then said in a very serious tone that we should be very careful not to mention *anything* about things falling out of windows. I quipped, "I think we can handle that; it's not a subject that comes up very often!"

That evening as we were gathering for cocktails, someone turned to me and said, "Nancy, you live in New York, don't you?" I nodded yes, and he continued, "Have you read about the poor man who was leaving the famous Pavillon restaurant and was hit on the head with a barbell and died?" "Of course," I said. "As a matter of fact, I can tell you how it happened. Arlene Francis and her husband live in the apartment building above the restaurant, and their teenage son left his barbell on the radiator in front of the open window. The maid was dusting and inadvertently pushed it, and . . . it . . . fell . . . out of the window." I became ashen and tried desperately to change the subject, but things got even worse. Someone said, "Well, what was the playwright's name who was walking along Central Park West, and someone accidentally pushed a potted plant out the window and hit him on the head, and the poor man has never been the same since?"

Actually, there was a good reason not to bring up this subject. I found out later that the writer and his wife had lost their only child when he climbed out of their apartment window and fell to his death.

But who was this man John Wayne? Although he had graduated from the University of Southern California, he did not seem educated in the academic sense, but he had an abundance of life experience that most people will never have. For all of his fame and fortune, he was surprisingly humble, completely at home with himself and others. But there was a hidden place within him that he would reveal only at unexpected moments. He showed his appreciation for women, but he did not flirt. I always thought there was a sexual mystery about him. Although he was married three times, it was always to a Latina. His wife at that time, Esperanza, was not beautiful; in fact, she was quite plain. She seemed to me to be the caretaker, the assistant, the accommodator, not the intimate.

But it was his inner rage that jumped out unexpectedly and seemed to come from a deeply emotional and disturbed place that startled me. I think he used politics as an outlet for this anger.

One beautiful Hawaiian night we had a small dinner with some of the cast on a terrace overlooking the sea. I'm not sure how the conversation drifted to a discussion about President Franklin Roosevelt, but John suddenly started to shake. He rose slowly from his chair with his fists clenched, his jaw trembling, his color changing to purple, and shouted, "That goddamned cripple!!"

Again, I was too young to be a convincing leading lady for John, who was more than twenty years older than I at the time. But it didn't matter; John and I retained an affection for one another that never seemed to diminish. Although I missed my baby so much, and although Alan came to Hawaii in the middle of shooting to spend some time with me, making the film was an unforgettable oasis from my marriage, and I accepted it as a gift for healing a troubled time. Thank you, John.

23

Starting Over

It's amazing to me how life and heartache can become repaired after a certain length of time. By the fall of 1952, Alan and I were back in the country with our little baby girl, and it seemed to be a quite tranquil and harmonious time. It allowed us to think of other things and get reconnected to what was going on in the rest of the world. We were ardent Democrats and were fascinated with politics.

I remember sitting in the little library in the early fall while Alan was working across the road in the studio. We had a television set installed in our house for the first time, and I remember wanting to watch the Democratic Convention in Chicago. President Truman was not going to run again, and the Democratic Party had chosen the unknown governor of Illinois, Adlai Stevenson, as their nominee. No one had any idea who he was or what he was all about. I sat there alone and listened to his acceptance speech and was startled by his brilliance and charisma. I ran down the path and burst into Alan's studio to tell him what had just occurred and urged him to join me to watch the reactions to the speech. We became enthusiastic Stevenson supporters and made ourselves available to help in any way we could.

A major fund-raiser for six thousand people was scheduled at Madison Square Garden in New York City. It was designed to have all the celebrities the party could find to support Adlai Stevenson. Humphrey and Betty Bogart were the hosts, and the comedian George Jessel was the emcee. The organizers asked me to attend and be introduced as a new, young, emerging star who was casting her first vote for Adlai Stevenson. Of course, I said yes, and Alan and I arrived at the arena in the early evening.

I wore a navy-blue wool cocktail dress that had cap sleeves and a boat-neck front with a bare back, perfect for a pearl-and-diamond clip on my right shoulder and masses of pearls on my wrist. The dress was very slim and didn't give much room when I walked with my high-heeled, navy-satin pumps. The

Garden was full and cheering with the introduction of each celebrity. Distinguished guests were seated in a row on the stage. Mrs. Roosevelt was at the center between New York State governor Herbert Lehman and secretary of state Carmine DeSapio. The emcee was speaking at the front of the half-moon stage, where he would introduce the next celebrity guest. The stairs leading up to the stage were placed just in front of the seated distinguished guests.

When I heard my name being called, I was excited and a little nervous. I ran up the stairs, tripped on the last stair, went flying across the stage, and landed on all fours in front of Mrs. Roosevelt. Six thousand people gasped! George Jessel took the mike out of the stand and came to my aid, saying things like, "Oh, the poor little girl. I hope she hasn't hurt herself too badly." Getting up was awkward and took an eternity; it even occurred to me that perhaps I should just lie there and pretend I was dead. But that was not an option, and I knew that I simply had to come up with something to recover.

I remembered reading that morning in the *New York Times* that Bette Davis was appearing in a play in Detroit and on opening night fell down at the beginning of the first act. The curtain came down, and after a few minutes she appeared again, looked at the audience, and said, "I fell for *you.*"

All the way to the front of the stage, limping and feeling that all was lost, my life and career and reputation over, I said to myself, "Use it, use it." I finally reached the microphone, took a deep breath, and said, "Well, I fell for Stevenson. How about all of you?," and walked off the stage to a heartwarming cheering applause. Thank God for the *New York Times!*

24

Alan Lerner's Family and Growing Up

If I were beginning a story about Alan's family and his early life, I would have to say that the story begins with a lie. You might consider the lie to be inconsequential, but it dominated Alan's entire family and poisoned every avenue they took. The problem with a lie is that it has to be nurtured and fed and supported by more lies. Sometimes it's difficult to keep track of what is the truth and what is not. Lying becomes an accepted way of life and is considered part of one's survival.

I remember the first month that Alan and I were married, he had an appointment in New York City, and I was in the country alone. I remember going to the drawer that contained his passport and, with my heart thumping in my chest, opening it to see the date of his birth. I breathed a sigh of relief when it confirmed the age that Alan said he was. I hadn't been sure whether he was lying to me.

The family's original lie was that they were not German Jews; they were from Russia. Part of the network of this lie consisted of changing the names of the boat they came over on and the town that they came from. I remember talking to Alan's youngest aunt and telling her I was thinking of writing a book about Alan and his family. I was shocked when she became panicky and said that it would kill her older sister and that I was not to think of pursuing this idea. What did she think I was going to write about that was going to be so devastating? It was Alan's cousin, with whom I was having lunch one day, who smiled and said, "Well, she doesn't want you to know that she is not German."

The stories of Alan's family are an intermingling of truth and fiction, and I cannot verify everything that I am about to relate. Somewhere there is the real story, a story that no one will ever know, but the essence of reality you will understand.

Alan's father, Joseph Lerner, had three brothers. I met only Joe and Michael. No one ever talked about the other one. They had two sisters, and all came over together to the United States from Russia (not Germany). Joe married Alan's mother, Edith, who came from a Jewish family that was quite Orthodox and fairly well educated. Joe and Edie had three children, Richard (Dick), Alan, and Robert (Bobby). Richard was the only son who was bar mitzvahed; the other two wanted to escape from the anti-Semitic atmosphere at that time.

Joe put a sign in his window advertising that he was a dentist and would pull a tooth for a fair price. I am not sure whether he ever attended any dental school, but he had the spirit of an entrepreneur and survivor.

The story that I heard was that Joe and his brothers went to Harlem for a prolonged poker game and won a small store in the neighborhood. They decided to sell reasonably priced women's clothing, an enterprise that was quickly successful, especially with Edith at the cash register. This eventually led to the opening of the Lerner Shops across the country. They moved to Park Avenue and sent their children to the best private schools and lived a very privileged life.

There was one terrible problem between Joe and Edie. His pursuit and abuse of women were legendary and inexcusable. Alan told me of family summer voyages on the *Queen Mary* to Europe with Joe's mistress in another stateroom. Joe made no attempt to disguise his infidelity and was quite uncaring of the embarrassment to his wife. He felt that as long as Edie was kept supplied with her diamond rings and brooches, what in the world more did she want?

Several years after I was married, I stayed with Edie in her New York apartment for one night when Alan was away. She had me sleep in the twin bed next to her, and when the lights were out and it was still and dark, she started to tell me stories of her life and marriage to Joe. She told me of waking in the middle of the night with Joe on top of her, raping her. In those days, unwanted pregnancies were handled by a woman who came to the apartment to give her a "curettage." We both were silent, but finally she whispered, "She came often."

I never learned what the last straw for Edie was, but she and Joe finally divorced, and Edie met Alan Lloyd and lived off her alimony and settlement from Joe for the rest of her life.

As a young boy, Alan was sent to England to a boarding school. He never talked about it, but a melancholy would come over him if it was ever mentioned. I think he and Fritz had something in common in their boyhood experiences. He did talk about Choate and was very forthcoming about his Harvard years.

Alan's stories of going to Harvard and graduating before the United States entered World War II in 1940, when anti-Semitism was rampant and accepted here, were shocking to me. Alan was obviously a gifted writer and longed to join the famous Hasty Pudding Club to write one of their infamous musicals, but he was not allowed because he was a Jew. One of his best friends, Ben Welles (son of Sumner Welles, the secretary of state under Franklin Roosevelt), was a member and managed to get Alan in through the back door. He could bring Alan to dinner only twice a year and somehow manipulated the club to let Alan participate in the writing. This bigotry was completely accepted and sanctioned by the university. These stories made me realize what a protected environment I had grown up in and helped me to understand how someone like Alan, whose ego was fragile at best, was forever damaged.

Bobby, Alan's younger brother and the one I knew the best, had possibly the most remarkable and heartrending story of the three boys.

When the family moved to Park Avenue, Edie had a weekly Canasta game with some of her Park Avenue friends. One of them was a very attractive woman in an unhappy marriage. All the families spent time together, and somehow Bobby, who was barely out of high school, and this thirty-something older woman became infatuated with each other. It is hard to imagine what possessed this woman to leave her marriage and run away with Bobby.

The Lerner family was disgraced and in despair. They completely disowned the couple and pretended Bobby never existed. This young boy and older woman were cut off from all family members and became almost destitute. Reminiscent of the plot of a great dramatic opera, the woman came down with infectious pneumonia and died. Bobby was beside himself with grief; the war had started, and he signed up to be a paratrooper, one of the most dangerous assignments in the army. Alan always felt that Bobby didn't care to live any longer. The family knew that he was in the army, and although they had no contact with him, they were devastated when he was declared missing in action.

Bobby's story of dropping down in front of the advancing Allied troops in France is almost unbelievable. The Germans were retreating as quickly as they could. Bobby entered a farmhouse that had been bombed and found a German soldier pinned under the collapsing roof. He was wearing a Red

Cross armband, and although Bobby had been told to take no prisoners and to shoot any Germans left behind, he helped free the soldier and released him.

The Germans suddenly regrouped and started to push the Allies back. The Battle of the Bulge was fierce, and Bobby was forced to retreat, taking refuge in the basement of a ruined building, which suddenly collapsed, a pillar piercing his hip. He was alone but heard the advancing Germans coming. A small group of soldiers searched the house but did not find him . . . except for one. It was the same German soldier that Bobby had helped to escape. They recognized each other, and the German slowly unpinned Bobby, who was severely injured. He looked at Bobby's dog tag and must have realized that this was a Jewish boy because the Star of David was engraved on the back. He ripped it off and took Bobby to a group of captured Allies to be imprisoned.

The prison was a nunnery; the cots were made of wood, the food consisted of boiled potato skins, and there was no medicine or any kind of medical care. The soldiers who could walk were forced into the fields; the soldiers who could not move simply lay there to die. The nuns realized that Bobby's wound was becoming gangrenous. Their solution was primitive but effective. They dropped leeches from their sleeves at night into the infected area, and the leeches did their work. Perhaps the most moving part of this entire story is one that Bobby himself told me. He said that a man across from his cot kept looking at him. One evening at dusk as the light slowly dissolved into night, he looked at Bobby and raised his eyebrows, and Bobby nodded yes—he was a fellow Jew.

There was no word about what had happened to Bobby, and the family was beside itself. When the liberation of the prison camps finally happened, there was a large picture of a group of American prisoners in *Life* magazine. There he was, barely seventy pounds, but, thank God, Bobby Lerner was alive!

Alan had graduated from Harvard and was eager to spend time with his younger brother. One of the things that changed Bobby's life was when Alan took him to see the just opened production of *Carousel*. The lead was Jan Clayton, an enchanting performer who captured Bobby's heart. It is not surprising that Jan was about seven or eight years older. They married, had several children, and did not divorce until many years later. It is important to tell you that every time Bobby came to New York, he visited the grave of his first love.

25

Joe Lerner

Perhaps nothing is more compelling than the story of Alan's father, Joe. He was a cigar-smoking lover of parties, women, and good wine. He was rich, successful, a terrible husband, and not the most involved father. However, nothing he ever did to hurt other people warranted his life sentence of horror and misery.

The first sign of Joe's health issues began when he had a toothache and his jaw hurt. He went to his dentist, who discovered a suspicious patch of tissue on his gum, which turned out to be a lethal form of cancer. From that moment on, he kept losing pieces of his head. It started with a part of his jaw, then his tongue, then another piece of his jaw, then the whole lower part of his face was gone. When we met, he wore a thick layer of gauze under his nose, with ties placed over his ears and around the back of his head and neck. This slow, agonizing process was spread over a period of many years. When we first met in 1950, he still had his voice box and was able to make sounds like laughter and could indicate yes or no.

He had a house on Long Island with a boat named *Brigadoon* that took him out every day on the sound, and when winter arrived, he would go to a house in Miami, Florida, right on the beach, his boat waiting to take him into the tropical waters. I'm not sure how his spirit survived, but he was curious about everything and seemed to be enjoying this bizarre life. There were pads of paper and pencils everywhere, so he was able to join the conversation, usually telling you what to think.

At the dinner hour, Joe would disappear and have his martini poured down the opening of his esophagus, along with exactly what we ate. The difference was his food had gone through a blender. One of the hazards of his existence was the gathering of phlegm in his upper esophagus. There were machines everywhere, including on his boat, that handled this nicely. I never entered his bedroom, but apparently his bed often had a young woman servicing him, and Alan admitted to me sadly that there were pornographic drawings everywhere in Joe's room. His piercing, startling blue eyes had a mischievous glint—nothing stopped him from pursuing his appetites and pleasures.

Joe finally lost his voice box and was forever silent thereafter. He had so many operations that after the seventy-ninth piece of his face and head was removed, he jokingly wrote on a piece of paper, "When it hits eighty, sell!"

It was the last operation that made it clear that he was about to die. Alan and I were in California when Alan got the phone call that his father was slipping away. It was in the spring of 1952, and Alan had been nominated for an Academy Award for Best Writer of an Original Screenplay for *An American in Paris*. Of course, we planned to go to the awards ceremony, but when Alan received the news about his father, he felt that he must fly to New York to be by his side.

I attended the ceremony alone, and when I was ushered to a reserved seat on the aisle near the front of the theater, I knew that Alan was going to win. I remember wearing a flaming-red, off-the-shoulder gown with a full skirt just covering the knee, gold sandals, gold-and-diamond Cartier earrings, and a large Cartier gold-and-diamond bracelet, but what in the world was I going to say? When it was announced that Alan Jay Lerner had won and that his wife, Nancy Olson, would accept for him, I marched up the aisle and up the steps to the microphone. I knew that Alan was in a hospital room listening to the radio with his father. I said, "On behalf of my husband, Alan Jay Lerner, I want to thank the Academy for this award and all of you who voted for him . . . and congratulations, darling!" I remember hearing a very warm applause and feeling, for just a moment, a sense of triumph.

Soon after that, Joe took his last breath. After he died, we attended his wake at the funeral home, and to my astonishment the infamous Cardinal Francis Spellman was there. Alan explained that his father had paid for one of the gold-engraved doors of the famous St. Patrick's Cathedral on Fifth Avenue. He laughed and said, "The old man was covering all his bases."

But it was the synagogue Temple Emanu-El, also on Fifth Avenue, that completely intrigued me. The service was conducted by the rabbi, and it was in classic Jewish tradition. How was it possible that I had never been in a synagogue before this funeral? I loved the mystery and intellectual beauty of the ceremony and whispered to Alan that it was important that we bring our daughters to experience this history of their ancestry. He looked at me with panic and dismissed the idea immediately.

As I am writing this, I am slowly realizing who Alan Jay Lerner was and how life, family, education, and religion had invaded and shaped him. His first wife, Ruth Boyd, came from a socially prominent family from New Jersey. I emphasize the word *prominent*, which was important and necessary for Alan and his self-image. She was also tiny; she had to look up to him. They had a beautiful little girl, Susan, and were divorced after about three years of marriage. I met Susan when she was about six years old and thought she was a delightful child. I know Alan loved her even though he rarely spent time with her. She visited us in Rockland County and was a darling older sister to Liza and Jenny. Her adoration for her father is something I will never forget. The depth of her longing to be close to him brings tears to my eyes, and there is much more to say about Susan later in my story.

Apparently, Alan had a history of romancing his leading ladies. It was all part of the script that he created for himself. Marion Bell had played the lead in *Brigadoon* and managed to elicit a marriage proposal and wedding. I never met her, and I know very little about her. Alan always made me feel that this was not a terribly important relationship in his life. He wooed the star of *Love Life*, Nanette Fabray, but this dance, thankfully, did not end with more nuptials.

Alan's next most serious relationship was ours. Actually, it was his longest marriage and produced two gorgeous children. It also was one of the most creative periods in Alan's career. I think every artist has an arc in his or her work; I experienced the apex of that arc with Alan in our years together. I'm not sure how much of a muse I was or how much I contributed to this extraordinary period; however, I do know that I provided stability and a foundation that was reliable and encouraging and allowed him to soar with his gift. I think Alan, in his most honest moments with himself, understood that, too, which was probably the strongest reason why he was so determined to continue our marriage after his sad relationship with Olga San Juan.

I knew life was precarious, and even though Alan showed a real resolve to be close again, I certainly never intended to have another child. So I was shocked when I found myself pregnant once again. If I were in the same circumstances today, I'm not sure whether I would continue that pregnancy. At that time, to get an abortion was almost impossible, unless, of course, you went to Cuba or one of those dark alleys somewhere in Miami or had a private arrangement with a doctor or an abortionist (as Edie had). I shudder when I think of it because one of the great joys of my life is Jenny Lerner. Liza and Jenny are two of the most special girls in the world.

Of course, Alan was ready to leave Fritz again. He thought that a partnership with Burton Lane or Arthur Schwartz was what he needed. He actually wrote a completely new score with Burton and an original screenplay for an enchanting film musical, *Royal Wedding*. In it, there is a beautiful ballad, "Too Late Now," and a delightful comedic song, "How Can You Believe Me When I Said I Love You When You Know I've Been a Liar All My Life?" Fred Astaire and Jane Powell sang and danced their way through this charming, very funny, and witty song. I laughed along with everyone else, oblivious to the fact that I should have been paying more attention to its message. Burton and Alan also wrote a score to Mark Twain's *Huckleberry Finn*, which was supposed to be made into a film but was never produced. Some of the songs were simply wonderful. I wonder where they are now.

Alan tried to find the right project with Arthur Schwartz as well. In fact, Arthur and his new wife, Mary, took Alan to dinner the night I went into the hospital to have Jenny. Alan was extremely solicitous and sweet to me at this time; I think he wanted to make up to me for the difficult period I had having Liza alone. In fact, when he kissed me goodbye to have dinner, I was just beginning to have mild labor pains. He said he'd be back to the hospital in an hour, but guess what? Jenny was born forty-five minutes later! Alan seemed to be devastated that his new daughter had already arrived without him, but after visiting the nursery and looking at Jenny, he seemed genuinely thrilled.

It was the end of the summer in 1953, immediately after Jenny was born, that we received an invitation to attend Jacqueline Bouvier and John F. Kennedy's wedding on September 12, 1953. Alan had been at Choate and Harvard with John Kennedy. Although Alan was a year behind Jack, and they were never close friends, they were nevertheless aware of each other and their accomplishments. Obviously, Jack remembered me, too. Frankly, it just seemed like too great an effort to travel to Newport, Rhode Island, for an event with hundreds of guests, so we quite cavalierly decided not to go. I regret that decision, and I particularly am sorry that I didn't even save the invitation.

Alan and I had reserved feelings about Jack, but we understood that he could possibly be a powerful leader. We were enthusiastic supporters of Adlai Stevenson and were devastated when Eisenhower won in 1952. In 1955, Jack was a senator from Massachusetts and made a bid to become Stevenson's vice president, but Estes Kefauver was chosen for that position. Alan and I and a small group had dinner with Jack shortly after the convention. I had never seen Jack seem the least bit vulnerable and was surprised to see his emotions about his failure so evident. There was a short period of time before the campaign started when it seemed that Stevenson and Kefauver had a good chance of winning. Jack was filled with regret about this lost opportunity. I remember making the point that 1960 could be his real chance. He looked at me without that incredible confidence he always used to have. He was wounded.

In the meantime, Alan himself was increasingly wounded. The partnership with Arthur was going nowhere. Burton Lane had deep psychological problems that made him extremely difficult to work with. Fritz Loewe was feeling rejected and betrayed and was proclaiming that he would never work with Alan again (he even went so far as to tell those around him not to mention Alan's name.). Nothing was working out for Alan Lerner—and Alan felt utterly lost.

26

My Fair Lady

A lan and I decided to shake up our lives. In September 1954, we left our country house and leased a townhouse on East Seventy-Fourth Street in New York City. We took our two baby girls, Liza and Jenny, with their nanny, a cook, and a maid and planned to stay for a year. By the time spring came, Alan was desperate. One Friday morning he sat on the edge of our bed and started to weep. He said his career was over. He had tried everything, but nothing was working. He said the rights of George Bernard Shaw's *Pygmalion* had become available, and he felt he knew exactly how to adapt this famous work into a musical. He said Fritz was the only composer who could do it, but of course Fritz was no longer talking to him.

I sat up in bed and handed Alan a Kleenex, put my arms around him, and said, "Don't you understand that Fritz is sitting by his telephone waiting for your call?" Alan said that was nonsense; he doubted that Fritz would answer the phone. I said, "I'll prove it to you." I picked up the phone and dialed Fritz's home. The minute he heard my voice, he said, "Nance!" (pronounced "Naahnce"). "How are you? How are the children?" I told him that we were going to the country the next morning and would love to see him. I explained that Alan had an idea for a new work and that there was only one person in the entire world who could compose the music, and that was him. Could he possibly join us for lunch tomorrow? He asked, "What time?" I answered, "One o'clock." He said, "I'll be there!"

I told our cook and nanny that we were going to the country for the weekend and expected a visitor for lunch. Fritz arrived at one o'clock, and the three of us sat in our small pine-paneled, early-American dining room chatting away, and it was obvious that Fritz was delighted to be there.

Alan explained that Dick Rodgers and Oscar Hammerstein had tried for a year to conquer George Bernard Shaw's play *Pygmalion*. They owned the rights but had decided to give them up and release them, stating that this work could never be transformed into a musical. Alan said they misunderstood how to approach the property. "They're writing songs for Alfred Drake!" (Alfred Drake was a theater actor most famous for his long-running role as Curly in Rodgers and Hammerstein's *Oklahoma!*) "They don't get it. Higgins is the key. The lyrics and music have to be an extension of Shaw's dialogue. A great Shavian actor like Rex Harrison should play Higgins. He doesn't even have to sing that well!" Fritz looked stricken. What did Alan mean when he said, "He didn't even have to sing well?" Alan smiled and said, "Don't worry, Fritz. There will be a place for your melodies. Freddie, who is smitten with Eliza, will sing the love songs, and Eliza has to have a great voice to be able to sing about her feelings of being transformed into a duchess."

Fritz was intrigued, and the two of them were so deeply engrossed with Alan's ideas that I might as well have been invisible. They got up from the table, left the dining room, walked out the front door, and crossed the road to the studio without even glancing at me, much less thanking me for lunch. By five o'clock that evening, Fritz had already rented the house at the top of our orchard, arranged for his mistress to join him, and for one year sat at our dining-room table every day for lunch and dinner.

Perhaps that year was the happiest Alan and I ever had together. The excitement ran high as he and Fritz plunged into the work. Both were at the top of their game, and they knew it. Alan was content and grateful for the loving atmosphere pervading our little house in the country with our two darling little girls. Sometimes I would wake up in the middle of the night to see him seated in the chair and ottoman in the far corner of our bedroom, working on a lyric. He seemed delighted that I was awake so that he could read to me what he was writing. I was always an enthusiastic listener.

One particularly cold and stormy winter night I was awakened abruptly by Alan and Fritz shaking my bed, telling me I had to get up. I was alarmed, thinking perhaps the house was on fire, and where were my children?! They said the house and children were fine, but I had to get up and come to the studio to hear what they had just composed and written. Fritz handed me my galoshes, Alan helped me put on my winter coat and muffler, and the three of us went down the stairs and out into one of the worst blizzards I had ever experienced. We trudged our way through the snow, down the driveway, across the road to the studio, already ablaze with light.

I walked in and was told to sit in the armchair facing the piano and a small settee. Very much like children playing, they set the stage and scene for me. Alan said he was both Higgins and Eliza, and Fritz was Pickering. Alan was an exasperated Higgins, who told Eliza to repeat and repeat and repeat the phrase "The rain in Spain stays mainly in the plain." Pickering told Higgins that perhaps they should go to bed and forget the whole exercise. Higgins was not about to give up, and suddenly Eliza said perfectly, "The rain in Spain stays mainly in the plain."

Fritz rushed to the piano, Alan said to Eliza to please say it again, which she did, and Fritz started quietly playing the phrase to music. Suddenly the two of them started singing and dancing and bullfighting, finally finishing by falling back on the settee in triumph.

I was stunned and speechless. Suddenly they were no longer Higgins and Pickering and Eliza and became Alan and Fritz looking at me with such expectation, both saying in chorus, "How do you like it?"

I looked at them very seriously and said, "You have created one problem." Fritz said in panic, "What is it, Nance?" I quietly said, "This number will stop the show. The actors will be unable to continue. There will be such a reaction from the audience that they may actually have to take a bow in the middle of the first act. Not just one bow, but many." As the wind howled outside, the glow of hope and excitement lit up all of Rockland County.

While the work continued, I spent time in New York looking to buy an apartment in the city. We chose a large condo on Fifth Avenue overlooking the park. There was a room for everybody—Alan, me, the children, the nanny, the cook, the chambermaid waitress—as well as a kitchen, a pantry, a laundry, a dressing room for both Alan and me, and a work studio one story beneath us. Of course, there was day help as well, and they all had to be fed and made happy. This sounds very grand, I know, but there is always a caveat. Somebody had to run this place and keep it going: that would be me. I have always said that I earned a PhD in keeping house, planning menus, picking the correct wines, as well as keeping everyone happy—a daunting task!

27

Battle Cry

While Alan and Fritz were busy completing the script and score for *My Fair Lady*, I got another call from Warner Bros. insisting that I play a role in *Battle Cry* opposite Aldo Ray. The household was running smoothly, and I felt tempted to leave everyone for a short time to make another movie. Alan encouraged me, too, and assured me that he and the children would survive very nicely, so off I went to another Hollywood adventure.

The script had many plots involving many actors, but the main love story was between Aldo's character and my own. Aldo had exploded on the screen with Judy Holliday in *The Marrying Kind* in 1952 and was considered a very hot commodity at that time. He had a kind of rough but sweet appeal, and I admired his performances. To me, there was a genuineness and a certain power in his presence. I was still extremely vulnerable emotionally, which I think Aldo picked up on.

The two of us couldn't have come from more different backgrounds and education; Aldo was not in the least sophisticated, but he was completely confident about what he could bring to his work. I liked him very much, and he became somewhat infatuated with me. I tried hard not to encourage him, but, still being in a rather fragile emotional state, I found his inability to keep his hands off me, even in the friendliest of gestures, reassuring. After Alan's indiscretions, it would have been so easy and so enjoyable to have a brief affair with Aldo, who seemed to be thinking about it every day. It was interesting to me that even Alan picked up on this situation via our phone calls, although I was so careful to hide it. *Battle Cry* became one of the biggest hits Warner Bros. ever had at that time, which was amazing to me.

It's hard for me to explain why I never wanted to work in Hollywood after this film with Aldo, but life in New York, marriage with Alan, raising two little girls—that was about all I could handle. I told my agents to stop submitting me for anything. *Battle Cry* put a period on my career, or so I thought. I don't regret making this decision, and I have retained the deepest affection for my friend and admirer Aldo. Many years later, one of his former girlfriends told me that he talked about me all the time, which saddened me greatly. My tears welled when I heard of his death in 1991, and a deep feeling of regret came over me.

28

Journey to Broadway

Eventually, *Pygmalion* became *My Fair Lady,* and we moved into the city. We put our little girls in the Town School for preschool and kindergarten classes. It was time to start thinking of who should play Higgins, and Rex Harrison was everyone's first choice. Alan, Fritz, and I flew to London to meet with him. We stayed at the Connaught Hotel and arranged for an extra room with a piano in it. There was a great deal of tension and anticipation. Alan was convinced that Rex could make *My Fair Lady* happen as well as be the key to creating the authenticity that he was searching for. Rex arrived one afternoon with his tweed hat in hand, already looking like Henry Higgins. He had played the role many times, so that was not an issue for him, but he had never sung a note on stage. Fritz said if he could sing "Happy Birthday" on key mildly well, he would be just fine.

They laid out the play, sang all the songs, and waited breathlessly for his response. Rex was obviously titillated and wondered aloud if he could actually pull it off. He called the next day and said he would like to do it. That night the three of us danced in the streets of London and the next day flew home on such a high we truly could have flown on our own.

The casting of Higgins was key, and now that it was going to be Rex, Alan and Fritz's first choice, it was time to find the perfect Eliza Doolittle. Who else? Well, of course, the incomparable Mary Martin!

Their confidence bolstered by Rex's reaction to the project, Alan and Fritz called Mary's agent-husband and arranged to play the entire score at the Plaza Hotel in a suite they reserved for this purpose. We decided that I should not attend, but I know Mary, her agent-husband, and their best friend, the legendary clothes designer Mainbocher, were there.

I met Alan and Fritz downstairs in the Oak Room after the meeting, very excited and anxious to hear about everyone's reaction. They were subdued and felt that it had not gone well. The next day Mary's husband called Alan and said how disappointed she was in the score and felt very sorry to have to turn them down. This was a setback, and an insecurity crept into the sensitive crevices of Alan's and Fritz's fragile egos (mine, too!). How could we all be so wrong? They had created the most innovative, brilliant, and delightful score ever written! What was wrong with that stupid woman that she did not understand this? It took several weeks before there was renewed energy and determination to make *My Fair Lady* happen.

They eventually recovered, and everything magically began to fall into place. Julie Andrews would play Eliza Doolittle, and the famous English music-hall performer Stanley Holloway would play Alfred P. Doolittle, her father. Moss Hart was signed to direct, Cecil Beaton to design the costumes, and Oliver Smith to design the sets. Hanya Holm was to be the choreographer, and CBS would underwrite the complete cost. It was scheduled to be the most expensive stage production in the history of the theater, $500,000, considered a mere pittance today.

The score was complete except for the last song to be sung by Higgins. It was the first real dilemma for Alan; he simply could not decide what kind of a song it should be. One late afternoon he buzzed me from the studio and asked me to join him. I went down the stairs and found him very quiet and troubled.

He said, "Nancy, as you know, Shaw absolutely would not allow Eliza and Higgins to fall in love. In fact, in the postscript of the play he wrote that Eliza married Freddie and lived above her flower shop. I cannot accept this. I know that Higgins cannot live without Eliza! I do not want to betray Shaw, and I do not want to betray myself. I have to write a love song that is not a love song, and I don't know where to begin."

I said, "Would you like a cup of tea?" He answered, "Great idea!"

I ran up the narrow, winding, open staircase, went to the kitchen, and put the tea tray together. As I came down the stairs slowly, carefully balancing the tray, he looked at me and said, "You know something, Nancy? You really are a very pretty girl!"

I looked at him severely and said, "Thank you very much for finally noticing. How many years have we been married?"

He said, "Oh, come on! I'm with you all day, I'm with you all night, we have breakfast, lunch, and dinner together, and I forget! It may be hard to believe, but I have become accustomed . . . to . . . your . . . face." He stopped and said, "Don't move." He ran over to his desk, sat down in his writing chair, and wrote in his tiny script, "I've grown accustomed to her face——She almost makes the day begin——." He was no longer conscious that I was there. I picked up the tray and quietly went up the stairs.

At about six o'clock that evening, the doorbell rang. It was Fritz saying that Alan had demanded that he come immediately and, by the way, had also invited him to stay for dinner. He went down the stairs, and when I rang them to join me in the dining room, they couldn't finish their meal fast enough—they were so excited to keep working.

I always said that Alan and Fritz had a partnership similar to that of Trilby and Svengali. Alan dominated the process. He would tell Fritz what the song was about, how it highlighted the drama, and what the essence of the music should be. He started by stating the first line of the lyric, and Fritz would sit at the piano working out the music and theme of that first line. When Alan liked what he heard, he would say, "That's it! Now repeat that theme. Now have the music go up and up again . . . ," and soon there was a completed melody. At about midnight that night, Fritz came up the stairs and said to me, as he always did, "Conception has taken place! I'll see you tomorrow."

Alan didn't come to bed until about 3:00 a.m. He was up at 7:00 the next morning and worked through the day. After dinner that evening, he called Fritz to tell him to come immediately. The two of them went down to the studio and after several hours buzzed me frantically. They demanded that I hear what they had completed. I remember sitting on the sofa, watching Fritz at the piano and Alan singing "I've Grown Accustomed to Her Face." I think that it is still one of the most touching and beautiful songs ever written. Here are Alan's lyrics—words that I heard for the first time that unforgettable night. Please read every word as I brush a tear or two from my eyes.

> *I've grown accustomed to her face.*
> *She almost makes the day begin.*
> *I've grown accustomed to the tune that*
> *She whistles night and noon.*
> *Her smiles, her frowns,*
> *Her ups, her downs*
> *Are second nature to me now;*
> *Like breathing out and breathing in.*
> *I was serenely independent and content before we met;*
> *Surely I could always be that way again—*
> *And yet*

104

I've grown accustomed to her look;
Accustomed to her voice;
Accustomed to her face.

But I'm so used to hear her say
"Good morning" ev'ry day.
Her joys, her woes,
Her highs, her lows,
Are second nature to me now;
Like breathing out and breathing in.
I'm very grateful she's a woman
And so easy to forget;
Rather like a habit
One can always break—
And yet,
I've grown accustomed to the trace
Of something in the air;
Accustomed to her face.

Many years later I thought about this song and wondered where in Alan's head it had come from. I decided to examine Shaw's play more closely to see if I could find a clue. Sure enough, there it was! In the last act, Higgins says to Eliza, "I have learnt something from your idiotic notions: I confess that humbly and gratefully. And I have grown accustomed to your voice and appearance. I like them rather." Alan used this dialogue in *My Fair Lady*, and the word *accustomed* was obviously rolling around in his head. Although it certainly is an awkward word to use in a love song, it was the solution for this love song.

Rehearsals began and went so smoothly that it scared everybody. The chemistry between Rex and Julie was absolutely magical. Moss Hart's direction could not have been any better. The sketches of the sets and costumes were breathtaking. I remember saying to my friends that if this production weren't a success, I didn't know what would become of Alan. He had an image in his mind that this musical would be the ultimate defining American musical and would encompass all the great works that came before it. He was going to put a period on the end of a great era.

Rex was feeling quite comfortable singing his songs and actually enjoying them! However, no one anticipated the problem that would confront them when they held their first rehearsal in New Haven with a full orchestra. It was the afternoon of the opening, and no one realized that Rex had been rehearsing with only a piano accompanying him and would now hear an orchestra for the first time. He panicked. Where was that nice young man who used to cue him from the piano bench? He walked off stage, announced that he could not possibly open that evening, went to his dressing room, and locked the door.

Everyone started to talk through the door in the most soothing tones, pleading with him to please come out. He refused. His former wife, Lilli Palmer, was in New Haven to attend the opening, and they summoned her to talk to Rex through the door. Nothing worked until Moss Hart took charge. He dismissed everyone from the theater—the cast, the producers, the writers, the dancers—except Julie and the orchestra. The theater was quiet, and Moss gently said, "Rex, please come out. Everyone is gone except for Julie and me." Rex slowly opened the door, and Julie took his hand and gently led him on stage. Moss and Julie and Rex went through every one of Higgins's songs with the full orchestra, and Rex finally began to feel confident.

That night there was a blizzard in New Haven, but the theater was packed with an audience that had already heard about the possibility of a tremendous hit; however, everything that could go wrong seemed to happen. The revolving stages got stuck and took forever to be fixed and moving again. Moss came out at eleven o'clock, apologized, and said that the production would go on, but if anyone in the audience felt it was too late, they could receive a refund. The audience went crazy and shouted, "We're not leaving!"

In the first act when Eliza finally masters "the rain in Spain stays mainly in the plain," and the three actors perform the song ending with falling back on the settee, the audience went wild. They stomped their feet, cheered, and stood up clapping. Rex was appalled and did not know how to go on. He whispered to Julie, "What are we going to do? How can we continue?" She whispered back, "We are all going to stand up, hold hands, and take a bow." They stood up and took their bow, and the audience went cuckoo all over again.

While Alan and Fritz were cleaning up the tiny loose ends in New Haven and then for the tryouts in Philadelphia, there was a great deal of excitement for the impending opening in New York. The word was out, and there were lines around the theater for weeks before it opened. But one of the most essential questions for me was, "What am I going to wear?!"

Kitty Hart introduced me to the designer Valentina in New York (as distinguished from Valentino). She was inspired to design the perfect dress. It was a soft-pink, silk-brocade sheath accenting my tiny waist with a charming little bow at the bottom of the zipper in the back, spaghetti straps, and a detachable overskirt lined in a luminous coral-red silk. I walked into the den where Alan was waiting with Fritz; I was wearing just the dress and a pair of small diamond-and-ruby earrings borrowed from Edie Lloyd. Alan exclaimed his appreciation as I had never heard before or would hear after. When I put the full skirt over the dress, picked up the bottom, and looped the red silk over my shoulders, there was more *ooohing* and *aaahing* from both gentlemen. The outfit was completed with a little pouched evening bag in the same coral-red silk. I do not think I have ever felt as satisfied with myself as we stepped into the limousine on our way to the theater.

It was March 15, 1956. *My Fair Lady* opened on Broadway and was revered as a brilliant and masterful piece of art. It was clearly an historic moment for the musical theater. Alan Jay Lerner and Frederick Loewe had created a masterpiece.

29

Gigi

Having the biggest hit in Broadway history is a very heady experience. Even I felt acknowledged when Alan brought home the published book of *My Fair Lady*. He pulled back the cover and showed me the printed dedication: "To Nancy, with love." Alan and Fritz were beside themselves with a mixture of joy, revenge, renewed egos, and shock! They had done it! But now what?

It seemed to me the only place to put all this energy was another project, and they agreed. Alan had always loved the story of *Gigi* by the extraordinary French writer Colette, and he persuaded Fritz to write a musical of it with him. Alan called Arthur Freed at MGM and suggested that they write an original movie musical. Of course, Arthur was thrilled at the opportunity to do a special film with two of the most successful writers on Broadway, and they all plunged in. The story was already so beautifully told by Colette that even Alan couldn't help but write a very good screenplay, and the score was absolutely perfect. I think my second most favorite lyric that Alan ever wrote was the song "Gigi."

It was clear to me, though, that Alan was restless and looking for something more—more validation, more adoration—than I could give after seven years of marriage and two children. I was thrilled with the writing of *Gigi* and made that very clear to both Alan and Fritz. In fact, I was fascinated at how they continued with their peak of brilliance, and I was as enthusiastic as I knew how to be, but he needed more.

What I never truly acknowledged was how insecure Alan felt socially. We were very much a part of the theater world, but Alan wanted to be part of the exclusive social world, too. Because of our celebrity, we were pursued by people such as Alfred and Jeanne (the first Jeanne) Vanderbilt and were invited to many parties and weekends at their Long Island estate.

I remember the first summer after the opening of *My Fair Lady*, Alan insisted on renting a house on Center Island. It was a huge housekeeping effort to move everyone to a rented estate, and I was not looking forward to it. However, it was an interesting time for me. Alan was going back and forth to New York, and I started to take time for myself to read some of the books that I had never explored. I remember reading Kafka's *Metamorphosis* and following Alan around the house reciting some of its prose. He wasn't terribly interested, being more concerned with the dinner party that we were invited to on Saturday night at the home of Marietta and Ronald Tree.

During this time, I received a call about auditioning to play the leading lady in a comedy on Broadway called *The Tunnel of Love,* written by Peter DeVries and Joe Fields and starring Tom Ewell. It was exactly what Alan was looking for! To get me out of the house and give him more freedom to find that elusive thing that would fill the empty space within him.

I decided to audition and found myself in rehearsals for my first role on Broadway. Tom Ewell was as insecure as most actors are, and I was happy to give him his space, allowing him to upstage me as often as he pleased. Any theatrical project is a growing experience, and most people in the theater are very much in touch with their inner child, knowing how to play and have fun. I am no exception.

When it came time for our first tryout in New Haven, Alan came for the opening night. Something in his behavior reminded me of the past. His mind was somewhere else, he couldn't wait to get back to New York, and I started to panic. I twisted my ankle the next day and was unable to perform that evening. My poor understudy had to take my place, and, unfortunately, because the ankle was not broken, I was persuaded to continue the run. I am sure that something inside of me wanted to prevent me from continuing, but I couldn't get out of it. The play opened, and it was a big hit, and I was trapped in a year's contract.

In the meantime, Alan and Fritz completed *Gigi.* Vincente Minnelli was to direct, and an incredible cast was assembled: Leslie Caron, Louis Jourdan, Maurice Chevalier, Hermione Gingold, and Eva Gabor. They were scheduled to shoot in Paris, and Alan couldn't wait to get on that plane. I was trapped in New York, going to the theater every night (except Sunday) and twice on Wednesday and Saturday. The children and I missed him very much and looked forward to his daily phone calls.

I enjoyed my relationship with Tom Ewell and especially the rest of the cast. We were buddies, and they helped fill my lonely space. Sydney Chaplin, the son of Charlie Chaplin, whom I had known in California before I married Alan, was appearing in *Bells Are Ringing* with Judy Holliday, which was also playing in a theater on Forty-Fifth Street. On matinee days, he would pick me up, and we would walk to Sardi's for dinner before the evening performance. Sydney was one of the most amusing human beings I have ever spent time with, truly a delight. There was no flirtation, just friendship. What I didn't realize was that Sydney had many friends in Paris and was aware of Alan's secret life there. He never hinted that he knew something that I was not aware of. However, looking back, I seem to recall an increased protective attitude and concern for me during this time that only now makes sense.

One night I went to a party with a group of people from the theater and bumped into my first real boyfriend, George Englund. George was a handsome and charming rogue, and I am blessed that we never actually became serious. But let me tell you that I have never been kissed as perfectly as when I was kissed by George. That first kiss many years ago was an introduction to what was yet to come. My sensory responses couldn't wait. Whatever he awakened was alive and waiting for the next step. It truly swept me away! Unfortunately, every boyfriend I ever had after George, their kisses had difficulty in measuring up to his.

He took me home from the party, and I invited him up to the apartment for a drink. We laughed and reminisced until it was time for him to leave, and, of course, he kissed me goodnight. It was meant to be a friendly gesture, but it reminded me of the past and how much I missed being kissed.

The phone rang about ten minutes after George left, and it was Alan. I said, "Alan, come home. If you care about this marriage, come home and come now." He became alarmed and said, "What is it, Nancy? I have never heard you sound like this." What I didn't realize was that he was panicking at the thought that I perhaps had heard some gossip about him, but what I was really trying to tell him was that this long separation made me extremely vulnerable and that I didn't quite trust myself and my own actions. About three days later, he came home.

I remember this time as being filled with fun, sex, love, and clinging to each other. Alan picked me up every night after the play, and we joined friends for drinks and a late supper or went to a party or simply wined and dined with each other. I wanted to know everything about *Gigi* and how things were going and was thrilled to hear that it was exactly how he dreamed it.

One night very late, as we were sitting in his studio and were about to go upstairs to bed, he started to tell me a little about Paris. He looked at me and said, "Nancy, do you know what the latest thing in Paris is?" I innocently said, "No, of course not. What is it?" He said, "When a woman loves a man, she allows him to watch her making love with another woman and then takes him in her bed." I was stunned and didn't know how to respond, but I do remember putting my finger down my throat and gagging as if to say, "How revolting!" I then, for some unknown reason, turned to him and said, "Alan, my darling, you have always wanted to open Pandora's box. It's important for you to close it, lock it, and throw away the key. Your salvation is your work." The next day he said he had had a call from Vincente Minnelli, who wanted him back in Paris—and he was gone.

30

The Music Stops

It was now the end of spring in 1957, and I received terrible news from my family. My father called and told me that my mother had massive tumors in her breast and under her arm, and she was scheduled for a mastectomy and cobalt radiation. He was clearly falling apart, and I knew that I had to go to California. I went to the producers of *The Tunnel of Love* and explained why I must leave the production, and they were wonderfully gracious and let me go. Of course, I was in touch with Alan about all of this and said that the children and I would be staying in Los Angeles, and as soon as he could join us, we all would spend the summer there.

I rented a large house on the Santa Monica beach and brought with me my entire staff—nanny, cook, maid—and my children. I think we were there about two weeks before Alan finally joined us. I met him at the airport, and he seemed genuinely concerned about my mother and very happy to see me and the children. We went to several parties, one of them given by Cole Porter, with Bogie and Betty Bogart and Gary Cooper and his wife, Rocky, also there as guests. I remember that evening and thought that Gary Cooper did not seem well. In fact, he was dying.

Cole Porter was a small, delicate man with impeccable manners. I had met him shortly after *My Fair Lady* opened in New York. He had reserved a seat on the aisle in the third row once every week for six weeks just so he could truly understand the genius of this work. I will never forget his going to the piano at a luncheon at his home in California. I thought, "Oh, my God! I'm going to hear Cole Porter play his own sweeping, pulsating melodies as I have never heard them before!" To my surprise, he played in the most provincial, mundane manner. The left hand kind of did an "oompa—oompa," which shocked me. Did he just hear in his head those melodies he had created? Genius remains a mystery to me and always will.

At Cole's party, Alan's distance was particularly evident to me. I was baffled (and stupid)! The next night we decided to have dinner at one of the restaurants at the beach. He didn't talk much, and it was evident that I had to challenge him sooner or later.

When we got home, we decided to take a walk on the beach. The fog was coming in, and I shuddered in the cool, damp wind. I decided this was the moment; I simply had to confront him. I turned to him and said, "Alan, you must talk to me. You are not here. Where are you?" With that, he started to weep, collapsed on the sand, and said, "I have fallen in love with someone in Paris, and I have to leave you." I sat on the ground next to him, he put his arms around me, and we wept together.

When someone is in shock, it's hard to know how to survive. I wondered in that moment, should I scream? Should I become hysterical? Should I be calm? Should I lie down and die?

We walked numbly back to the house, and while Alan was taking a shower, I went out on the balcony overlooking the ocean. I think one of the survival mechanisms we humans have is to be able to remove ourselves from a catastrophe and focus on something else. I remember thinking as the fog engulfed me, "I know life changes and yet somehow goes on. . . . I wonder where we all will be ten years from tonight?" Alan came back from his shower, and we got in bed together. I needed comforting and had nowhere else to go. We clung to each other until finally we went mercifully to sleep.

The next morning I said to Alan that I was not going to allow him to end our marriage and our family. I suggested we go back to New York and talk to our psychologists to see if we could save our future. He was noncommittal but was willing to go back to New York immediately. The staff and the children would join us a week later. I remember that I had been reading the J. D. Salinger *Franny and Zooey* stories in the *New Yorker* and was dazzled by the writing. I could not help myself but simply felt compelled to share this work with Alan and followed him around the house reading from the magazine. He actually listened with a certain amount of interest.

I don't remember much else except getting on a plane, flying to New York, going to the apartment, and making the appointment to visit Dr. Frank, who had been working with me at the time of *Paint Your Wagon*. Alan was supposed to talk to him first and would meet me after my session in the Palm Court of the Plaza Hotel, which was across the street.

Dr. Frank said to me that Alan was determined to leave and that there was very little that I could do about it. I remember him saying that this was not easy for Alan, that his attachment to me was quite profound, but he simply had to go. I went to the Palm Court and said that I still was going to resist his leaving. This made him angry, and we said very little in the cab ride to our apartment. When I got into bed that evening, I looked at him as he walked in the room, and I knew there was absolutely nothing I could do to change his mind. I told him that it was OK—he could go.

It is very hard for me to write about this and very difficult to explain why for one week the two of us became such desperate and passionate lovers that it took our breath away. We went to dinner and came home and made love— I thought I was losing my mind. Looking back, I think it might have been the happiest Alan had ever been. His phone calls to Paris at dawn kept his lover happy there, and his nights with me helped fill whatever sad, vacant place he had within him. He had both of us—how perfect!

It was Sunday morning, and we were invited to lunch in the country at Katrina and Don Ettlinger's. It was decided that I would go alone, and the car would bring me back home for dinner and another evening with Alan. His new French love, Micheline, was arriving from Paris the following Tuesday.

That morning I woke up and said to myself, "Enough!" I got up and fixed breakfast trays for us, got the *New York Times* at the front door, and walked into the bedroom. Alan had just awakened and reminded me to tell Katrina that I was not staying for dinner. I didn't say anything. I simply sat on the edge of my bed, picked up the phone, and called the car company. I said that I needed the car at 11:00 a.m. Alan reminded me to tell the car to wait for me and bring me back to the city for dinner, but I said I didn't need the car to bring me back and would be returning Monday morning with one of the Ettlingers.

Alan was silent. I turned to him and said, "I am now leaving. I will come back Monday morning and will expect you to be gone." I have never seen him look like that; I think it was finally dawning on him that this was not a play. This was his life and mine. There was no turning back—the decision was final.

I washed the dishes, took a shower, dressed, and packed an overnight bag. Alan was not in the bedroom or his dressing room—Where was he? I found him wandering around the children's bedrooms. I told him that the car was waiting for me and just wanted to say goodbye.

Alan could never make me understand who I was; everyone has to learn that for themselves. And no one in the universe could have saved Alan Jay Lerner, least of all himself. Actually, when I look back, I think I came as close to saving him as anyone, and I think he knew that, too, but he couldn't help destroying what was worthwhile in his life for the endless pursuit of finding someone to fall in love with him. He felt whole only when looking into the eyes of someone who worshipped him.

On Monday morning, I returned to an empty, silent apartment. There was a note from Alan on the table in the foyer saying that he was at the Hampshire House in case I needed him. It was signed "Love, Alan." I called Dr. Frank and asked him to recommend a lawyer. I also had stopped eating and was becoming seriously thin.

31

Divorce

Within a week, the news was out and written about in many columns. I woke up every morning in a fetal position, knowing something terrible had happened, but for an instant I couldn't remember what it was, and then, of course, it was clear—I knew what it was. The children and staff came back from Los Angeles, where they had remained for the summer while my mother recovered from her cancer surgery. Their return only made everything more heart-wrenching. I started getting phone calls from friends who knew or heard about Micheline: Alan might be in some kind of terrible trouble, and did he realize what he was getting into? I communicated some of this to Alan in the gentlest way possible, but of course my warnings were only taken as incendiary criticism, especially by Micheline!

I must have been in a very fragile state because when Alan called and asked me to go to his mother's apartment with him to tell her that we were getting a divorce, I should have known better and said, "No, tell her yourself." But for some reason I was still protecting him.

The plan was that I would meet him in the lobby of 480 Park Avenue at three o'clock the next day. The only delightful thing about this event was that at one o'clock I went to the shoe salon at Bergdorf Goodman. I picked out a pair of pumps that had the highest heels in the whole store—so high that I literally wobbled my way over to Park Avenue. I knew that Alan would either be on time or a little late, so I got there at about 2:50. I sat on the couch in the lobby and waited. At about 3:15 p.m., Alan arrived, breathlessly telling me how sorry he was to be late. He said, "Well, let's go up." I nodded and stood up; he was shocked and confused. He said, "You've grown!" I smiled and said, "Yes, I have."

It was important for me to talk to someone. Katrina and Don Ettlinger were as loving and supportive as two friends could possibly be. Their concern for me and the children was so real and resonated so deeply; I remember both of them with loving gratitude. I also continued to meet with Dr. Frank, especially for guidance on how to deal with my children.

I will never forget sitting down at the little table in Liza's bedroom with her and Jenny. I told them that I wanted to tell them something and tried to tell them the truth in as protective a way as I could. Liza was just turning six and was deeply affected. When she saw that my eyes became teary, she quietly got up, walked across the room, picked up a Kleenex box, and brought it to me. She said, "Don't daddies know how much their children need them?" I will never forget this question or forgive Alan for being so cavalier about his family. Dr. Frank told me that it was important to keep emphasizing to the girls that this was a problem between grown-ups and was not their fault. Liza was extremely upset by her father leaving, and it breaks my heart to write of this so many years later.

The children's older half-sister, Susan, was also deeply affected by her father's new divorce, and Micheline was obviously threatened by me (which was ridiculous). She insisted that I never have any contact with Susan ever again. I was stunned when Alan told me this; it seemed as if I were being punished for something I had not done and was never going to do. Alan assured me that he would see that Susan saw Liza and Jenny regularly, and that was most important to me. However, it occurred to me that cutting off my very sweet relationship with Susan would be hurtful to her as well, so I sat down and wrote her a letter and sent it to her mother to be the judge of whether to give it to Susan. In it, I said that grown-ups have problems that have nothing to do with their children but sometimes affect them deeply. I told her that it might be hard for her to understand, but that we had decided that her daddy would be the one to see to it that she continue to be the wonderful big sister to Liza and Jenny that she had always been. I wrote that I would always think of her in a loving way and that I knew Liza and Jenny would always keep me up to date on how her life was going. Above all, I wanted her to know that she was loved, admired, and special. I never found out whether her mother gave her the letter.

I was slowly gaining a tiny bit of strength as the days went on. I knew that it was important for Edie Lloyd to remain loyal and protective of her relationship with her son, especially her famous son! She played perfectly into the script that Micheline was being attacked and increasingly becoming a martyr. Nevertheless, I was not quite prepared when Edie called me and said she was coming to the apartment to retrieve the gifts she had given me over the years. I was dumbfounded. What was she talking about? Did she mean the little porcelain vases and dishes that were part of our home? Weren't they part of Liza and Jenny's heritage and meant to be in their homes some-day? I am pleased with myself when I remember telling her that she was not to come to my apartment ever again and that she would receive none of the items she thought still belonged to her.

Have you ever experienced knowing that somebody wished you would die or just simply disappear? It seemed to be more important for Alan and Micheline to make their mark in New York and be accepted as the real and true Mr. and Mrs. Alan Lerner. The image of "Alan and Nancy" had to be erased forever and as quickly as possible. This was cruel and unnecessary. They had nothing to fear from me. Micheline had a questionable reputation that followed her to New York and had nothing to do with me. Her despera-tion to be acknowledged was somewhat pathetic and sad to me, although that is not what I felt at the time. There is an incident that I hesitate to write about, but I can't resist. . . .

George Axelrod (author of *The Seven-Year Itch*) and his wife, Joan, were very much a part of the theater scene in New York. Their children attended the Town School with Liza and Jenny, and although Joan and I were never close friends, we knew each other socially and were on a school committee together.

One late afternoon Joan called ostensibly about our committee work and then said, "By the way, guess who we met last night?" I knew what was com-ing as I had experienced it many times before. I settled back on the sofa and waited to hear how dreadful Micheline was. To my dismay, she said, "Well, she is simply fantastic. Not only is she wonderfully attractive and bright, but she is probably the most exciting person that has hit this town in a long time! Nancy, if I were you, I would be sure that she spend as much time with your children as possible. They will gain so much. Oh, and by the way, if you think *I'm* raving, you should hear George!"

Her last statement, "If you think I'm raving . . . ," is etched in my mind so deeply that it is impossible for me to erase and will be there for the rest of my life. I stammered my goodbye and hung up, barely able to breathe. What had I ever done to this woman to make her revenge so vicious and devastating? About five minutes later the phone rang again, and it was Jeanne Vanderbilt, who said, "Nancy, guess who we met last night?" I could not bear to hear this twice and tried to stop Jeanne from going on, but instead I heard, "What is

Alan thinking of? How can he be leaving *you* for this fraudulent woman? Doesn't he know what he's getting into?" This conversation helped . . . a little . . . and I whispered through my tears about the earlier conversation. Jeanne was incredulous and said, "Joan's crazy, or there is something going on that we don't know about."

Life has a way of being almost perfect. I think it was about two months later that I attended a large party at the Axelrods' townhouse. I had not been personally invited but went with Sydney Chaplin. About a half hour after our arrival, I saw George making his way across the room toward me. I tried to evade him and backed up until I hit the wall, and there he was towering over me. Dear God, did I have to listen all over again to how wonderful Micheline was? George looked into my eyes and said, "Nancy, I have something to tell you." I thought to myself, "Oh, God, here it comes." He started to smile and said, "I think you are the most beautiful, smart, and interesting woman in New York, and if I were single, you wouldn't have a chance. I would pursue you until you were mine!"

My life was dramatically changing.

One afternoon, I returned to my apartment and found a message from Oleg Cassini, whom I had met only very casually in large groups. It was obvious to me that he had read about the divorce and was interested in the "new single girl in New York." Although I still maintained my creative and professional friends after the divorce, Oleg brought me into a different world—"New York society."

Jackie Kennedy and her sister, Lee Radziwill, were part of that group. I loved watching them arrive at a party. Jackie had the instincts of a great movie star. Everyone in the room was aware that she had arrived, and every woman in the room immediately felt they were wearing the wrong things. Jackie set the standard, and it was a distinctly personal, understated elegance. Her sister tried but was never quite as successful. Jackie's sense of style was uniquely perfect for her. She was only self-conscious about her hands, which were square and blunt. We bought our shoes at the same Italian boutique. I was amazed that she had extremely large feet but somehow made them seem delicate and elegant. There is an old-fashioned adjective that I associate with Jackie: the word is *fey*. She was a big girl with incredible eyes placed at the very edges of her face. They glowed with a cultured, feminine intelligence.

Oleg and I became good friends, and I still retain an affection for him. He was close to Jack and Jackie and arranged for the four of us to have dinner. Jackie was pregnant with Caroline at the time. I look back at that evening with sadness. I was still so stunned at Alan leaving me and our children for a Corsican woman that he met in Paris. (It would have helped if I had known he would marry four more times.) Why is it that our fragile egos go into high gear when we have been rejected, many times for reasons that have nothing to do with who we are? We waste so much time proving that we are really wonderful, and aren't they stupid not to know that?

I recently read an excerpt of a letter Jackie Kennedy wrote to a seventy-three-year-old Irish priest in 1952, a year before she married Jack. She wrote, "He's like my father in a way—loves the chase, and is bored with the conquest—and once married, needs proof he's still attractive, so he flirts with other women and resents you." She also comments that this behavior exhibited by her father nearly killed her mother. Did Jackie marry Jack Kennedy, whose behavior resembled her father's, in order to solve her internal conflict about men—as I married Alan Lerner to solve my original problem with my father?

I actively supported Jack's campaign in 1960. At the bottom of my costume-jewelry drawer is a blue-metal lapel button with the name "Kennedy" printed in white letters across it. I received many of these buttons at the various events I attended. It was so clear to me that he could be an exceptional president and that our country was ready for this young man. I don't know why I saved this one button, but I am pleased that it is there for my grandchildren.

32

Sydney Chaplin

One of the most fortuitous invasions into my life was my old friend Sydney Chaplin. Of course, he knew of Micheline long before I did and was waiting for the moment that Alan would leave. I think he had spent enough time with me in the last months of our marriage to understand how vulnerable I was and how devastated I would be. About three weeks after Alan left, I had just tucked my children in bed and was climbing into my own when the phone rang. It was Sydney.

He said, "Nancy, I will be finished at the theater and at your apartment around 11:20 p.m. I am picking you up, and the two of us are going to get a little supper and a little drunk."

"Sydney, you darling man, you are doing no such thing," I said. "I am in bed and incapable of getting myself organized to join you."

He simply answered, "I'll see you later," and hung up.

We didn't have cell phones in those days, so there was no way for me to call him back and tell him to please not come. At about 11:20, he persuaded the doorman to let him come up to my apartment's vestibule, where he insistently kept ringing the doorbell. Sonya, my cook and housekeeper, got out of bed and answered the door. He swept past her and walked down the long bedroom hall to my room. Sydney was very tall and extremely handsome and possibly one of the truly nicest human beings I have ever known. I hesitate to refer to a man as sweet, but he was. There I was, lying in bed, and he came and put his arms around me, picked me up, and said, "Where do you keep your clothes?" He took me into my bathroom and turned on the cold water and handed me a washcloth and said, "Wash your face, brush your hair, put some lipstick on, and throw on a sweater and pair of pants and don't forget your shoes." He stood there as I went through the motions, turned his back as I slowly got dressed, helped me brush my hair, told me how beautiful I was, and marched me down to the front-hall closet to get a warm coat. Sonya stood there not knowing what to do, but he turned to her and simply said, "I will bring Mrs. Lerner home in a few hours." And we left.

After that, Sydney and I saw each other almost every night after the theater and on weekends. He was adorable with the children, who agreed that Sydney Chaplin was possibly the funniest human being on the planet. If he could make us laugh at this terrible time of our lives, then he surely must be a genuine genius. He would describe Alan Lerner in elevator shoes and have us all on the floor. Sydney was irreverent in an honest and accurate way and incapable of deceit. How refreshing after what I had been going through for so many years.

It was fun, and it was sad. Sydney was a gentle lover and unfortunately became extremely smitten with me. The last thing I wanted to do was ever hurt him, but I think I did. I could not see a life with Sydney as more than just what it was at that moment, and I know he felt rejected. I still smile to myself when I think of him and always hope that his life was satisfying and happy.

33

Emmet Hughes

In the meantime, it seemed New York realized there was a new single girl in their midst, and they were intrigued. I suddenly was not only part of the theater world but pursued by "New York society"; it seems they always were looking for a new face. One of the interesting things about New York social life is the overlapping of all the worlds. It is a fascinating amalgamation of social, theater, government, publishing, Wall Street, politics, and writers writing everything. It is possibly the most stimulating place to be in the entire world, and I feel extremely grateful that I spent a number of years enjoying it all. It is so different from Los Angeles, which has a tendency to be much more provincial, each group staying within its own boundaries.

I attended many parties and was pursued by all kinds of men who never interested me until I met Emmet Hughes. Emmet was of black Irish descent, a twice married conflicted Catholic who possessed a brilliant intelligence. He was an only son of a judge and a deeply religious mother who had wanted him to become a priest. He graduated from Princeton summa cum laude and was a member of Phi Beta Kappa. When I met him, he was the *Time* magazine bureau chief for Europe and the United States. He was extremely handsome with a kind of dark seductiveness, and only now do I realize how dangerous he actually was, even to himself. Please don't laugh when I tell you that his kisses reminded me of George Englund's—very addictive. My insecurities dovetailed perfectly with his needful ego. His need to seduce and win women's emotions was somewhat comparable to Alan Lerner's needs.

Emmet and his first wife were married in Spain in a very orthodox Catholic ceremony, and they had one son. Of course, this marriage was not enough, and he fell in love and pursued his second wife, with whom he had two little girls. In order for him to marry a second time, the first marriage had to be annulled, and I believe it went all the way up to the pope to make this happen. He was only legally separated from his second wife, and it was quite clear that he would never get a divorce and marry again until both of his parents were gone. And, indeed, that happened, but after he and I broke up, and I was already happily married to someone else.

Please understand that Emmet's attractive and irresistible seduction of me was not the only addition he brought to my life. Emmet opened a door to another world of people in New York—the political and publishing world. Although I had met many of these people socially while married to Alan Lerner, I had never spent any time with them.

Theodore (Teddy) H. White was one of the leading journalists in New York, culminating his enormous successes with his famous series of books, *The Making of the President*. Alan Lerner and I had known Teddy, but it was only after meeting Emmet that I really spent time with both Teddy and his fabulous wife, Nancy. I loved their dinners with every major journalist in town, from Walter Cronkite to Ben Bradlee, Richard Clurman, James Reston, and, of course, the man whom Emmet worked for, the eminent Henry R. Luce.

I remember going to Marion and Jack Javits's wonderful parties, with such a remarkable mixture of people. I particularly remember one evening going up the elevator with the artist Salvador Dali and his murmuring to me, "Has anyone ever painted you?" It was a black-tie party, and I wore a black-velvet dress with a tiny, fitted bodice and a tulip skirt that opened to the knee and was lined in white satin. I put masses of pearls around my neck, wore pearl earrings, and, of course, my shoes were white satin, the color of the lining of my skirt.

That night I danced with Jack and said that I had a question that has never been answered to my satisfaction. "Jack, you have been a senator for over twenty years. Why has there never been realistic and sensible gun-control legislation?" He said, "Nancy, you will never get it, and I will tell you why. People are emotionally involved with their guns. Their guns are their balls!"

I have never forgotten this response. I was reminded of it some years ago when Barack Obama was reprimanded for commenting about the less-educated people in Pennsylvania, "They cling to guns or religion." He was right. People, especially men who feel diminished, need to augment their sense of being in control and powerful, and guns help them feel that way.

34

Nelson Rockefeller

Emmet was one of the speechwriters for President Eisenhower. It was Emmet who wrote the famous line "I will go to Korea" that probably was the determining factor that led to Eisenhower's winning the presidency in 1952. Emmet's knowledge and expertise in politics were always something he pursued. He supported Nelson Rockefeller for governor of New York in 1958 and wrote some of Rockefeller's major speeches.

I will never forget an evening with Emmet, Mary and Nelson Rockefeller, and another couple, a Dr. Murphy and his wife, Happy. It was a black-tie Republican event at the Waldorf-Astoria. Emmet wrote the speech for Nelson, who was the principal speaker. We were invited to attend the event and afterward join the governor, his wife, and the Murphys for a drink at the Rockefellers' Fifth Avenue apartment.

I remember wearing one of my favorite outfits. I chose my burgundy-velvet dress with a matching short-fitted jacket with large rhinestone buttons, diamond earrings, white kid gloves, and, of course, shoes and a small satin handbag dyed to the exact color of the dress.

I don't remember the speech very well, but I vividly remember what happened afterward. We all were tucked into a large comfortable limousine, arriving at the Rockefellers' apartment to many open doors and greeters. The apartment was not enormous, except for a large gallery filled with extraordinary paintings on the first floor. From the gallery, we were directed up a winding staircase to a small sitting room adjacent to Nelson and Mary's bedroom. On the way up the stairs, there were windows with amazing pre-Colombian art in 24-karat gold behind them. There was a series of these windows, each beautifully lit and filled with dazzling treasures. I literally gasped when I saw them. The sitting room had a rather low ceiling and was furnished with comfortable, somewhat worn leather sofas and chairs.

At one point, I asked if I could use the ladies' room and was directed to go through their bedroom to their bathroom. I have been in many grand homes and have observed various degrees of pampered wealth, including two twin beds with turned-down sheets and blankets, fresh nightgown and pajamas carefully placed on top, but I never encountered what I saw on the Rockefellers' sinks. A toothbrush was laid out for each next to the cold-water handle, very carefully squeezed toothpaste on its bristles, ready to be picked up and put in their mouths. On my way back to the sitting room, I almost tripped on Mrs. Rockefeller's slippers, which were placed neatly on the side of her bed and astonished me with their size.

Happy and her husband, Dr. Murphy, were animated and extremely flattering about the speech—especially Happy. It was revealed in the conversation that she worked for the governor, which I assumed was the reason for such enthusiasm. At one point, the governor turned to me and said, "Nancy, you seemed so interested in the art on the stairway. Would you like to look at the art in the gallery downstairs? As a matter of fact, why don't Happy and I take you there?" I was thrilled and jumped out of my chair and ran down the stairs with Happy and Nelson behind me.

I assumed that they would conduct a tour and tell me all about what I was about to see, but to my amazement the minute we entered the room, they disappeared. They quickly walked to the far, far other end and started to whisper and laugh; their intimacy and pleasure to be with each other were palpitating. I politely looked at a few of the paintings, and after an awkward ten minutes or so I went back up the stairs to join Dr. Murphy, Emmet, and Mrs. Rockefeller. Dr. Murphy looked at me a little anxiously; however, Emmet and Mrs. Rockefeller continued their conversation as if they had not noticed that I had entered the room alone.

Finally, Happy and the governor joined us. It was time to leave. Emmet and I thanked the Rockefellers for their hospitality, said good night to the Murphys, and climbed into their limousine, which they so kindly kept waiting for us to use on our journey home. I turned to Emmet and said, "Do you have any idea what's going on between Happy and the governor?" It was hard to believe that Emmet never picked up on their relationship, but I find men can sometimes be rather obtuse about these things. It simply never occurred to him. However, it became clear about six months later when it was announced that Nelson Rockefeller was getting a divorce. A year after that he married Happy. They had two children and about sixteen years of marriage.

In telling the end of this story, I want to emphasize how I keep finding the symmetry and perfection in how our actions predict the inevitable ending of the events in our lives. On Friday, January 26, 1979, Nelson had dinner with Happy and their two sons. After dinner, he excused himself to go to his office—actually, he went to his townhouse on Fifty-Fourth Street to meet his twenty-six-year-old aide, Megan Marshak. He had a major heart attack while they were in bed and died. Every time I think of Happy, I am reminded of the biblical phrase, "You live by the sword, you die by the sword."

35

Life as a Single Parent

The first summer after I was divorced, Alan and Micheline invited Liza and Jenny to spend a month with them in the south of France. Emmet and I decided that after I delivered the children to Alan in Zurich, Switzerland, I would go on to London and meet him there. Emmet spoke Italian and Spanish perfectly, and his French was pretty good, too. This was a business trip for him, but it was combined with a pleasure trip for the two of us.

It was very surreal to escort my two little girls off the airplane and walk them into the terminal in Zurich and hand them over to Alan. For their sake, I was enthusiastic and tried to be joyful for them and their wonderful new adventure. Alan had a copy of my itinerary with all the telephone numbers of the various hotels I would be staying at. After he left, I sat in the airport waiting for my connection to London, silently weeping.

When I arrived at the Connaught Hotel, there was a telegram waiting for me from Alan. I was not prepared for its cruelty, but it did prepare me for future relations with Alan and Micheline. It said, "Nancy, I hope you are not registered as Mrs. Alan J. Lerner. Signed, Alan." All Alan had to do was call the Connaught and ask for me, and he would have discovered that I was registered as Mrs. Nancy Lerner. Poor Micheline—she was so desperately afraid that I would be misconstrued as the "real" Mrs. Alan J. Lerner. It's pathetic when I think of it today; it was so unnecessary to go to such lengths.

This was a very difficult transition time for me, and I thank Emmet for the gift of this magical trip he helped plan. After a lot of theater, parties, dinners, and enjoying London, Emmet had to go to Vienna to work with the *Time* magazine bureau. We arranged to meet in Vienna at the train station, where we were to board together for the trip to Venice, Italy.

I flew alone to Vienna in the morning and checked into the Grand Hotel. I was meeting Emmet at 6:30 in the evening, so I had the day to explore Vienna. It was a beautiful summer day, and I found the city enchanting. I am not a sweets lover, but I never tasted anything as delicious as the cream puff I bought from a charming little bakery around the corner from the hotel. I arrived at the train station with my luggage and only the number of the train and its destination to guide me.

It was also very confusing and difficult for me to find someone to communicate with in English. In fact, it was getting late, and I began to panic just a little, thinking that I might miss our train. Eventually, I found the platform. Steam was already coming from the bottom of the cars, people were rushing around me, it was getting later and later, but something wonderful happened. One of the windows of a car was open, and Emmet was leaning out, watching me. He casually said, "Looking for someone?"

I could not help thinking that I was in the middle of a movie; it seemed to me that I had seen this on film before. He helped me get my luggage inside and directed me to our little compartment, where he had a bottle of wine and some delicious Austrian rolls with cheese and jam; it was all we needed. We arrived the next morning in Venice with the sun shining. We got into a boat with our luggage and entered the city. I don't think there is any experience quite like visiting this extraordinary place for the first time.

I think it's important to tell you that I never stayed in the same hotel with Emmet for most of this trip. It was not only expected at that time, but I felt it was important for my children. I did not want them to be exposed to any criticism of their mother that might hurt them. Emmet and I traveled down the coast to Florence, Rome, and eventually to the most unbelievably special place on earth, Ravello. We did stay at the same hotel in Ravello but maintained separate rooms. When I think of this trip, I want to say, "Thank you, Emmet."

It was time to go home. I flew to Zurich and met the girls in the terminal. They raced across the room into my arms; I don't think the three of us were ever so happy to be together as we were at that moment. I had the feeling that this "vacation" with their father and stepmother was not as much fun or as loving as they had hoped. I heard bits and pieces that sounded strange. Apparently, Micheline was critical of their clothes, implying that their mother did not really have very good taste. Again, all I can say is, "Poor Micheline." Did she really feel so inadequate or insecure? Did it make her feel comforted to be superior? Perhaps I should have felt "poor Alan" as well.

We returned to New York, and I put the girls back in school and resumed my single life. It was briefly interrupted with a play on Broadway. I was offered the lead opposite David Wayne in a play titled *Send Me No Flowers*. It was quite a charming comedy, and I enjoyed working with David very much, although he had a somewhat volatile and emotional temper. I will never forget one moment during rehearsals when he turned to me and shouted, "You are always so accommodating! Don't you ever get angry at anything?!" I was startled and wondered, "Did I?"—that was a good question! The play lasted only six weeks on Broadway but was immediately sold to Universal Studios to be made into a movie starring Doris Day and Rock Hudson.

It occurred to me that I might never do another film, which was perfectly OK. I never thought of myself as an "actress" exclusively. Life was far more complex and fascinating to conquer and explore.

The second summer of my divorce presented a problem. I was going to be alone for a month without the children, who would be visiting Alan and Micheline and their two-year-old son, Michael, in Antibes. Emmet and I decided to go to Europe again while the children were away. This time we met in Spain. Barcelona and Madrid were spectacular, but the best of all was spending time on the island of Majorca.

One afternoon I received a phone call from Los Angeles. The operator said a Mr. Walt Disney was on the line. "Really?" I said, not quite believing her. Actually, it *was* Mr. Disney, who said, "Nancy, we are doing a motion picture and spending more money than in the history of the studio with a star-studded cast, and we want you in it. The picture is the classic story *Pollyanna*." He said, "When are you coming back, and what are your plans for the rest of the summer?" "Well," I said, "as a matter of fact I am going to be in Los Angeles in a couple of weeks to visit my parents, and I am bringing my children with me." "Perfect," he said, "we are starting to shoot at the end of July and will be through in time for you to put the children back in school in New York."

I never asked him about salary; as a matter of fact, I never considered it. It wasn't that I thought of myself as being so wealthy; it just was not the issue. Actually, making this film was the perfect solution for the rest of the summer, and I thought it might be fun for the children to be part of it, too. So after I picked them up in Paris, we went directly to Los Angeles.

36

Disney

Walking on the Disney lot was an entirely new experience, so different from any studio I ever worked at. It was so clean and orderly, and everyone called each other by their first names, even Mr. Disney, or Walt, as he insisted. The studio had produced a group of works of art beginning with the legendary *Snow White and the Seven Dwarfs* and followed by *Pinocchio, Fantasia, Dumbo, Bambi,* and then the magnificent *Cinderella* and *Sleeping Beauty.* I remember *Snow White* was one of the first films I ever saw, and I never have quite recovered from being stunned by its beauty and artistry. All of these films represent a lifetime of superior achievement, and they will live forever. Walt was a genius, a surprising one. He actually was quite provincial in his own life and tastes.

While films like *Treasure Island* and *20,000 Leagues under the Sea* were very successful releases for Disney, in the early 1960s the studio was more well known for its animation than it was for its live-action movies. Walt Disney decided to change that with his rendition of *Pollyanna,* which was a well-known children's classic. He decided he might gamble with a larger budget and a more star-studded cast.

Mary and John Mills's daughter Hayley was chosen to play Pollyanna. Jane Wyman was contracted to play her aunt; Richard Egan, Karl Malden, Adolphe Menjou, Agnes Moorehead, and I completed the cast. All of us were distinguished actors, and the director, David Swift, was exactly the right person to put this charming story on film. One of the joys of making this movie was my friendship with the Mills family, who were absolutely delightful people. Hayley was a darling girl and a very intuitive performer. I think anyone who has young children should get the DVD; I know they will love every minute of it.

While I was making this film, I remember one afternoon one of the assistant directors said that I was wanted on the phone by a man named Clifford

Odets. I couldn't imagine why Mr. Odets, whom I had never met, would be calling me. He was very polite and said that he would like to take me out to dinner later in the week; he had something he wanted to discuss with me.

I knew that Clifford Odets had been a very celebrated writer for theater and films. In fact, *Golden Boy* was considered one of the greatest American plays ever written and had made William Holden a star in the film version. . . . I was intrigued.

The following Saturday night he picked me up at my parents' home and said we were going to visit Marlon Brando before we went to dinner. I had never met Marlon, but I was a great admirer of his talent. We drove to the top of Mulholland Drive and walked into a very contemporary, rather sparsely furnished house. Marlon's wife, Anna, was a beautiful Asian woman, but there was something disturbing in the air. Marlon was in his bare feet, wearing dark pants and an open white shirt, and seemed to be playing a game with his wife and with us. They insisted that we go into the bedroom and look at their beautiful son, Christian, but Marlon seemed strangely removed from all of us. We amused him from a distance; his lack of caring for or interest in any of us was obvious. He was like the stage manager of a play, moving us all around the set (his house) and directing us, but we all remained distant players. He moved like a dancer in his bare feet, choreographing everything.

Clifford and I had dinner, and he never told me why he wanted to see me. It was a somewhat awkward evening, and, frankly, the whole thing seemed bizarre. He insisted on taking me to dinner again several nights later. We talked about the world, the theater, politics, and life in general. It was still not clear to me what he wanted—that is, until he walked me to my parents' front door. He grabbed me and pulled me into an impassioned embrace, almost sobbing desperately. Breathlessly he said, "I know what you did for Alan Lerner! Please, please help me to write again—I have one more great work within me, and I need you to help me make it happen."

I felt immensely sorry for him and felt that this encounter was possibly one of the strangest moments in my life. Extricating myself as delicately as I could, I explained that I could not possibly produce the magic that he was looking for. I also told him that I was involved with a man in New York and could not have anything more than the most platonic relationship with him. He did not take me to dinner again; however, I received a long, rambling letter from what seemed to me . . . to be a lost soul.

Liza and Jenny enjoyed being in California and especially spending time with my parents. Emmet came out to visit for a long weekend and, I think, was intrigued with visiting me on the set. I established a lovely relationship with everyone at the Disney studio and was not surprised when I got another call, this time from my agent, asking me to make *The Absent-Minded Professor* with Fred MacMurray. It never ceases to amaze me how doors keep opening and completely and unexpectedly change our lives and the direction we seem to be going.

It was early in 1960 when I received that call from my agent, and although it seemed to me that Fred MacMurray was a little too old for me (I was thirty-two, he was fifty-two), I thought the film was the perfect solution for my summer plans. I would shoot the first half of it while Liza and Jenny were in Europe visiting their father and Micheline. I would stay with my parents until the children and their governess, Miss Stocker, joined me in California.

When they arrived, I rented an apartment in Santa Monica at the Oceana, which overlooks the Pacific. My parents adored the children and loved spending time with them. Miss Stocker was a fabulous caretaker, and I was having another film adventure in the most delightful project, *The Absent-Minded Professor,* now considered a classic.

The Disney Studios was changing, especially after the success of *Pollyanna*. Bill Walsh, the producer and cowriter of this new film, was I think a true genius. His whimsical and fanciful sensibility created some of the most delightful Disney films of that era.

Fred MacMurray was a master comedian and had an intuitive, natural, and effective presence on the screen. I marveled at his technique, which seemed so utterly effortless.

He married June Haver after his first wife died. June was a very pretty woman and extremely religious. In fact, she had joined a nunnery after a short career in films but, thank goodness for Fred, decided that that life was not for her. They adopted twin girls, and Fred seemed more concerned about what he was going to cook everyone for dinner that night than how to approach the next scene. He was also a Republican, which pleased Walt Disney but not me. However, his awareness of my loneliness was apparent, and his kindness to me I shall never forget. We exchanged stories of growing up in Wisconsin and made each other laugh all the time. We seemed to look at the world through the same midwestern looking glass.

When *The Absent-Minded Professor* was released in March 1961, it was the Easter week in New York. It was playing at Radio City Music Hall and was such a huge hit that a front-page story appeared in the *New York Times* about the traffic jam it created on Sixth Avenue.

One night Emmet and I attended a dinner at the 21 Club. On the way up Sixth Avenue, we passed the theater. It was late, and Emmet looked at the marquee, exclaiming, "There you are!" I said, "What do you mean?" He said, "Your name. It says, 'Starring Fred MacMurray and Nancy Olson.'" I was stunned. It never occurred to me that they would bother to put my name next to Fred's. Even though I was costarring in the film, I assumed that because I had worked so seldom, my name was not important enough. We humans are such an interesting mixture of egos and non-egos; in my case, a positive and confident outlook combined with an assumption that nobody cares.

My life with Emmet, New York, raising two children alone, and trying to set a course for the future were beginning to challenge me more and more. I resumed taking piano lessons and enjoyed exploring Schubert's extraordinary piano pieces, but I obviously was not going to ever debut in Carnegie Hall. Where was I going? Where was this life taking me?

I remember the last meeting that I had with Dr. Frank. He said to me, "Nancy, someday you have to figure out why you married Alan Lerner in the first place, and your life will not be satisfying or happy until you find that out." I thought he was crazy. It seemed to me pretty obvious why I had been so compelled to marry Alan Jay. And yet here I was trapped in a somewhat similar relationship. I actually was determined that Emmet should write a book and knew that he would not be completely happy with his talents until he did. Can you believe that I found myself sitting in his apartment while he sat at the typewriter and handed me the pages as he completed them? I honestly feel that the book would never have been written if it had not been for my encouragement and nurturing. The book was *America the Vincible*. When it was published, he handed me a copy and turned to the dedication page. It said, "To my mother and father," and in his own hand he had written, "And to Nancy with gratitude and love."

37

The Inauguration of JFK

It's amazing to me how John F. Kennedy keeps interrupting this story. Emmet and I decided to go to Washington for his inauguration. The day John Fitzgerald Kennedy was inaugurated as the thirty-fifth president of the United States was dark, damp, and cold, with a sky ready to unleash big, lumpy, wet snowflakes. Who can forget the young, beautiful couple, the picture of Robert Frost with his hair blowing in the icy wind as he recited his masterful poem "The Gift Outright"? Anyone who was there or saw it on television will always remember the young president's historic speech and be haunted by these images.

Emmet and I attended receptions, parties, and many of the balls. We ended up on a bus with friends and some of the Kennedy clan. I remember Teddy joined us for a short time between ballrooms. One of our group was Afdera Fonda, Henry's wife. He was appearing on Broadway in *Critic's Choice* and could not be with us. Earl Smith, who had been ambassador to Cuba during the revolution, and his wife, Flo, were with us—they were Palm Beach neighbors of the Kennedys—and I remember the young pianist Peter Duchin was with us. There were about twelve or thirteen people in our immediate party.

Joe Alsop, the newspaper columnist, was attending the festivities separately along with his house guest, the historian and Kennedy adviser Arthur Schlesinger Jr. Mr. Alsop gave someone in our group the key to his home with the understanding that whoever reached the house first would turn on the lights, light a fire, and open a bottle of brandy.

Around midnight, we arrived at the house, cold and exhausted, and did as Joe had asked. A few went into the kitchen to search for something to eat as well. The kitchen was on the other side of the front hall, and as I was on my way to help, I heard a rather desperate pounding on the front door. I called out that someone was at the front door, and the others called back to please open it!

The door seemed to be stuck, so I gave it a good yank. It opened, and there was Jack. He was standing alone—no coat, no hat—the snow billowing around him. Behind him at the curb were only two limousines—no Secret Service, police, or security of any kind. He walked in, took my trembling hand, and said, "Good evening, Nancy." I stammered, "Good evening, Mr. President," and "Congratulations, Mr. President."

Everyone was stunned; however, I noticed Afdera standing behind me not seeming the least surprised. I learned later that Afdera had managed to get into the presidential box at one of the balls and had whispered into Jack's ear, "We're going to Joe's."

The president sat in an armchair facing the fire. He was eager to reminisce and share some of the impressions of this historic day. He talked about going to the White House in the morning and meeting President Eisenhower wearing a top hat. With great glee, he said that the outgoing president had looked like a real "mick"! He talked about how Robert Frost's poem had touched him, but he seemed the most interested in what happened that day to Richard Nixon, the outgoing vice president, whom Kennedy had just defeated in the election: he wanted to know if it was true that Nixon had taken a train back to California and was planning to run for governor.

He talked to Afdera about her visit to see his new baby boy, John. He said he was sorry that Henry wasn't there. To my astonishment, he turned to me and said, "Nancy, when I saw *Critics' Choice*, I thought of you. You should have played opposite Henry."

Before I end this story, I want to share a picture that remains in my mind. A young president, knees crossed, a cigar in his right hand, a glass of brandy in his left, beginning to drift with his thoughts. He stared into the fire and said quietly, "I was briefed by the State Department yesterday." Shaking his head slowly, he almost whispered, "They left a mess in Vietnam. . . . "

There was a moment of silence before Jack stood up and said it was getting late and he should get to the White House. He'd been there for almost an hour. We all walked him to the front door, saying our goodbyes, and watched him descend the steps to the open door of one of the limousines. When it disappeared, there was commotion and exhilaration—some went to get another drink, and some of us were too paralyzed to leave the front hall. Suddenly we heard a key twisting in the front-door lock. The door opened, and Joe and Arthur walked in.

I have never witnessed another human being suffer such intense devastation as when Joe Alsop slowly absorbed the fact that the president of the

United States had come to his house on the night of the inauguration, but he had not been there to witness it.

Isn't it interesting, though, that Joe Alsop dined out for years on his famous evening with Jack Kennedy the night of the inaugural and how they talked until dawn at his house—he wrote about it many times, and the evening is even described in a play, the last scene showing the headlights of limousines, Secret Service vehicles, and police motorcycles arriving at his house—it never happened.

One evening later that year, I was in a taxi crossing Seventy-Sixth Street between Park Avenue and Madison Avenue when I casually looked out the window and I saw a man walking alone near the side entrance of the Carlyle Hotel. I almost asked the driver to stop immediately. It was twilight, but I could swear that I had just seen Jack Kennedy. It seemed too ludicrous. What would the president be doing walking alone on Seventy-Sixth Street? So I continued my journey home, where about half an hour later the phone rang. It was my and Jack's mutual friend Chuck Spalding. He apologized for calling on such short notice, but he wondered if I could possibly join him and some friends for dinner. Unfortunately, I wasn't free, and after we chatted amicably for a minute or two, we said goodbye.

The next day when I had my hair done, one of the hairdressers who was famous for doing most of the models in New York commented, "Hey, guess what? The president was in town last night partying!"

I guess it was time for another piece of chocolate.

38

Mrs. Kemeny

In the meantime, Emmet, of course, was flirting with all kinds of other women in New York, and only after finally acknowledging how devastating this relationship was did I understand that I had come to a real impasse. I actually woke up one morning and said out loud to no one but myself, "I'm willing to give it up."

On my bedside table was the telephone number of a woman psychologist, Diana Kemeny. It had been given to me by a very close friend who said that she was tired of listening to my tales of woe; she just couldn't listen any longer. That morning I picked up the telephone and dialed Mrs. Kemeny. She answered the phone and said that she had a cancellation that afternoon and would be happy to see me.

At three o'clock, I stepped into her office and met the most incredible person I have ever known. She was in her sixties, with white hair and an intense gaze, and she was a profoundly gifted listener. She had studied with Jung and was completely familiar with all of Freud's theories as well; she combined everything into her own genius. I told her what I had said that morning, and she looked at me intently and asked if I knew what that meant. I could not answer precisely, but I knew that it was important that I give up whatever it was that was destroying my life.

She asked me if I had any recent dreams that I could remember. I said, "Yes, I dreamed that I was walking up some wide winding stairs and reached a plateau, and there were no more stairs to climb." She looked at her watch and said our time was over, but she wanted to see me every Tuesday and Thursday at three o'clock. Like a professor giving a student an assignment, she asked me to dream. She also suggested that I write down my dreams when I awakened in the morning so that I could remember details. We said goodbye.

What an incredible life-altering experience I had working with Diana Kemeny! Apparently, I had taken her assignment very seriously; I began having the most vivid and detailed dreams, and because I am an actress, I was able to describe them perfectly. In fact, I never had to write them down; they were as real and unforgettable as any movie, play, or book that I have ever seen or read.

Our routine was for me to sit down and describe my dreams at the beginning of each session. Then Mrs. Kemeny would start to critique and unravel a story that became as fascinating and real to me as anything that I ever experienced. My dreams became so intense that I began to have two every night. The second dream started with my taking care of a baby, a baby that I kept trying to prop up as it continually slumped over the minute I let go. I kept putting the baby in a corner, which I thought might help, but to no avail. Slowly, though, the baby began to sit up by itself.

As Mrs. Kemeny explained the meaning of the first dream I had, the dream about the baby began to change. The baby was now three years old and walking by herself. Soon she was riding a three-wheeler and eventually a real bicycle. One of the last dreams I had was her walking across the street by herself to the park.

I hesitate to oversimplify this experience, but I think it's important for everyone to understand how we humans put ourselves in unsolvable positions in order to exorcise a problem that confronted us when we were children. And, of course, because we were children when presented with this original problem, we could not possibly solve it because we were not in authority. And as adults, if we confront this problem, it is duplicated in absolutely unsolvable circumstances. Therefore, we are stuck. The only possible solution is to understand that we could not solve this problem as children, and we don't have to experience it over and over and over again; we just have to understand it. I will oversimplify my own dilemma growing up, but only so that you might understand what I am saying.

My father adored me but was intimidated by my mother, especially since as I grew older and more independent, she felt threatened and treated me more like a sibling rival than her child. There was always the presence of the "other woman" in the relationship between my father and me. I am sad to acknowledge that as fortunate as I was to have two very special parents, I somehow was damaged by them, and I put myself through unnecessary unhappiness as an adult because of it. How fragile we humans are.

While I was struggling with my own failures and sadness, my children's longing for a father in their life, the three of us searching for a happier future and determined to create something new, my life continued in an ever-fascinating and evolving mixture of experiences. I was still seeing Emmet, but not exclusively. I was also making myself part of the rest of the world.

There is one evening that I remember in detail to this day.

39

A Special Memory

On a cold, darkening November afternoon, my phone rang. It was my friend Bennett Cerf, cofounder and publisher of Random House. He and his wife, Phyllis, were friends of Alan and me, and we had continued our relationship after my divorce. Phyllis was a formidable woman and not overly gracious or friendly to me; however, Bennett was my champion and dear friend.

I picked up the phone, and Bennett said, "Nancy! I hate to call you with such short notice, but our friend Bill Faulkner is in town, and we're taking him to dinner tonight with another couple. Can you possibly join us?" Of course I was busy. I was busy every single night of the week, but something told me that I shouldn't miss this evening, so I said I would love to join them. "Splendid!" he said. "Meet us at our house for a drink at seven, and I've arranged for a car to take us all to Côte Basque for dinner."

Can you remember exactly what dress you wore, what jewelry you used, what shoes, what handbag, the winter coat that you put on more than fifty years ago? I do. I wore a quite beautiful, sleeveless, silk-satin, knee-length sheath in a lustrously rich, ripe raspberry color, a delicate antique gold chain with an oval locket and a large diamond in the center, matching earrings, and an antique 22-carat gold bracelet embedded with multiple garnets. Of course, at that time everyone had satin pumps matched to the color of their dress. My hair was pulled back in a simple twist. A mink coat, white kid gloves, and a small gold handbag completed my costume.

I arrived by taxi at the Cerfs' townhouse on East Sixty-Eighth Street. Of course, I was a little apprehensive. I wasn't sure that I could completely handle the evening with a legendary author as well as Phyllis! I was greeted by a butler, who took my coat and escorted me up the stairs to the second landing, where I was told Mrs. Cerf and her guest were waiting for me in the library. As I entered, I saw Mr. Faulkner at the far end of the room in an animated conversation with Phyllis. Hesitatingly, I walked over to them and extended my hand to Mr. Faulkner. There was no response from Phyllis to please pull up another chair and join them, so I quickly retreated to the couch on the other side of the room. I accepted a glass of wine from the butler and waited anxiously for Bennett to join us and save me.

Bennett Cerf was known for his exuberant friendliness. He made everyone feel welcome and accepted with such genuine and unique warmth. It was a treat to be invited to their home. I remember an evening sitting at the same table with John Steinbeck and John O'Hara (I wore a pale-blue satin cocktail dress, with masses of pearls around my neck and satin shoes to match the color of my dress, of course!)

I was so glad to see Bennett, and he seemed genuinely happy to have me there. The butler announced that the car was waiting, and the four of us went down the stairs and began our journey to one of the great restaurants in New York City. We were joined there by the author of *I Can Get It for You Wholesale*, Jerome Weidman, and his wife, Peggy.

There was a lot of conversation, laughter, gossip, politics, and wonderful food. I did not overintrude, not only because I was intrinsically shy but also because it was important to keep my place with Phyllis. Before dessert was served, I excused myself to go to the powder room. When I came back, Mr. Faulkner greeted me with a warm smile.

After dinner, we climbed into the limousine and headed back to Sixty-Eighth Street. Phyllis and Bennett insisted that we join them for a nightcap before saying goodbye. I climbed up the stairs and was about to join everyone in the library, when suddenly Mr. Faulkner gently took my arm and guided me into the front sitting room. He said he wanted to talk to me. I don't know if it was the wine, his demeanor, the loneliness I was constantly feeling then, but I was so pleased to be alone with him. He asked for a glass of brandy and started to ask me questions. After about half an hour, he said, "Why don't I take you home, and we can have another glass of brandy there?" I quickly agreed.

William Faulkner was a small, slight gentleman. He couldn't have been more than five foot six or seven. He was clearly not in the greatest health, and although he was only in his early sixties, he seemed much older. He was extremely frail. Life was draining away from him; he was whittled down to his very essence and yet seemed so utterly comfortable and at peace. It is hard to describe his gaze, although I remember it perfectly. It was intensely interested, without judgment, without regret, only a profound, thoughtful wisdom. He was a famous stranger, and there was no reason on earth why he should want to listen to me, and yet I wanted desperately to talk to him. I had been rejected by my husband, the father of my children. I had found myself in another relationship that was also fraught with rejection and betrayal. I was lonely and worried about my two darling daughters, Liza and Jenny, not having a complete family to grow up with. I was in despair and for the first time in my life wondered what was going to become of me.

We sat together in my living room at the Beresford on the deep-blue, Scalamandre silk-velvet sofa, a glass of brandy for each of us on the coffee table. He began the conversation with his description of my entering the Cerf library. He said, "You came in so soigné, so beautiful, and yet with your mind made up that we were not the least bit interested in you, and so you walked to the other side of the room."

This comment so surprised me that I began to open our conversation to another level. I told him that Phyllis always scared me to death, and she looked as if she was completely enjoying her conversation with him and not welcoming anyone to interrupt. I asked him what he thought of Phyllis. He hesitated a moment and bent his elbows, the palms of his hands facing away from him, slowly bending his fingers into claws. He said slowly, "I am always careful of Phyllis."

Inevitably, our conversation turned to what I was longing for the most: I wanted to talk about love. I asked him if he remembered being in love. It was an audacious and naive question, but he sat silently contemplating how to answer. He said it was no longer relevant to him. He struggled to give me an answer that would enlighten me, but all he could say was that at this time in his life love was an abstraction for him. Perhaps, as I think about it today, he was trying to make the issue less powerful and overwhelming.

There was a moment that I recall with a degree of embarrassment. He asked me about my children, my little girls, my precious little girls. I described my older daughter Liza and said she was inherently an artist. She also was the most affected by her father's leaving, and I was desperate to help her. I don't know what I was thinking, but I leaped to my feet and went into her room to find a poem she had recently written. Liza was about nine years old and was fascinated with Greek mythology. She had written a poem entitled "Helen of Troy," which I found to be quite remarkable. Believe it or not, I gave it to William Faulkner to read. He accepted the piece of paper like a college professor about to examine a doctoral dissertation. He was serious and respectful. He studied it carefully, put it down on the table, and said, "You know who this poem is about, don't you? . . . It's about you."

143

There was a moment soon after our second brandy when we both became silent. His right hand was resting on his knee, and it slowly began to move toward my knee. I literally stopped breathing. His hand seemed to be suspended in space for an eternity and quite slowly changed its mind and moved back to his own knee. Tears filled my eyes.

It was about 4:30 a.m. We knew the evening was coming to an end. I walked him across the long foyer to the front door. He took my hand and said, "I want you to do me a favor. I want you to send me a postcard with a message of only two words." I looked at him expectantly. What could I possibly write in two words in a message to William Faulkner?

I told him I would be pleased to send him a postcard with only two words, but I couldn't imagine what they might be. He said, "The words I want you to write are—'I'm happy.'"

The next morning I woke up and started to weep. For some reason I couldn't stop. The phone rang, and it was Bennett. "Nancy, thank you so much for joining us last night. I thought you would like to know that Bill loved being with you. It was interesting. At the restaurant when you left the table to go to the powder room, he turned to me and said, 'Why is that lovely young woman in so much pain?'" Bennett was being his very gracious self. I struggled to keep my voice from betraying me, thanked him, and said, "It was a wonderful evening for me, too."

It is now the twenty-first century, and this memory still haunts me. I remember my tears. In fact, I think I cried for three days. I tried then to describe this encounter to my psychologist, Diana Kemeny. I told her, "He was like a GRAND father"—not a grandfather but a father who was grand. I never sent Bill that postcard. He died in July 1962, and it wasn't until September 1 of that year—the day I married Alan Livingston—that I finally found true and lasting happiness. If only Bill had lived a few months longer, he would have received that postcard.

It's amazing to me that I now, after all these years, understand why I wept and why I was so moved by the gift of his presence. People always assumed that I had everything—wonderful children, a career, beauty, wealth, many men admirers—What could I possibly need more of? Bill Faulkner understood that what I needed most . . . was kindness.

40

A Shocking Story

It was the summer of 1961 that marked a complete change in the direction of my life and destiny. I was spending another summer in California at our same apartment in the Oceana to be near my parents, not only for them but for the children as well. Liza and Jenny visited their father and Micheline in Biarritz, France. Miss Stocker picked them up in Paris and flew directly to Los Angeles, arriving at eleven o'clock at night. The minute I saw the children, I knew something terrible had happened during their visit. Jenny flew into my arms and sobbed and sobbed and sobbed. She desperately held on to me, and between her sobs she whispered, "Mommy, would you please buy me a little house with furniture in it?" I was stunned and immediately deeply concerned about what had taken place on their trip.

I assured her that of course I would get her a little house with furniture in it, but it was time now for her and Liza to come back to the apartment and get some sleep.

Jenny shared one bedroom with Miss Stocker in twin beds; Liza shared the other bedroom and a queen-size bed with me. Liza seemed equally needful but not as desperate as Jenny.

The next morning we could not get Jenny to eat her breakfast. She just wanted to sit on my lap and quietly weep. My father and mother were alarmed as much as I was, and we all were determined to find out what happened.

One night Liza climbed into bed next to me; I took her in my arms and said, "Liza, please, please tell me what happened to Jenny." She whimpered, "Mommy, it was awful."

Slowly Liza began to feel safe with me at night in our bed, and she started to tell me what happened in the last weeks of their visit in Biarritz.

Apparently, they all went to the beach one afternoon, and when they returned to the house, Jenny exuberantly raced into her room and flung her sandy body on top of the bed. Micheline was behind her and became enraged, shouting, "How dare you have such little regard for my house! Look at how you have ruined the bedspread! You shall be punished for this!" She stalked out of the room, calling for Alan to come to her immediately.

Liza said Jenny was trembling and ran into the bathroom to clean herself. All of a sudden Alan came into the room and said that Liza was to leave immediately; he told Jenny that she was to go to Micheline and apologize. Alan pushed Jenny through the door and took her to Micheline, but by this time Jenny was sobbing so hysterically that she could not utter the words "I'm sorry." She tried and tried but was unsuccessful. Alan took her back to the room, shoved her inside, and locked the door behind her.

Liza told me that from that moment on Jenny was targeted by Micheline as the most undisciplined and rude child she had ever experienced. And every time Alan locked Jenny in her room, Liza would lie on the floor and talk to her through the space between the carpeting and the door, begging Jenny to stop crying.

One evening Alan announced that he had to go to Paris for two days and wanted to bring presents for everyone when he came home. Jenny said she wanted a group of books that were recently published by an English author whose name I do not remember; Liza wanted some yarn to knit with; and Michael asked for a little house with furniture in it.

When Alan returned from Paris, Micheline said that Jenny had been rude to her again. Alan invited the children into the living room and gave Michael and Liza their presents but said that Jenny would not be receiving hers. Jenny sat silently, saying nothing. Liza told her father that she thought she shouldn't accept her gift either.

Apparently, Jenny eventually received the books before she left.

I found this story to be so heartbreaking. I remember the morning Jenny left to go to Biarritz and said to Senya, our cook, "Senya, I'm going to visit my daddy! I can't wait to see him!"

Now that I knew what had happened, my mother, my father, Miss Stocker, Liza, and I slowly nursed and loved Jenny back to feeling more like herself, and she even started to eat a little. Of course, she opened a big box with a doll house in it and lots of furniture.

When I look back, I have to thank Liza for not only supporting Jenny and helping her as best she could but also sharing this horrific story of what happened.

It was impossible for Alan to stand up to Micheline; her need to hurt and punish Liza and Jenny for nothing more than being my daughters was overwhelming, and he was paralyzed. That was not an excuse, as far as I was concerned, and I made it clear to him and to the girls that they would never be treated like this ever, ever again!

Somehow we put the children's visit with their father behind us. Liza, Jenny, and I didn't realize that it was the second half of our California visit that was going to change our lives forever.

41

A New Beginning

One afternoon I received a phone call from a woman who had been a great friend of Alan Lerner and now was equally my friend as well, Lilly Messanger. She had been a powerful presence in the Hollywood community as Louis B. Mayer's assistant. I saw her several times a year and found her to be always interested in me and the children as much as she was fascinated with Alan Lerner and his work. After Louis B. Mayer retired, she started to work at NBC Television.

Lilly was a short, plump, red-haired Jewish matron who was married to Prince Alex Thurn-Taxis, a very strange union indeed! One afternoon Lilly called me at the Oceana and said she would like to drop by to visit the children and take me to dinner with a friend. I suspected she was doing a little match-making, which did not interest me, but I was delighted to join them for dinner.

Lilly and Alex picked me up, and after chatting with the children, we went to a private club in Beverly Hills (I don't remember the name, but I do know it no longer exists). They had reserved a booth and for some reason put themselves in the middle and me at one end, reserving the other end for Lilly's mysterious friend.

Suddenly, I caught a glimpse of a man walking toward the booth. He was very tall and slender and moved with a kind of elegant ease. As he sat down to join us, I quickly assessed that he was quite handsome: dark wavy hair, a lovely full-lipped smile, and dark, dark, soft-brown eyes. He was shy but also comfortable with himself and seemed unpretentious in a friendly midwestern way. Lilly said to me, "Nancy, this is Alan Livingston, my boss." He appraised me and seemed pleased but not overly so. I don't remember what we talked about, but I do remember I had a very nice time. Lilly and Alex asked Alan to please take me home, and he seemed happy to oblige.

As we drove down Wilshire Boulevard toward the ocean, we chatted about what was happening in the world, and when we arrived at my apartment building, he got out of the car to escort me to the door. I turned to say goodnight, and he paused before he said something astonishing: he enjoyed meeting me very much but wanted me to understand that if he did not call me, it was not because he didn't find me very lovely; it was because he was involved with another woman. I was so ingratiated by his honesty and felt so comfortable in telling him that I did not want him to worry about my feelings because I was also involved with another man. We said goodnight.

The next day I received a delightful spring floral arrangement in a charming basket with a note. It said, "You are beautiful, Alan."

As my internal life was coming into focus, my external life was dramatically changing, too. It became so obvious to me that I had to permanently extricate myself from Emmet, and I took steps to do so. This made him crazy: What happened to make me so independent and unresponsive to his tactics? In fact, it made him so upset that he made an appointment to visit Dr. Kemeny. The first thing he said to her was, "What are you doing to her?" I think he realized that he might have to look at himself differently as well. That didn't matter as I had already separated my emotions from him; I truly was no longer interested.

In the meantime, my phone kept ringing with pursuing suitors. One of them was a very fascinating and attractive man who was a successful and brilliant scientist. He was somewhat a man about town, and every time we were in the same room, I was aware of his glances. When it was clear to everyone in New York that I was no longer Emmet's girlfriend, he called and invited me to dinner. We had a very friendly time; he was interesting and attentive, but he was certainly not the man for me. I told Dr. Kemeny the next day about our date and said that I think I had finally graduated from her class. I told her that the gentleman said to me: "What has happened to you? A year ago I knew that if I ever had the chance, I could make you so exquisitely unhappy, but you are no longer interested!" I told her that I felt as if I were in the twilight zone; I could no longer react to anyone. I asked Kemeny if I was doomed to remain in this state forever. She said, "No, you are exactly where you should be."

Soon after we returned to New York, I received a phone call from Alan Livingston. He said he was no longer at NBC and had returned to Capitol Records as its president. He was in New York for the opening of the new Noel

Coward musical *Sail Away*. He asked if by any chance I might be free to join him for the theater and the supper party at Sardi's afterward. I surprised him by answering, "As a matter of fact, I am free."

He picked me up at my apartment, met the children, and off we went. The musical was not a great success, but the evening was. At Sardi's, he took my hand and whispered to the maître d' that he wanted the booth at the far end of the room, where we could talk more privately, and talk we did. When he took me home, I mentioned that if he were free, why didn't he come to the apartment the next night for a drink? He said he would.

Unfortunately, the next night was a disaster. I had arranged to stay at home with the children for dinner, and after receiving a call from my friend Katrina Ettlinger, who was coming into town from the country, I foolishly invited her to join us. When the doorbell rang, I realized that I had forgotten that I had invited Alan, too, and Jenny became upset that our special evening together was being ruined. She started to cry, and I wondered how my life had become so chaotic. It was clear to Alan when I opened the door that I was not prepared to be with him. I tried my best to please everyone (one of my main faults!), but it was evident to him that he had been dropped through the cracks. He stayed a half hour or so and left—I felt terrible.

I kept working with Kemeny and adapting to giving up my addiction for the wrong men. Emmet was already very involved with another woman, and I kept dating a variety of other suitors. I even decided to start entertaining again. I remember one particular party I gave sometime in November. It was one of my classic cocktail and light-buffet evenings. My guest list was always chosen with great care. In fact, it reminded me of creating a play in which superstars mingle with the cast and crew.

I don't remember who it was, but one of my guests brought Lady Jean Campbell and her latest love, the author Norman Mailer. Jean had been having a notorious affair with publisher Henry Luce, who refused to divorce his wife, Clare Boothe Luce. I was not surprised that Jean had picked another celebrity to be with. However, I was startled to see Norman so shortly after the stabbing of his wife; he had barely posted bail before his court appearance. I was particularly worried when I saw him start to drink heavily.

The evening was long, and guests slowly said goodnight and left my apartment. I was alarmed when I walked into the dining room and saw

Norman sitting in a chair facing the wall. I gently approached him, and when I was about six feet away, he said loudly, "Leave me alone!" Which I did.

I asked Jean if she could persuade him to leave with her as most of the guests were gone, and I was concerned about being left alone with him. In fact, I asked two of my extra male guests to stay a little longer. Jean went into the dining room and after about ten minutes came out and said to me, "I'm afraid he won't budge. But, please, Nancy, he is such a darling person. Don't worry—eventually he'll just get up and go. It's very important that I go now." And with that, she left.

I panicked and pleaded with the two young men to stay with me in the library. In the meantime, the phone rang. It was Jean, who said, "I'm in a phone booth around the corner. How are things going?" I answered, "He's still here!"

Then I had an inspired thought. I slowly went into the dining room and said to Norman, who was still staring at the wall, "Norman, my boyfriend is here, and we want to be alone. Will you please leave so that we can be together?" He replied, "I will be leaving soon." I went back to the library and pleaded with one of the men to stay with me. I explained that I had just told Norman that we needed to be alone. He panicked! (I never saw that young man again.)

Finally, Norman, without saying a word, walked through my front door into the vestibule and rang for the elevator. My heart was pounding with relief, but no faster than the heart of the young man who had agreed to stay.

There is a postscript to this story. Many years later I was living in California and invited to a party at Arianna Huffington's home. Arianna always adorned her evenings with as many celebrities as she could find. On this particular night, one of them was Norman Mailer. About halfway through the evening, Norman came up to me and said, "Oh my god, you're Nancy. I think I owe you an apology for something that happened in your apartment many years ago."

Christmas was approaching, and the children and I decided to spend it in California with my parents—again fate intervened.

42

A Christmas Gift

Liza and Jenny loved being with Grandma and Grandpa for the holidays; however, I increasingly felt sad and lost. Of course, the phone was still ringing with my California suitors.

One night, one of them took me to the famous restaurant Dominick's in Beverly Hills. As we were leaving, I passed a table with two men who were very involved in conversation. Suddenly I realized that one of them was Alan Livingston, and I said, "Hello!" He looked up and realized who it was. He said, "Nancy, what are you doing in California?" I told him that the children and I were staying with my parents for the holidays, and he asked, "May I call you?" I answered, much to the disappointment of my date, "Of course. I'd love to hear from you!" His companion immediately took out a pen and paper and carefully wrote down my telephone number for Alan. We said goodnight, and I thought to myself, "I wonder if I will ever hear from him."

The next afternoon the phone rang, and it was Alan, who said, "Nancy, by any chance are you free tomorrow night? I have to show up at a Capitol Records Christmas gathering, and we can go to Chasen's for dinner after that." I responded that I would love to join him and told him how to get to my parents' home.

I didn't realize it at the time, but that night was the real beginning of our relationship. I wore a pale-blue, nubby wool suit. The skirt skimmed the middle of my knees; the jacket was short and fitted, with a pale-blue, brocaded shell. I added pearl earrings, a multistranded pearl bracelet, black patent-leather low-cut pumps, and I carried a small patent-leather bag. After the party, we went to Chasen's, one of the great, established restaurants in Los Angeles at that time, and sat in a deep, quilted-leather booth and talked, laughed, argued, agreed, and enjoyed each other. After dinner, he took me home and again said that he was sorry that he was not going to call me before I left California, but he left open the possibility of seeing each other again in New York.

The night that I arrived from California at the New York apartment alone with my children is an evening that stays with me all these years. I put the children to bed and walked to the windows of my empty living room. Looking at the skyline of New York City, the lights sparkling with the life of all its people—everyone searching to be a vital part of its promise—I had never felt such loneliness. I walked from room to room and thought, "This is one of the saddest places I have ever been in." The past was filled with painful pictures of tortured unhappiness and failure. I started to weep and could not stop. I was alone! Period! I could not see the future. I went to bed.

43

Mary, Mary

B ut life is never over unless you are gasping for your last breath. About a
week after I returned home, the phone rang. It was Roger Stevens, the
famous entrepreneur and Broadway producer. He said, "Nancy, we need you!
We have the biggest hit on Broadway, *Mary, Mary,* and our leading lady, Barbara Bel Geddes, is on the verge of a nervous breakdown and needs a break.
We don't want to stop the momentum of our success and need a star to step
in. It's not a huge commitment; we figure you'll need two weeks of rehearsal
and hope you can stay with the play for six more weeks. We can't think of
anyone that could step into this role better than you. Please, please do it!" I
quickly realized that this was probably the best thing that could possibly happen to me at this time. *Mary, Mary* was a comedy that could lift my spirits
and a challenge that could erase my troubles for at least two months.

I never enjoyed being on stage as much as I did playing Mary. There is
nothing more rewarding than evoking laughter from a large group of people.
I had great fun making some of Jean Kerr's jokes come to life, ones that Barbara somehow had missed. However, I was totally frustrated that I never con-
quered the timing of one of the biggest laughs in the first act. It was a line that
Barbara had effortlessly nailed. It was when Mary picks up something odd
from a porcelain bowl on the desk and asks her exhusband innocently, "What
are these?" He answers, "Dried apricots. What do you think they are?" Mary
examines them and answers, "Ears!"

Coming home at midnight to my quiet, lonely apartment was not as devastating as it used to be. I poured a glass of wine for myself and sat in my
library trying to figure out how to nail that laugh. To this day, I think to
myself, "Perhaps if I tried it this way, it would work!"

The nice thing was that Jean Kerr seemed thrilled and grateful for my
performance. Apparently, the first night I was on stage, she saw me get a huge
laugh from one of her favorite lines that Barbara used to ignore. It was at the

end of the second act when Mary and her exhusband start to review their marriage. The husband, played by Barry Nelson, said to Mary, "I always told you you were beautiful!" Playing Mary, I started to cry and blubbered through my tears, "Yes! You told me I was beautiful . . . like Mrs. Roosevelt!" The audience went absolutely crazy with laughter. Jean turned to her husband, the noted theater critic Walter Kerr, and said, "She got it!" Walter answered, "And so did they!"

While I was doing this play, a couple of interesting things happened that I must share. The first occurred one Sunday morning, when the doorbell rang at about ten o'clock. Miss Stocker had taken the children to the park, and Senya, my housekeeper-cook, was gone for the day. I put on my robe and slippers and went to the door. When I opened it, there was Susan Lerner, my stepdaughter. I was stunned. She put her arms around me and said that she had missed me, and she was now old enough to have a relationship that pleased her without her father's approval or disapproval. I was overwhelmed with emotion and so eager to know all about her life. We talked and talked and waited for the children to return; it was a joyful reunion, and we all vowed that we would stay close for the rest of our lives . . . and we did.

I also will never forget what happened one afternoon involving Liza and Jenny's half-brother, Michael, Alan and Micheline's son. Apparently, Liza and Jenny had been told by Micheline that whenever they visited, they must never mention me in front of Michael. This was a difficult assignment because Michael would ask them when they were picked up by Miss Stocker, "Where are you going?" I will never forget how incredibly inventive and sensitive they were in responding: "We're going home. We live with a very nice lady!"

One afternoon I was sitting in my bedroom working at my desk when I heard the children and Miss Stocker laughing and talking in the foyer. They had just come home from lunch with their father. The Lerner chauffer had been instructed to drop off Liza, Jenny, and Miss Stocker at our apartment and then take Michael and the nanny immediately to the park. But when they reached the Beresford, Liza and Jenny said to Michael, "Would you like to see where we live?" Michael eagerly answered yes and came up the elevator with his nanny to finally solve the mystery of Liza and Jenny's life.

When I came into the foyer to greet the children, there was Michael. Liza quickly said, "Michael, this is the very nice lady we live with." Michael was fascinated and accepted my hand when I asked him if he would like to see the children's rooms and toys. He examined everything and then turned to me and said, "I'd like to see your room, too." We walked down the hall, and I sat in my chair and put him on my lap. I told him that I had heard all about what a wonderful boy he was and what a very special brother he was to Liza and Jenny. The nanny was fascinated with this adventure almost as much as Michael was, but I'm so sorry that her penalty for allowing Michael to visit our apartment was that she was fired the minute they got home.

I want to end this chapter with one additional story about Micheline. When Michael eventually graduated from Harvard, Alan asked Liza to go to Boston with him for the graduation ceremony. Micheline and Alan were long divorced by that time, and I think he was already at least two marriages beyond theirs. Micheline stayed at a separate hotel. She was registered as "Mrs. Alan Jay Lerner."

44

A Rainbow Emerging

The spring of 1962 was beginning to show signs of new growth—sprouts of green were emerging and with them all the signs of a fresh beginning. Alan Livingston was coming to New York more and more frequently and calling from California to check in on Liza, Jenny, and me. I don't remember exactly what night it was, but I remember the doorbell ringing one evening, and Alan was there. It was as if I truly looked at him for the first time. I thought to myself, "I like this man—I really like this man."

One night he took me to dinner at one of my favorite restaurants, Orsini's, on Sixth Street between Fifth Avenue and the Avenue of the Americas. This used to be a haunt of Emmet's and mine. If you were well known, you always sat in the back room lined with leather booths. Alan and I walked in, and there was Emmet at the number-one booth on the right with his new lady. The maître d' quickly escorted us to the far end of the room.

At first, I was somewhat disoriented, all kinds of emotions swirling through me, but they gradually disappeared, and I found myself totally focused on Alan. In fact, by the time I looked at the other end of the room, Emmet was gone. I hadn't even noticed that he had left. I remember this night with a sense that I had finally graduated from the past.

After dinner, we decided to walk up Fifth Avenue; the air was warm and sensual; holding hands, we stopped to sit on the edge of a pool of water in front of a large store. At one point, I put my head on Alan's shoulder and felt protected and happy. Nothing was promised, nothing was certain, but something had shifted in the warm night air. When Alan took me back to the apartment, he gently kissed me and held me for a long, long time. We simply said good night.

Things were getting serious. Alan started to share with me his life, his career, his early years growing up in a small town in western Pennsylvania, his time in college at the University of Pennsylvania, his marriages, and, most importantly, he told me about his two children by Elaine (Elaine Osterweil), his first wife. They had married when they were very young, Alan just drafted into the army and Elaine recently graduated from Vassar. There was obvious great concern and pain regarding his son, Peter, who was born with hemophilia, and his daughter, Laurie, who missed him desperately. I selfishly was very grateful that Elaine had already remarried and assumed she was not waiting for him to return.

His second marriage, on the rebound from the first, was to the absolutely crazy, undeniably talented, needy to the point of being psychotic—the incomparable Betty Hutton. I asked him many times over the years, "Tell me again! Why did you marry Betty Hutton?" It took me a long time before I finally understood that strange alliance.

It was obvious that both Alan and I had been battered by deep disappointments—victims of our own mistakes and very cautious about taking major steps for our future. We both were in no hurry, and yet we both sensed that we were on a path that might lead to a future together. Events had a way of pushing us along; I accepted an offer from Disney to come to California in the late spring and early summer to make *Son of Flubber*, a sequel to *The Absent-Minded Professor*. That settled the matter of spending more concentrated time together. I arranged to lease a house in Brentwood near my parents, which came with a live-in housekeeper and more than enough room for Miss Stocker, the children, and me. Alan in the meantime was signing the Beach Boys at Capitol Records and was obviously excited and happy that I was going to spend some time with him in California. Nothing was certain—nothing was stated—and yet something was happening. Our journey of the next forty-seven years together had begun.

Alan was waiting for me at the gate of American Airlines. He was smiling, gave me a quick hug, helped with my bags, and we headed for Brentwood. I was going to stay with my parents for several weeks before I moved into my rented house. The first thing I learned about Alan and his driving was that he had absolutely no sense of direction. I couldn't believe he had been living in Los Angeles for most of his adult life and didn't know how to get to Brentwood Park! He accepted my instructions with grace, and I learned to accept this handicap of his, although it took me many years. We were excited, we were explorers in a new dimension of life—each of us wondered in his or her own way if we were finally being rescued.

Alan invited me for a weekend in Palm Springs, and lovemaking finally began. It was tentative, shy, tender, and sweet. It had been such a long time for both of us. Our feelings were guarded—it took time before our passions emerged and overwhelmed us. I think it was the second weekend in Palm Springs that Alan parked the car in front of a restaurant, turned to me, and absolutely shocked me when he said, "Nancy, I think we should think about getting married." I was so surprised that I quickly said, "Really? Don't you think we should think about this a little more?" We had a lovely dinner and a lovely night together, but he didn't mention it again.

The following weekend in Palm Springs we were in the pool swimming and playing. I swam up to him and said, "Alan, I've been thinking about what you said last weekend. . . . I would like to marry you." He gave me a chlorinated kiss, took my hand as we climbed up the steps of the pool, and took me into our room, where we consummated our agreement.

It was time for me to meet his children. He was very nervous about this, and when I met them, I realized why. Peter was about to be thirteen, and Laurie was Liza's age, eleven. They both were very beautiful, with dark-brown eyes and hair like their father—complete physical opposites of my children, who were so fair and blue-eyed.

Peter had been tortured with his illness, as all little boys with hemophilia are. Their instinct is to run and play and physically compete, but with hemophilia they do not dare. You and I might trip and twist our ankle, and our response would be to say, "Ouch!," and move on. For a hemophiliac, it would mean a small capillary in that ankle is ruptured and continues to bleed internally until he has to be hospitalized and receive an IV of blood plasma, which restores the normal clotting response for about forty-eight hours—that is, of course, if he doesn't move or rerupture the capillary with any normal activity. Peter was brilliant as well as beautiful and seemed to me to have an intuitive understanding that his life would end tragically.

Laurie was shrewd, cunning, and manipulative. It took her many years to understand that her life could be saved and made happy only by giving up her competitiveness and truly and honestly finding her inner integrity. I don't know too many people who have been able to completely change their view of the world and shed the resentments of unhappy childhoods, but Laurie was one of those people who did. It didn't surprise me that when this transformation took place, she changed her name from "Laurie" to "Laura."

I used to literally become paralyzed with anxiety when Alan announced that Laurie was coming to visit. I soon welcomed Laura into my life, though, and accepted her friendship as a gift.

45

My Second Wedding

It was decided that Alan and I would marry on September 1, 1962. My second wedding would take place in the same location as my first, my parents' home, although I insisted that we change rooms. Alan Lerner and I had married in front of the fireplace in the living room; Alan Livingston and I were married in front of the fireplace in the library.

Alan's brother, Jay, and Jay's wife, Lynn, with their daughter, Trav; my mother, Evelyn, father, Henry, and brother, David; my aunt Ethel, uncle Dutch, and their daughter, Cynthia; Liza, Jenny, and Miss Stocker were in attendance, along with the new minister of the Unitarian church my parents attended, Ernie Pipes. Alan arrived in a dark-blue suit, looking so handsome; I was in a pale-beige suit with a patterned-taffeta shell in soft colors and wore a small pillbox hat in the same fabric.

My father was smiling this time, and my mother was in her usual frantic mode. In fact, when I arrived, she had not completed setting the table with the cake and teacups. I helped her get it together and felt sorry that she was so scattered but grateful that she was happy with my new marriage.

I gave Alan a hug after we said, "I do," and I will never forget the next moment. I thought a hug would do, but for him, even with his shyness, it would not. He pulled me up and kissed me so exquisitely that I remember the tingle of that kiss to this day.

I was finally ready for my last session with Diana Kemeny. I was now married to Alan Livingston; not only was he extremely attractive and darling but also possibly one of the few truly adult men in the world.

I told her that when I had first met Alan, I was not particularly interested; he was much too nice for me. That was before I fell in love with him and finally realized that he was exactly the perfect partner I could ever have. She told me that she had never had a patient who was as ready as I was to give up the issue that was destroying her happiness. She warned me not to send anyone to her that might expect the same result.

She then asked me if I had any recent dreams. I told her that the previous night I had a glorious dream in vivid Technicolor. The baby in my second dream was now a young woman, standing on the bluff above the Wisconsin lake where I had spent all my summers growing up. Suddenly the small pier that I used to jump off of became a giant wharf, and the lake began to expand into a great ocean, with ships coming in from all over the world. It was a thrilling dream, and I realized that my world had finally opened itself to endless exploration, adventure, and possibilities.

POSTCARD

STAMP
HERE

Dear Bill,
I'm happy

Nancy

Mr. William Faulkner

Somewhere

In the Universe

Book 2

Introduction

This is the letter I wrote to my son, Christopher, the day his father, my wonderful husband, Alan W. Livingston, died.

March 13, 2009

Dear Chris,

As you and I held Dad in our arms and watched him take his last breath, the air seemed to throb around him—absorbing his being, his soul. We held him for over an hour before they came for his body. Jenny and our beloved housekeeper, Ruth, stood beside the bed. No one said anything as we watched the mystery and miracle of life dissolving—joining every cell in the universe. Alan Wendell Livingston no longer needed his body; in fact, we could've thrown it in the trash—it wouldn't have mattered—it was no longer of any consequence.

When they came to pick up his remains, he was still here with us. I kept thinking about my young, gorgeous husband walking in and taking me in his arms and holding me. The memory of that embrace has sustained me in the last months.

I remember a conversation with Alan when he said that he wondered what qualities he possessed that took him to the success he had. He wondered what he could tell his children or anyone who asked him for advice in building a career.

As a young man just out of the army and joining an equally young record company, Capitol Records, he found immediate success creating Bozo the Clown and many historic children's albums. He rescued Frank Sinatra from impending obscurity, paired him with arranger-conductor Nelson Riddle, and created the most memorable repertoire of Frank's career.

He helped Nat King Cole find the courage to become a solo artist at a time when Black artists were not accepted or played on mainstream radio. He took a leap of faith and left Capitol to go to NBC Television and created *Bonanza,* then went back to Capitol as president in 1960, signed the Beach Boys, the Beatles, and the Band.

Your father never stopped taking chances. In 1968, he left Capitol again and created his own small company, signed Don McLean, and produced the legendary single "American Pie"; wrote a young-adult novel published by Random House; and became a senior vice president and president of the Entertainment Group of 20th Century-Fox during the making of *Star Wars.* He ended his career by establishing and owning the first wholly owned American company in China, an animation company.

I have told you the story of how we met and fell in love and made the commitment to live together forever. I now want to tell you about our life together, my own journey of self-discovery, and how I had to rediscover and redefine who I really was.

I managed to go from being the wife of a celebrated theater legend in New York who had an insatiable need for ego fulfillment to being the wife of a man with incredible integrity who somehow survived and succeeded in the cruelly competitive culture of the corporate world.

I didn't realize the challenges I was about to face in creating a family in an entirely new environment and being the partner of someone in the closely regulated business world—all while watching your incredible father become a leader and legendary creator who contributed to defining the twentieth century.

The truth is, as much as I had found happiness, life and learning never stopped—success stories only led to new challenges.

A recurring dream I had at the beginning of our marriage suggested what I was about to face.

I was being given an exam that I knew I had not properly prepared for and, of course, always failed. Shortly after your father and I married, I had the same dream, only this time I was prepared and I received an A. When the professors looked at me and said that I had done the exam perfectly, they then startled me by demanding that I now take the exam in French!

When I look back at this dream, I realize that one's learning and growing and deepening never end. The preparation for taking the exam in "French" was just beginning.

I know you know how much we loved you—we made mistakes, as all parents do, but you rose above them and returned our love with such purity. You made our union complete; you gave us a joyful goal and taught us how to be a real family.

I hope you will find the next pages not only interesting but revealing and will learn from them. To be in the universe is an incredible, mysterious, and glorious experience. Live every moment with awareness, lovingness, and joy.

Here is the rest of my story.

Love,
Mother

46

Mr. and Mrs. Alan W. Livingston

After the ceremony, cake and champagne, and many hugs with the children and family, Alan and I climbed into the waiting limousine and went to the airport to catch a plane to New York. As we were about to enter the plane, a small group of people from Capitol Records descended upon us and showered us with rice. Everyone seemed genuinely happy for us, especially for Alan, whose personal problems and sadness they had witnessed firsthand. As we floated above the clouds, we kept holding hands and smiling at each other. "What have we done? Were we crazy? Did we just jump off a cliff into the abyss?" We knew we were taking an enormous leap of faith, but we somehow also knew that we were absolutely on the right path.

We had a suite waiting for us at the Hampshire House on Central Park South. It was a balmy, warm evening, and we walked down to the Plaza Hotel for supper at our favorite place, the Oak Room. Every moment of that night was filled with bliss.

It was very important that we plan a special moment for Alan's children, Laurie and Peter, who lived in New York. The next morning, my dear friend Malla Moss arranged for a brunch at her charming apartment and invited Alan's sister, Vera, who lived in Connecticut; Alan's father, who was visiting Vera; and Alan's children to join us. We had a photographer to capture this important occasion. Malla had put together a beautiful buffet, including cake and champagne. Everything seemed exactly right. That night we were on a jet flying over the Atlantic Ocean to London.

Waiting for us was a small suite at Claridge's overlooking the rooftops of London. Alan was on the board of EMI, which owned Capitol Records. He had meetings all day, and we had dinners to attend every night with members of the board. One afternoon he came back to the hotel and said he had been with Ernie Martin and Cy Feuer to discuss an album for their next Broadway musical.

Apparently, Alan Lerner was in London at the same time and also met with Cy and Ernie. They said that Alan Lerner had spent their entire meeting talking about me and my new marriage and was demanding to know everything he could about my new husband. I was fascinated to hear that he was particularly interested in knowing if they had seen us together. I'm quite sure that Alan was not trying to find out if I was finally happy with the right partner. My guess is he was just looking for some clue that I might be missing him.

After London, we flew to Cannes and started our real honeymoon. We had a little cottage overlooking the Mediterranean, and with the rising tide we could hear the pebbles being pushed onto the small beach beneath us. We rented a small convertible and never put up the top. We sat on the flat rocks and jumped into the water, made love, ate delicious breakfasts, lunches, and dinners. It was a slow, measured beginning of exploring intimacy and trust.

There were times when Alan seemed distant, which sometimes alarmed me. But I slowly pulled him back and realized this man had been deeply wounded and was not taking joy or success for granted. I also became increasingly aware of his delicious sense of humor—it wasn't raucous or obvious but clever and mischievous and fun. I was a great audience because I loved to laugh; his humor made me appreciate and love him all the more.

After about ten days, we went back to New York and started facing the reality of marriage, children, stepchildren, exhusbands, exwives, and the future. This time we stayed at my apartment. The children, Miss Stocker, and Senya, the cook, were waiting for us, all wondering what their own future would be.

I'll never forget climbing into my own king-size bed and Alan lying next to me. He was the first man who had ever shared this bed with me, and it was a little scary. In the morning, the children shyly knocked on our door and peered in. They were shocked, too! Mommy was in bed with a man in pajamas, someone they had only seen fully dressed in the living room or den. Poor Alan wasn't completely comfortable either.

47

Moving

It was time to say goodbye to Senya and Miss Stocker. I was going to take over the supervision of my children without any help for the first time.

The original plan was to leave my New York apartment and everything in it intact. My friend Judy Balaban, who was married to Tony Franciosa, had to come to New York with Tony for a Broadway play he was contracted for. She was leaving her large Beverly Hills house intact for us and would move her family into my apartment at the Beresford.

Unfortunately, the play was canceled at the last minute, and so were our plans. Judy felt so guilty about this that she frantically searched for another dwelling for the new Livingston family and found for us a charming, completely furnished house on Camden Drive. It was surrounded by a white picket fence and was decorated with amazing taste, including incredible antique posters and Metropolitan Museum of Art copies of Degas sculptures. It was completely furnished and supplied with linens, towels, dishes, silverware—everything you needed to run a household. All we had to do was move in our clothes and personal items.

There was only one problem: the house was incredibly small! Please remember that Liza and Jenny and I lived in a very large apartment, each of us having our own bedroom and bathroom. In the house on Camden Drive, Liza and Jenny shared a bedroom with each other and a bathroom with me. Alan had a small room in the back of the house where he could keep his clothes, and he had a tiny bathroom with a little sink, a toilet, and a shower stall. Period.

Also, do not forget that when we lived in New York, we were surrounded by people who took care of every little thing we needed. This would be the first time I would actually run the house, take care of the children, cook, clean, organize, and do everything with only one maid who did not live in . . . there was no room for her!

Moving

Because Liza and Jenny had attended only private schools in New York, I automatically put them into the John Thomas Dye School in Los Angeles. I'd planned everything ahead as well as I could and hoped for the best.

I will never forget the first night we were together on Camden Drive. Jenny and Liza had settled in their room and were doing their homework. I was preparing dinner, making meatloaf (which is about all I knew how to do at the time) with baked potatoes, broccoli, and a first course of a very tart and quite delicious salad.

Alan came home around six o'clock and went up the stairs directly to the back bedroom to shower and put on a change of clothes—slacks, sport shirt, and his monogrammed velvet slippers. I soon learned this was a pattern of behavior he would maintain for his entire life; nothing would deter him.

Jenny kept running down the stairs to watch me make the meatloaf. She then would gleefully run up the stairs, shouting, "Liza—Liza, guess what Mommy's doing?! She's making meatloaf and setting the table!" She then would slowly come down the stairs to review my progress. Finally, I started to light the candles and told Jenny to please tell Liza and Alan to come downstairs—dinner was ready.

On that very first night in our new home, Alan came down the stairs and established another ritual. He asked me to stop lighting the candles and told Jenny that he would call her and Liza to come down for dinner a little later. Jenny, looking a little downcast, slowly walked back up the stairs.

Alan asked me to fill the ice bucket with fresh ice and meet him in the den. He went behind the small bar and filled a cocktail shaker with vodka and a tiny drop of vermouth. He very carefully filled two glasses with delicious, cold martinis and, after handing me one, sat down and said, "Now, Nancy, tell me about your day."

Suddenly we heard Jenny coming down the stairs and then saw her peeking around the corner at the two of us. I explained to her that Alan and I were going to have a little cocktail before dinner and promised that it wouldn't be long but to please not interrupt us until we called her. Jenny looked a little disappointed, but I think when she saw the two of us sitting together in such peacefulness, her mother with a man in a relationship always dreamed of but never experienced, she seemed content and said, "OK."

As it turned out, this cocktail time just before dinner became sacred to both of us. In fact, it might have been the happiest part of our day. We shared this time before our dinner until two days before he died. And because of our love of music, and because Alan was in the music business, we had an extensive collection of classical records that we listened to every night. Alan had played the violin when he was growing up and was especially fond of violin concertos. I had played the piano and always looked forward to the piano concertos. We played music during our cocktail time and usually through dinner. I always felt it was a gift for our children to grow up with this music in the background of their lives.

After our cocktail together, we called the children and walked into the dining room. I lit the candles and told everyone where to sit. The salad was already at each place, and there was a moment of silence—it wasn't awkward—it wasn't uncomfortable—it was more a moment of peacefulness. We all knew that this night was precious; it was the beginning of a new life. Suddenly Jenny just sighed and said very quietly, "Oh, Mommy, I'm so glad I'm not a princess!"

48

A Sad Story

Liza and Jenny loved the Dye School and made many friends, but I will never forget the day Liza came home extremely distressed. She asked if she could speak to me privately. I couldn't imagine what was wrong.

She sat me down and said she had something to ask me. I responded, "What is it?! What's wrong?!" With tears in her eyes, Liza said, "Mommy, there is a little girl in my school who is very unhappy. She cries all the time, even on the playground. She hates her mother and says that her mother opens all her drawers and spies on her and accuses her of things she hasn't done. Mommy, do you think it's possible to invite her to live with us?"

I was enormously touched by Liza's concern and of course explained to her that children have to live with their own parents, so this girl would never be allowed to live with us.

That little girl was Patti Reagan.

49

My Second Husband

When I heard Alan talk about his childhood, I slowly began to put together the pieces of who he was, with awe and wonder and a deep appreciation for the struggles that helped create the amazing man I was married to. Both of my husbands had outstanding careers. Both were extremely smart and talented. Both of their families had survived the Depression. The main difference is the Lerners serendipitously became rich, and the Livingstons struggled to survive.

What astonished me the most about Alan Livingston was how he maintained a genuine modesty even with the excessive heights he managed to accomplish in his career. Christopher, our son, used to tell me that while growing up, he knew nothing about his father; he learned everything about Alan's remarkable accomplishments by hearing details from other people.

The story of how Alan and his older brother, Jay, grew up in the tiny town of McDonald, Pennsylvania, and managed to change the face of pop music is an interesting one.

Looking back at the beginning of our marriage, I realize now that Alan and I did not know that much about each other—our families, how we grew up, our dreams. We knew we both came from immigrant grandparents who had come to this country willing to work as hard as they could to become successful and upstanding Americans. We knew that our mothers and fathers understood the value of education and making a constructive contribution to this nation. Our genes were complementary, both of us coming from northern European ancestry, mine Swedish and Norwegian, Alan's Russian and German. But there was a cultural difference between us that might have been our undoing if our parents hadn't made choices that affected our upbringing similarly.

My paternal grandparents held a devoted Lutheran view of the world; Alan's came from a Jewish heritage, seeped in all the orthodoxy that came with it. Luckily for us, our mothers and fathers rejected their religious roots, and both Alan and I grew up viewing the world through nonsectarian eyes.

That is not to say that Alan's heritage and upbringing did not affect him.

Alan Wendell Levison was born at 11:30 p.m. on October 15, 1917, in McDonald, Pennsylvania, a small town outside of Pittsburgh. He was the last child of Maurice and Rose Wachtell Levison's union; his sister, Vera, was the first, followed by his brother, Jay.

Alan's early life, particularly some of the challenges he faced growing up, made his rise to prominence and success all that more compelling.

His father, whom I had the pleasure of meeting before he died, was a very shy and retiring man—sweet, unassuming, caring, and very handsome. He was extremely tall, with white hair and dark-brown eyes, the eyes that I loved so much in Alan.

Alan's mother, who died of leukemia in her late fifties and whom I never met, was described to me by Alan as a strong, determined, and very smart woman. She ruled the roost and took it upon herself to push her children to be the best they could possibly be. They were. Alan had some qualities that came from his father—a real gentleman—but he also had an iron will that came from his mother. (Alan enjoyed my strength and dominance in certain areas. It was perfectly all right with him for me to take over conversation, points of view, social schedules, planning trips, and overseeing the children. He felt comfortable with a strong female. In fact, he encouraged it—thank God!)

As Alan was growing up, his father ran a small shoe store, and Alan communicated to me that he admired his father's diligence and commitment and how he made a success of it, drawing business from small towns around McDonald. I think by local standards they were considered well off, with a home in the better part of town known as Dude Hill, but in actuality they would have been considered lower middle class by most big-city residents.

Alan's brother, Jay, was sickly and fragile with an asthmatic condition that plagued him all his life. He stuttered as a teenager but showed an early gift for music and writing that would serve him well in his later years.

I found it interesting that Alan remembered his parents' insistence that their children speak only proper English, very much like my family. They were very disdainful of the language spoken around them in the small town. Alan sometimes jokingly used some of the townspeople's euphemisms: "Where you'se goin'?" and "I awready seen 'at 'ere pitcher show." As Alan explained, "Nobody ever saw anything. They only 'seen' it." He was fascinated that this abuse of the language went right through high school. He described to me his second-year French class, where one of his girlfriends said "vooz" and "nooz" for *vous* and *nous*.

One of Alan's favorite stories about his upbringing was the time his brother and he put up a lemonade stand outside their house. The sign said, "Lemonade—3 cents a glass, two for a nickel." Their friend four houses up the street decided to do the same but to cut the price. The rivaling neighbor opened up his stand, and his sign read, "Lemonade—2 cents a glass, two for a nickel!"

One might wonder how, coming from a town of limited resources and a largely uneducated populace, a young, skinny kid and his frail older brother were able to rise to such prominence in one of the toughest industries in the world.

Alan credited several sources for his success, one being his teachers at McDonald High School, who gave him a fantastic foundation in writing. Miss Kirk, his English teacher, drilled grammar and sentence construction and proper pronunciation relentlessly. Alan credited her, along with his own creative imagination, with his getting straight A's in English composition classes later in college—even an A+ once.

He also admired Mr. McKibben, the science teacher, who introduced the theory of evolution until the local churches forced him to stop. Alan remembered a girl in his class, the daughter of a prominent doctor in town, raising her hand and saying to Mr. McKibben, "My father said that's not the way life developed. It was created by God." Mr. McKibben answered, "Well, I asked the garbage man this morning, and he said he wasn't sure." Alan said Mr. McKibben was an unusual man for the little town of McDonald, and it always amazed him how he survived because the churches were out to get him.

One thing I did know about Alan that may have contributed to his success was that he had a deep-seated belief that, as he put it, "you can have anything you want in this world if you want it badly enough."

An interesting story that perhaps explains how Alan came to this conclusion, was strangely the result of his sex drive. Alan was born with a tremendous amount of testosterone, which remained with him for the rest of his life. As his sexual hormones developed in his early teenage years, he told me about the suffering that plagued him. He had tremendously strong sexual desires, and one of his fantasies involved his high school French teacher. The woman was amply endowed and often wore a transparent blouse to school. What was underneath was covered with a large brassiere. Alan wanted desperately for that brassiere to fall off, and often daydreamed in class that if he just concentrated hard enough, he could will one of the straps to break. Believe it or not, one day when he was focusing really hard, one of the straps snapped, and Alan described to me a large breast becoming totally exposed and visible. The only words he could utter then were, "Hot damn!"

Another, more obvious factor that contributed to the trajectory of Alan's life was that he and Jay took music lessons for years as children. These lessons meant being driven into Pittsburgh once a week. Jay played the piano, and Alan started on the violin, eventually transitioning to a saxophone. After their lessons, Jay and Alan would go to one of two theaters in Pittsburgh, the Penn or the Stanley, both of which showed movies and had live stage shows, one with Dick Powell as master of ceremonies. All the talent they saw inspired them to be in the entertainment business—and, of course, that's exactly where they wound up.

But it was not just small-town life in McDonald that created hurdles for Alan and his brother and sister; it was the family's religious background.

McDonald was the name of the man who founded the small, midwestern town in which they grew up, and it was mostly a Scotch-Irish community. Alan's parents were Jewish.

Having no synagogue and no other Jews in their school made the kids' upbringing particularly difficult. Alan's parents were not religious; in fact, the kids grew up with no religious training whatsoever. The closest proximity they had to any kind of religious experience was that they lived next door to the minister of a Presbyterian church, with whom they were friendly. They sometimes even attended church affairs with him, but none of that stopped prejudice from rearing its ugly head.

Alan told a story of how his mother was once on the back porch mixing a cake batter when the minister from his back door said, "What are you making? A Jew cake?" "It's devil's food," said his mother. "Same thing," the minister replied. Although it was said in fun, this comment in fact represented the attitudes of the Christians there.

Just imagine, there were seven churches in this small town, including two Catholic, a Methodist, and a Baptist. Alan said there was less of a problem with anti-Semitism for him in grade school, but it existed for his parents. They couldn't join the little six-hole golf club, nor could his father join the Elks Club, where the local businessmen socialized.

Alan was named president of his class every year through the eighth grade, but when he attended high school, that office went to the football players. It was right about this time that Alan first began to recognize he was considered an outsider.

He came to hate being classified as Jewish in spite of the fact that he felt no relationship with the religion. When he was around seven, one of the kids at school said to him, "You killed Christ." Alan answered, "Who? Me?" He remembered seeing the Ku Klux Klan in white robes burning a cross on the football field on more than one occasion.

Nevertheless, Alan managed to have two good friends in high school as well as a girlfriend—the best-looking and most popular girl in town. Her name was Frances Shanbon, but everyone called her "Franny."

As was the case when I was growing up, there was to be absolutely no sex in teen relationships—that was for the wrong people who occasionally got pregnant and had to get married. Franny's mother accepted Alan but once said to her cleaning lady, "He is such a nice boy. Isn't a shame he's Jewish?" One friend's father said to him, "There are Kikes, and there are Sheenies, but you are a Jew." Alan did not appreciate the "compliment."

His best friend's name was Cameron, a good Scotsman. His other best friend was Quinton Cunningham, who, along with Alan, received top grades at their high school.

One of the things Alan and Jay did have going for them was an innate streak of creativity. Since television, computers, Facebook, Twitter, and the ever-present cell phones were not available at that time, people had to create their own fun and challenges.

Alan and Quinton had a great desire to have a big telescope and explore the heavens but, of course, couldn't afford one. With Alan's urging, each of them bought two six-inch Pyrex glass pipes, got a book of instructions, and met in Alan's attic every afternoon or evening, where they ground and polished telescope mirrors perfect to one ten millionth of an inch. The test to determine the shape of their mirrors, known as the Foucault test, was in their case a tin can with a pinhole in it and a lightbulb set up at the focal-point distance from the mirror. They used an old razor blade to cut the focus in front of one eye. They polished endlessly with opticians' rouge. It took six months to get perfect mirrors (a credit to Alan's tenacity), which they then had aluminum-coated for five dollars each. The rest of the project involved putting together a tube and a stand made of old pipes and pipe fittings and then acquiring a prism to bend the image into an eyepiece in the side of the tube.

Our family still has that telescope to this day, and we bring it out of the closet on clear summer nights to peruse the heavens. We have looked at the moons of Jupiter, the rings of Saturn, and the polar caps of Mars. Alan said that he and Quinn used to point it at the lady across the street, sitting on her porch reading the newspaper, and they could literally see the pores in her skin.

On the night Neil Armstrong took the first walk by man on the lunar surface, we took out the telescope and focused it on the moon, which was full and bright. As we listened to Neil's voice declaring, "One giant leap for mankind," we peered through the eyepiece of Alan's telescope and imagined we could actually see this magical moment happening.

I think one of the most wonderful stories that Alan and Jay told me that offers a window into where their lives were headed was the time their parents, who never put up a Christmas tree but did share gifts during the holidays, asked the two boys what they would like. It was the height of the Depression, and Maurice and Rose held their breath, hoping and praying that what the kids wished for wouldn't be an expensive bicycle or a set of golf clubs or anything that was out of reach economically. Thankfully, the boys said that all they wanted was three hundred feet of wire! Their parents were so relieved that they didn't even inquire as to what in God's name the boys would ever do with it!

But Alan and Jay had a plan. Being music lovers, they had managed to acquire a bunch of old records, mostly from a store in town that stopped handling them and wanted to get rid of its inventory. They had everything from Ruth Etting and Rudy Vallee to Fanny Brice. They were not satisfied to just play the records, though. They got a used seventy-eight RPM phonograph motor, mounted it on a wooden crate, put the assembly in a tiny, closet-size room upstairs, and ran the wire down through the wall to the radio in the living room, which fortunately was located directly below.

They had discovered that an old speaker they had—the large kind that the RCA Victor dog peered into—would act as a microphone if plugged into a particular slot on a radio. The result was a studio from which they could act as announcers and play records into the radio down below. They often used to fool guests, carrying on a complete show that included conversation and the announcements of guests visiting their house as if it were a news item being broadcast on the radio. Alan said the guests bought it every time.

It was a foreshadowing of things to come.

But perhaps the biggest factor in Alan and Jay's successful career trajectory was their mother, Rose. She was determined to give her children exposure to the arts and especially music.

Once a month she would drive Alan, Jay, and Vera into Pittsburgh to hear the Pittsburgh Symphony. It was a highly regarded orchestra, and I'm sure the tickets were very expensive. They sat in the third-row center of the highest balcony, and Alan always wondered what this beautiful music would sound like if he had a seat in the third-row center of the orchestra. He never got the chance to find out.

Years later, when he was a vice president at Capitol Records in charge of the Artists and Repertoire Division, he signed the Pittsburgh Symphony and Fritz Reiner, the conductor. He took his engineers to the Syria Mosque auditorium in Pittsburgh and instructed them to find the most perfect acoustical spot to place the microphones.

Alan went to lunch, and when he returned, he was astonished to find the microphones placed over the seats in the third-row center of the highest balcony. They were Alan's and Jay's original seats. I think there's a moral here— something like, "Be careful what you wish for. You may lose something precious if you give up what you already have."

Alan Livingston graduated in 1940 from one of the most distinguished Ivy League universities in America, the Wharton School at Penn (he was accepted at Yale as well but wanted to be with his brother at Penn). All the Ivy League schools had quotas for Jews, and one's religion was identified on the application. Getting accepted to an Ivy League college was not easy, but both Jay and Alan had been number one in their classes in high school.

Joining a fraternity was essential for a comfortable social existence. There were two classes of fraternities at these schools: Class A fraternities and Class B fraternities, each with different regulations. Jews could join only the Class B group. Jews were also not permitted to join Penn's Mask and Wig Club, which put on shows every year. Much like Alan Lerner, who was excluded from joining the Hasty Pudding Club at Harvard, Jay and Alan could not write for the Mask and Wig Club.

Jews were also not permitted to work at the *Pennsylvanian*, the school paper. Were they qualified? Of course. Jay became a top songwriter in Hollywood later and earned three Academy Awards. Alan became head of Capitol Records, where he did a great deal of writing and was accepted as a member of the American Society of Composers, Authors, and Publishers before becoming its president. Ray Evans, Jay's writing partner, managed to get on the *Pennsylvanian*, but when it was discovered he was Jewish, he was told to leave. There was no pretense about it—Alan never forgave the school.

Many years later Alan wrote about how all of this changed:

Strangely enough, you might thank Hitler. With his unbelievable atrocities on the Jews, and World War II, anti-Semitism became an unacceptable thing to openly acknowledge on anyone's part. Quotas were abolished everywhere, Israel became a country to respect and admire, and anti-Semitic attitudes went deep underground where they emerged and were acknowledged only by the few ignorant participants today. With no religious training as a child, I could look on it all objectively. Some of my Jewish friends today are critical of my lack of participation in Jewish affairs and not joining a temple. As to my Christian friends, particularly the Catholics, I could envy their faith. That must be very comforting, but beyond my ability to accept. Besides, it all didn't work in the world. Where was the Pope during Hitler and Mussolini? I never understood it all. History has identified religion as the basic cause of many wars, torture, and murder. Start with the Spanish Inquisition and go on to Christian Germany under Hitler. Any different today? The Pope recently visited India, and the Hindus reacted by murdering Catholics and raping nuns. The teachings of all religions are ignored in the face of, "I'm right and you're wrong." As to the Jews, there are the English, German, French, Swedish, Semitic, the ex-Catholic Crypto Jews of Spain and Portugal, and even African and Ethiopian Jews. What do they all have in common? Only one thing—their religion—from which Christianity emerged through a Jew named Jesus—whose teachings are ignored in Christian man's treatment of man. Amazing!

I think this paragraph describes perfectly Alan's assessment of his religion—as a matter of fact, his feeling about all religions. It was completely compatible with my own views. I think what we valued in each other was the recognition of how important it was for both of us to observe the teachings of moral behavior we had learned early in our lives and to strive to do our best as sensitive, honest, trustworthy, loving, and—maybe the hardest of all—forgiving human beings. I do believe that we have been good role models for our children, and as I watch them now living their lives as adults, I am filled with awe and admiration for who they are.

As a victim of the anti-Semitism that prevailed during his years at Penn, Alan never responded to the university's requests for a donation. Walter O'Malley, owner of the Los Angeles Dodgers and a prominent Penn alumnus, once visited Alan at his office at Capitol Records. He was concerned that

Alan had never given a donation of any kind. Alan described his painful experience at Penn because he was Jewish and found it hard to be generous to an institution that condoned that behavior. Walter was upset with Alan's description. He said, "Alan, do you realize the ratio of the Jewish students at our university today? Almost fifty percent are Jewish!" Alan responded, "Walter, you let one in, and you see what happens!"

After Alan graduated from Penn, he was inducted into the army and served as a private in the infantry; however, he could never accept being one of thousands directed by a sergeant who told the group when they had to turn out the lights, use the bathroom, and obey his command no matter how ridiculous and trivial it seemed. He was determined to become an officer, but there was one small problem. He was nearsighted and knew he would never pass the eye test.

Alan's ingenuity and resourcefulness have always astounded me. He somehow managed to get a photograph of the eye chart and memorized it so thoroughly that he could read any line forward or backward. After he completed the recitation of the letters perfectly, the doctor took his instrument and peered into Alan's pupil, murmuring, "This is amazing. You are clearly near-sighted, but you have adjusted your eyesight to compensate. You are one in a million people who can accomplish this." Alan became a lieutenant.

It was at this time, in 1942, that he married Elaine Osterweil. They decided they would like to have a short honeymoon at a resort in the Bahamas, and when Alan called to make a reservation for Mr. and Mrs. Alan Levison, the hotel replied, "We are a restricted resort and cannot accept your reservation." Alan waited twenty minutes before he called back and made a reservation for Mr. and Mrs. Alan Livingston, which was arranged immediately. He then called Jay and said, "Your name is now Jay Livingston," and said to his father and mother, "You are now Mr. and Mrs. Maurice Livingston." Right or wrong, Alan couldn't be persuaded otherwise, and everyone in the family applied for a new birth certificate in their new name.

When I met Alan, he was as deeply unhappy with his life as I was with mine. But our commitment to each other started the moment we said, "I do." When I look at the pictures of our wedding day, one in particular touches me deeply. Liza and Jenny are hugging me passionately, and Alan, leaning over us, is smiling like the Cheshire cat. I would like to imagine that he was thinking, "Look what I just got—the jackpot!"

The Bergstrom family. *Bottom row, left to right:* Nancy's maternal grandfather, John Victor Bergstrom; Carl Bergstrom; Bill Bergstrom; and Nancy's maternal grandmother, Matilda Bergstrom. *Top row, left to right:* Nancy's mother, Evelyn Bergstrom; Edith Bergstrom; and Ethel Bergstrom.

Nancy and her father, Henry Olson, on the set of the movie *Submarine Command* (1951).

Henry Olson, Evelyn Olson, Nancy, and her brother, David, in the house in which Nancy grew up in Milwaukee, Wisconsin.

Nancy with her father, Henry Olson, and her mother, Evelyn Olson.

Nancy when she was a junior in high school in a photo taken for the group she describes as the Cherubs.

Nancy's paternal grandfather, John Olson, and his second wife, Bess.

Left: The Olsons' house on Enterprise Lake near the tiny town of Elcho, Wisconsin. *Right:* The house built by Nancy's maternal aunt and uncle, Ethel and Dutch Keithley.

Nancy performing the role of Buttercup in *H.M.S. Pinafore* by Gilbert and Sullivan in high school.

Nancy as a little girl with her baby brother, David.

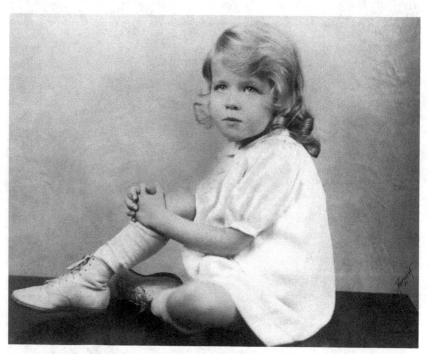

Nancy as a toddler (*full shot*).

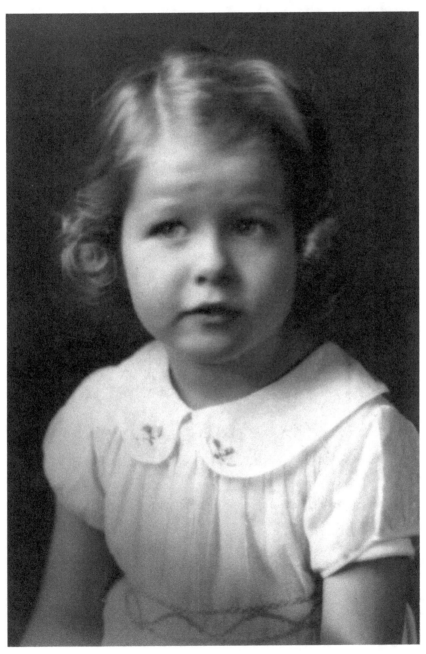

Nancy as a toddler (*close-up*).

Nancy on stage in high school playing Elizabeth in Jane Austen's *Pride and Prejudice.*

Looking through the window of the Olsons' lake house at Enterprise Lake.

Los Angeles Times photo of Nancy with her father, Henry, just after the plane crash with Liz Taylor.

Alan Jay Lerner and Nancy with their daughter, Liza Lerner, at her birthday.

Alan Jay Lerner and Nancy with their daughters, Liza (*left atop fence*) and Jenny (*right atop fence*).

Liza Lerner (*left*) and Jenny Lerner (*right*).

Jenny Lerner (*left*) and Liza Lerner (*right*).

Nancy with her daughters by Alan Lerner, Liza (*top middle*) and Jenny (*left*).

Paul McCartney, George Harrison, and John Lennon with Alan Livingston as the Beatles arrive at the party in Nancy's mother's garden in Brentwood, California.

Alan Livingston with the cast of *Bonanza*.

Alan Livingston performing the part of the circus ringleader with Bozo the Clown.

Laura Livingston (*left*), Liza Lerner (*center*), Jenny Lerner (*right*), and Nancy in the lobby of Capitol Records picking out photos from the Beatles garden party.

The Beatles party for the Hemophilia Foundation. Next to the Beatles are a six months' pregnant Nancy; Alan Livingston (*behind Nancy*); Nancy's mother, Evelyn; and Nancy's brother, David (*behind Evelyn*).

Alan Livingston working with Frank Sinatra on arrangements. We're pretty sure Nelson Riddle is the person in between them.

Nancy with Grace Kelly and Prince Rainier in Monaco at a Twentieth Century-Fox board meeting.

Nancy (*far left*) on stage with Dean Martin at a Share Show.

Alan Livingston and Nancy on their honeymoon in the south of France.

Alan Livingston and Nancy with her two daughters, Liza Lerner (*left*) and Jenny
Lerner (*right*), on their wedding day.

Young Chris Livingston and Nancy.

Baby Chris Livingston with Nancy.

Laura Livingston on her wedding day, with Liza Lerner (*left*), Jenny Lerner (*second from right*), and Patty Livingston, Peter Livingston's wife (*right*).

Peter and Patty Livingston.

The Livingston-Lerner family combined, minus Christopher. *Left to right:* Alan Livingston; Nancy; Gary Gibson, Laura's husband; Laura; Jenny Lerner; Patty Livingston, Peter's wife; Peter Livingston; Elaine Livingston, Alan's first wife; and Liza Lerner.

A group photo of Blue Ribbon executive presidents over the years. *Front row, left to right:* Nancy Olson Livingston, Joanne Kozberg, Joni J. Smith, Phyllis Hennigan. *Back row, left to right:* Helen Wolford, Joan Hotchkis, Margaret Wetzel, Sandra Ausman.

Buff Chandler (*center*) and Nancy, with an unknown third person.

BEVERLY HILLS

PEOPLE

Nancy Livingston and
First Lady Nancy
Reagan at the Amazing
Blue Ribbon luncheon
honoring the First Lady.

FIRST EXCLUSIVE PHOTO

VOLUME 1, NUMBER 8   JANUARY 8, 1985   85 CENTS

Nancy Livingston and Nancy Reagan on the cover of *Beverly Hills People*.

To Nancy Livingston
With best wishes, Sincerely
Nancy & Ronald Reagan

Ronald Reagan with Nancy.

Playbill for *Mary, Mary.*

Nancy and Bing Crosby in *Mr. Music* (1950). © Paramount Pictures Corp. All rights reserved.

Nancy and William Holden in *Sunset Boulevard* (1950). © Paramount Pictures
Corp. All rights reserved.

Nancy opening the front door of her home.

Nancy in profile in grainy black-and-white.

50

Laurie and Peter and Alan Jay

Nothing seemed more perfect than life in our little house on Camden Drive. Our realization that our marriage was the most perfect partnership that anyone could possibly ask for both stunned and amazed us, and we were so grateful for our good fortune. I had several offers to work on live television; in fact, before Mary Tyler Moore was cast in *The Dick Van Dyke Show,* there was great interest in my playing the part of Laura Petrie. Phil Silvers was also beginning a new series, and I was called to see if I had any interest in joining him. Without a moment of hesitation, I said I was absolutely not available. There could be no trade-off for my life exactly as it was.

Of course, it is true about life in general that there are always new challenges and problems to solve. The most momentous of those challenges was how to integrate Alan's children, Peter and Laurie, into our lives.

Alan and his first wife, Elaine, had had a daughter who died several months after being born with an incurable brain tumor. They decided to have another child, and Peter Livingston was born. Peter was a beautiful child, as all of Alan's children were, but after discovering blood in his crib from a source they could not identify, Peter and Elaine faced their second tragedy with a child. Peter was chewing on a toy that scratched his lip, and he began to bleed excessively, which is how they learned he was born with hemophilia.

Hemophiliacs are missing the gene that provides normal clotting of their blood following a superficial cut or wound. It is especially dangerous when it involves a bruise or an injured joint. It is the internal bleeding that is the most difficult to control. The hemophiliac gene is carried by the mother and is transferred only to a male fetus. Elaine had no idea that she was a carrier because there had not been a male child in her family history in a long time. Her mother must have been a carrier and passed this gene to Elaine. All female carriers have a fifty–fifty chance of bearing a hemophiliac son and a fifty–fifty chance of passing this gene on to their daughter. If the daughter is also a carrier, she again has the possibility of having a hemophiliac son and possibly daughters who will be carriers.

As they were discovering all of this, Elaine was pregnant again and gave birth to a beautiful little girl, Laurie, but the real focus of their emotions and attention was Peter, who, as he started to crawl and walk, would fall and then start to bleed internally.

When Alan and I married, Peter was turning thirteen. It was hard for me to even imagine what it was like for a little boy who wanted to run, jump, ride bicycles but didn't dare because he would end up in the hospital with endless plasma dripping into his veins, which had to be done slowly so as not to increase the volume of fluid in his arteries. He then had to keep his ankle, knee, hip, or elbow—whatever joint was involved—immobile for at least forty-eight hours.

This tragedy for Peter and his mother and father never abated for Alan and was made even worse because Peter's stepfather, Elaine's new husband, treated Peter brutally. Several years before we got married, Alan tried to get custody of Peter and was challenged in court by Elaine, who would not give him up.

As blissful as our life on Camden Drive was, we were now faced with the challenge of incorporating Alan's children into this new life. Laurie and Peter were living in New York with their mother and stepfather. Peter only wanted to be with us in Beverly Hills, and it was the most deeply painful obstacle that I have ever faced. And to make matters worse, Laurie only wanted to be with us as well, especially since her father was with two little girls her age.

Laurie didn't handle having two new stepsisters well—How could she? She was only twelve years old and wanted her father to be hers alone. One thing that helped us explain things to Peter and Laura was that we simply did not have room for the two of them to come at the same time. Camden Drive was just not big enough. They had to share the back bedroom and shower stall with Alan. How did we manage? And all of these children, including Liza and Jenny, were entering adolescence! I think Alan's and my deepening gratitude and love for each other saw us through.

It was also clear that although Laurie and Peter had a very good relationship with their mother, their stepfather was a cruel invasion into their young lives. Peter's hemophilia presented huge psychological problems for him, and his stepfather was particularly resentful of Peter's needs. Of course, when they came to visit us, the contrast of a loving harmonious environment compared to their chaotic and insecure environment in New York made them more needful to be with us than ever, which was especially difficult for me.

Both Peter and Laurie were far more independent, streetwise, and calculating than my girls, who were completely innocent by comparison. Laurie was impossible for me to deal with, even though I understood how hard all of this was for her. Peter broke my heart, particularly when it was time to say goodbye and send him back to New York, knowing that he didn't want to leave. It was a time of such conflicted emotions for me. I pretended not to see the tears in his eyes, but I will never forget them.

All of this was not made easier by their mother, who, to me, always seemed somewhat helpless. She loved her children and wanted them to be with her, and she also knew that she had married the wrong stepfather for them. Several times a week our phone would ring at around seven in the evening (cocktail and dinner time). It was Elaine asking for Alan to intervene in a fight the children were having at that moment or to deal with a problem she couldn't handle alone, making plans for their next visit, or simply reaching out for help.

I think Alan's desire to help Elaine was genuine and empathetic, and I look back with admiration at his integrity, even if at the time I resented her constant intrusion. It's kind of amazing, but Alan encouraged Elaine to see my psychologist, Diana Kemeny! He was so impressed with my stories of what Dr. Kemeny had done for me that in desperation he thought perhaps Elaine could be helped as well. I think Dr. Kemeny was deeply touched by Elaine's anguish and helped her to leave her abusive marriage and start a new and better life.

As far as Liza and Jenny were concerned, life was turning out for the better. They did not overly miss their father as they assumed correctly that he was quite preoccupied somewhere else. By this time, Alan Jay and Micheline were breaking up, and Micheline was giving him a notoriously difficult separation.

Obviously, another hurdle for our family was how to incorporate Alan Jay Lerner into our new existence. He was apparently very curious about my new husband and the children's new stepfather. Although he had almost removed himself from our life with the absolute madness that his marriage with Micheline had created, he tried to find out everything he could about Alan

Livingston and was very anxious to meet him. He called me from New York, and said he was coming to California on business and naturally wanted to see the children and meet their new stepfather. I will never forget this evening as long as I live.

Liza was still emotionally attached to her father; Jenny had long ago left those feelings behind, knowing how unreliable he was. Although Alan Livingston encouraged the girls to call him "Alan," not "Daddy," Jenny in particular felt supported by him and had a deep and growing affection for him.

Alan Jay was to arrive at 6:30; Liza was already waiting at the front door, but where was Jenny? Jenny was standing next to her stepfather's sink watching him brush his hair. She was talking nonstop, describing her father to Alan. Apparently, she said, "Really, Alan, my father is really, really short!" Alan just smiled, and she insisted, "Alan, I know you don't believe me, but he really, really is short!" She took his hand and walked down the stairs with him.

In the meantime, Alan Jay had arrived and was sitting on the couch talking to Liza and me while waiting for Jenny and Alan to join us. As they entered the living room, Jenny never let go of Alan's hand and said, "Oh, hi, Daddy." Whereupon Alan desperately tried to release her hand, but she held on tight, walked with him to the chair facing the couch, and proceeded to place herself on his lap.

Liza watched this display with panic and disapproval and tried desperately to motion to Jenny to please come over and sit on the other side of Daddy. Jenny firmly put her arm around Alan's neck, started to swing one of her legs, and began to hum. Poor Alan Livingston was squirming and didn't know what to do. I must give Alan Lerner credit; he smiled at Jenny with a reassuring attitude that communicated to her that her behavior was perfectly OK. I think he was genuinely amused and didn't want to make Jenny wrong. Thank God.

I am sad to say that Alan Lerner's life at that moment was crumbling. Micheline had no real interest in Alan any longer other than what he could buy for her. He had started to see Dr. "Feelgood" Max Jacobson, who distributed drugs to his very famous clients, including Eddie Fisher, Truman Capote, Tennessee Williams, Marlene Dietrich, and even Jack Kennedy, who was looking for relief from his intense back pain and fatigue. The drugs were a combination of amphetamines and painkillers, which were highly addictive.

That's when Alan Jay's work truly began to suffer because these drugs give one a sense of accomplishment that is not real. He was also about to marry for the fifth time, which was a relief for Liza and Jenny because they wouldn't have to deal with Micheline any longer. However, it was going to be difficult to adjust to another stepmother.

In the meantime, Alan Livingston and I had wonderful problems to solve. Obviously, the house on Camden Drive was perfect for the beginning of our marriage, but we needed a bigger and more permanent place of our own. We scoured the entire west side of Los Angeles and found nothing that we liked.

One afternoon we were on North Alpine Drive above Sunset Boulevard looking at a very big house that was clearly not for us. We walked out of the front door and saw an empty lot across the street. Alan took my hand, and without saying a word, we walked out to the edge of the empty lot overlooking the city. On this very clear day, we could even see the ocean. There was a "for sale" sign, and Alan turned to me and said, "How would you like to build a house?" Without hesitation, I said, "I think I would love it! Especially if we could build it right where we are standing." The next day he bought the lot.

51

Life in a Whirlwind on Camden Drive

Huge decisions were about to be made. We had no ideas or expertise in hiring an architect, but our good fortune continued to follow us, and we chose a young man by the name of Paul Wuesthoff, who was highly recommended by Alan's business manager, Edward Traubner.

We looked at several of Paul's completed projects, and although we were impressed with much of his design, he seemed to be too contemporary for what we had in mind. The house was going to be furnished with the art, porcelain, silver, and antiques from my New York apartment, and we couldn't quite see them in one of his very modern settings.

We sat down and explained this to him. We visited the lot together, and Alan said, "First of all, we have to have a one-story house." He assumed that we were going to grow old together, and he didn't want either one of us to deal with stairs. Obviously, we wanted to take advantage of the view, so how the house was to be situated was extremely important. I said the house should be a contemporary California structure with many windows facing the garden, the pool, and the world. I loved the idea of windows from floor to ceiling that would correspond with the doors as high as the windows. This followed a more contemporary design, but I wanted the windows to be structured as if they were a copy of a French antique door.

We also wanted high ceilings, and I insisted on a square dining room because I already owned a beautiful large round dining-room table. In fact, we took Paul at our expense to New York City and walked him through my apartment. It was clear to him that he should design a modern California house that would provide the perfect setting for all my treasures. He was inspired and gave us possibly the most beautiful home we could imagine, and through the years it has given both of us pleasure simply to wake up there and walk through the rooms. But building the house was going to take time and therefore extended our squashed life in the little house on Camden Drive.

The next decision was even more serious. I wanted to have a child with Alan. I was approaching my midthirties as he was approaching his midforties, so this was a decision we had to make sooner rather than later. To my surprise, I did not have to overly persuade him. We saw the value of what a child would do to bond our marriage and bring all the children together with a half-brother or half-sister. I, of course, insisted that we would have a boy and seduced Alan at exactly the moment I was ovulating, which gave the male sperm a higher chance of reaching one of my eggs first. It didn't happen right away, but the drama of life never stopped.

52

Dad

One afternoon I came home from the market at about four o'clock and found, to my surprise, that Alan was home from the office waiting for me. He had had a call at his office from my mother that my father had just suffered a major stroke, and she and my brother were waiting for us at UCLA in intensive care.

We raced to the hospital and embraced the family. My father died that afternoon.

Nothing prepared me for this sadness or having to take charge of my mother and my brother. David was still living at home and was not yet emotionally separated from our parents, even though he was by now a lawyer and working in the grown-up world. My mother completely fell apart and looked to me and Alan for everything.

Liza and Jenny were devastated to lose their beloved grandpa. Their feelings for him, as his were for them, were incredibly deep and loving. I could not have handled any of this without Alan at my side. Could I ever repay my wonderful husband for standing by me as he did?

Somehow, we got my mother back in her house in Brentwood; David got himself into some therapy and was able to make the break and find a place to live on his own. He even started to date some wonderful young women and picked the best when he married Katherine (Kitsy) Snow.

I was so busy supervising everything that my own tears had to be postponed—it was almost a year later before I could confront my own feelings. One afternoon I went to my father's grave and started to weep. I told him how much I loved him and how much I valued his being my father and would never forget the gift of his being my dad.

In the meantime, Alan's career was skyrocketing, but neither of us could predict the kind of turn it was about to take.

53

Capitol Records

A lan signed the Beach Boys to Capitol Records about the time we got married (the fall of 1962), and by this point he had taken what began as a small label and made it the most competitive record company in the world. The genius songwriter Johnny Mercer, songwriter and producer Buddy DeSylva, and the world's simplest man, Glen Wallichs, had started a tiny record company in a suite of offices in Hollywood in 1942 and had a great deal of success immediately.

Alan's career at Capitol ironically started with his taking a job that had nothing to do with music.

In 1946, Alan was just out of the army and wanted to find a job in Los Angeles. He went to a local employment agency and asked if Capitol had any job openings and what specific type of positions it needed to fill. He promised to pay the agency if this information resulted in his employment. He was told Capitol needed a copywriter in the advertising department.

Alan managed to get an appointment with Capitol Records, but when he arrived for the job interview, he unfortunately discovered that the company had just hired someone else five minutes before he got there. The people he talked to liked Alan, though. He remembered the advertising director saying, "You seem like a bright young man. I'm going to send you over to Jim Conkling, the Artists and Repertoire director. Maybe he will have something for you."

That's exactly where Alan wanted to be in the first place, but the only opening at that time was for a producer of children's records. He had no experience working with kids, but his early years of creativity gave him the confidence he needed to convince Jim Conkling that he would be perfect for the job.

Alan started his first day at Capitol Records staring at a blank piece of paper, thinking, "How in the world am I going to make a hit children's record?" He had always been fascinated with records growing up, experimenting by taking his finger and speeding them up to create a cartoon sound or slowing them down to a bare growl. Once he even bored an off-center hole in the middle of an album and enjoyed the wowing sounds that resulted. It occurred to him that "funny sounds" might be a key to intriguing children's imaginations. But how could he get them in the script? He then thought perhaps having animals talk might be the answer. Animals could make any kind of sound he wanted. So where should he start with animals? The circus, of course! Who would take the kids through the circus? A clown! And kids love clowns. What should he call him? "Bozo!" And so Bozo the Clown was born.

In those days, if a children's record sold fifty thousand copies, it was considered a hit. *Bozo at the Circus* sold a million copies! One thing that contributed to the record's success was something Alan created called a "record reader," in which kids could follow the story by turning a page in a book whenever Bozo blew his whistle. There were pictures of the action and a text of the dialogue to help children learn how to read.

"Bozo" became a household name. Much later, a national survey named Bozo the best-known clown in the world. This record set off a string of unprecedented successes in the field of children's records, including albums that Alan created for Disney and Warner Bros. cartoon characters. Alan even wrote and released songs featuring some of these characters: "That's All Folks!" sung by Porky Pig and Wee Bonnie Baker and "I Tawt I Taw a Puddy Tat" by Tweety Bird and Sylvester, which cracked the top ten on the Billboard pop charts in 1951 and inspired a short film released by Warner Bros. sixty years later in 2011. (I have always joked to the children that I left the man who wrote "I Could Have Danced All Night" for the man who wrote "I Tawt I Taw a Puddy Tat!")

Alan also wanted children to be inspired to listen to classical music, so he produced the albums *Rusty in Orchestraville* and *Sparky's Magic Piano* (which became the number-one record in England at that time), among many other hit records.

54

Nat Cole

With all of Alan's success in producing children's records for Capitol (at one time he had eight of the top-ten children's records on Billboard), he could not help but start to pay attention to what was happening with the adult records at Capitol as well. He was very interested in all of Capitol's artists, in particular the King Cole Trio, featuring Nat King Cole as the pianist. He heard Nat sing a few phrases with the group and realized Nat could be a soloist.

Alan approached Nat about the idea, but Nat was not receptive. Nat honestly believed that he was a very able pianist but did not believe he could pull off singing a hit record. But Alan kept insisting until Nat finally said, "OK, I'll record one single."

It was "Nature Boy," one of the biggest hits Capitol had at that time—yet another example of Alan's creative genius.

It was shortly after 1950 that Alan moved up to the adult Artists and Repertoire Division, and that's when he began to work closely with Nat.

Before Nat Cole, all Black artists' records were called "race records." For some reason, Nat bridged that gap, and even a white couple out on a date would play his love songs in the background during their courtship. It was still impossible, however, for Nat to get a concert date in the South, even though his records were uniquely accepted by the white audience. Alan always said that if Nat had been white, he would have been a movie star in five minutes, but prejudice was alive and well in America.

One of the most shocking incidents I remember Alan telling me about was a time he brought Nat to the Brown Derby restaurant. Alan ate lunch at the Brown Derby in Hollywood almost every day because it was only a two-block walk from the Capitol Records Building. The front booth was always waiting for him. One day he called George, the maître d', to say he was coming in and added, "George, just so you know, I'm bringing Nat Cole." All he got was a groan in response. Alan said, "George, I'm bringing Nat Cole, and

I don't want any problem." He hung up. George gave him a booth—at the very back of the restaurant next to the kitchen.

Around that time, Nat bought a home. He had just married Maria, a beautiful and lovely lady.

The house they moved into, a period English traditional, was in the Holmby Park area—older LA, very WASP, certainly not populated by entertainment people. The residents were mostly downtown bankers, lawyers, and corporate executives. There was a furor when Nat moved in. A neighborhood committee even visited Nat and offered to buy his house at a profit. He refused, and he and Maria lived and entertained there for many years. Fortunately, there was no violence. That's where Natalie Cole grew up to become a singing star in her own right.

Alan was always cautious about pushing songs by his brother, Jay, and Jay's partner, Ray Evans, even though they were winning Oscars, and their records were number one on the hit list. But when their publisher gave Alan a copy of their song "Mona Lisa," Alan was determined to have Nat Cole sing it. When Nat heard the song, however, he didn't truly understand it or want to record it. As a favor to Alan, he put "Mona Lisa" on the B side of a single and on the A side a song he was eager to record, "The Greatest of Them All (God)." To Nat's amazement, the disc jockeys turned over the single and played "Mona Lisa" instead; it became one of his most dynamic standards and is still played today.

I met Nat and Maria several times after Alan and I were married. Because Alan and I were jammed into our tiny little house on Camden Drive, it was impossible for me to do any major entertaining, but I looked forward to including them in my future dinner parties in our new home. But fate had another turn for Nat Cole's life. Alan said he never saw him without a cigarette in his hand, and the inevitable lung cancer was diagnosed sometime in 1964. Finally, he was hospitalized at Saint John's Hospital in Santa Monica to receive intense radiation and chemotherapy. It was sometime in January 1965 that Alan and I went to the hospital to visit him.

Nat gave Alan a hug and promised that he would be back at work very soon. I will never forget his color. Under Nat's dark skin was a pale gray that pervaded his lips, his eyes, and even his fingernails. I remember when we left, Maria was there holding his hand as we walked to the elevator.

On Valentine's Day, February 14, 1965, Nat did a radio interview, stating, "I am feeling better than ever. I think I've finally got this cancer licked." He died the next day.

55

Up the Ladder

After Alan became vice president in charge of the Artists and Repertoire Division at Capitol, he produced albums not only with Nat Cole but also with Margaret Whiting, Jo Stafford, Stan Kenton, Freddie Slack, Ella Mae Morse, and Gordon MacRae. He had decided to bring Benny Goodman back in some way to redo his classic hits, although it was thought that swing was pretty much dead. He signed Benny and called his first album *BG in Hi-Fi*. They were then recording on tape (with LPs pressed later to release on the market). Alan felt the big-band fans would like their favorites in high quality. He was right. He did the same with Glen Gray and the old Casa Loma Orchestra as well as others. He tried with Tommy Dorsey, but Dorsey turned him down. However, he did get Harry James, and Artie Shaw agreed if someone else would play the clarinet parts because he had sworn off playing. Alan never learned why.

Alan told me the story of Benny Goodman recording some of the classic songs that Fred Astaire was not only dancing to but singing as well at MGM. Alan was determined to record Fred with Benny's band. Fred was eager to work with Benny, but Benny was somewhat hesitant to work with Fred. Alan somehow got them together, but during their first recording session Alan got an SOS call to come down to the studio immediately. As he walked into the recording booth, Benny looked at Alan and said, "This dude can dance, but he can't sing." Alan calmed Benny down and explained that Fred was a true artist, especially in creating his own style with the lyrics. Suddenly Benny understood and accommodated the music to work with Fred.

Alan's endeavors at Capitol didn't include just music. Alan heard a comedy album released by a small label, Colonial Records, in North Carolina. It had sold a modest quantity, fifty thousand records, but Alan liked what he heard. It was by a little-known comedian, Andy Griffith, and was titled *What It Was, Was Football*, a monologue about the game.

197

Alan bought the rights to the record and rereleased it the same year. It soon sold nearly eight hundred thousand copies and was instrumental in launching Griffith's career in television, stage, and film. The record is still one of the biggest-selling comedy records of all time. On the original single, the monologue is credited to "Deacon Andy Griffith."

56

Frank Sinatra

Though it's difficult to believe today, in 1952 Frank Sinatra was let go by his longtime label, Columbia Records, with an announcement from then president Mitch Miller that Sinatra's career was over. He was not selling any records; in fact, he couldn't even get a club date, let alone a movie or a television spot. On top of all that, he was broke and in debt, Ava Gardner had left him, he was drinking too much, and no one would touch him.

Alan got a phone call from his friend Sam Weisbord at the William Morris Agency, who asked if Alan and Capitol would be interested in signing Frank. Alan answered immediately, "I would."

Sam replied in astonishment, "You would?"

"Yes, Sam," Alan said. "He is the most gifted singer in America. He needs a new arranger and conductor and definitely a new repertoire."

When Alan and Frank met, Frank was quite subdued, and they readily made a deal for a one-year contract with six one-year options. It was a union-scale advance against a 5 percent royalty.

When Alan told his producers about the deal, they were totally negative, and none of them wanted to work with Frank. He finally persuaded Voyle Gilmore to act as his producer and started planning the first record session.

Alan suggested that Frank might work well with Nelson Riddle, a talented young arranger-conductor, but Frank immediately rejected that idea, saying he worked only with Axel Stordahl. He was very determined, so Alan, in his typically low-key style, told Sinatra, "Fine. Let's put out a few singles and see what happens."

Alan attended the yearly meeting with the whole Capitol sales force and their district and regional managers and presented the upcoming new artists and recording plans. At the end of this meeting, he quietly said, "And we have just signed Frank Sinatra." One hundred twenty-five people let out a groan. Alan told me he was taken aback but responded to them clearly: "I deal in talent, and Frank is the most talented singer I have ever heard. Whatever his problems and lack of success in the past, they don't interest me now. He needs a new arranger-conductor and fresh material. You just stand by!"

The first several records did not sell at all, but in the meantime a music publisher brought in a song titled "Young at Heart." Alan felt immediately it was for Frank, and Frank agreed. Alan very shrewdly chose to discuss this recording with Frank when Axel Stordahl was in New York.

He told Frank that other artists were going to record the song immediately, but he wanted Frank to be the first. He explained he had reserved a studio for the coming Sunday afternoon and asked Frank to please use Nelson, just this once, and then he could go back to Axel.

Alan attended that recording session.

Every time I hear that record, which is played over and over again all over the world, I imagine my handsome husband standing in the corner of the studio, his arms folded, a very large smile on his face. He knew Frank was about to explode in the record business. And of course he did.

I can't resist adding that Alan was also instrumental in creating the famous circular Capitol Records building, resembling a stack of records. Not many people know this, but it was Alan's suggestion that a red light be put at the top that would blink "Hollywood" in Morse code. It was done and became a much talked about gimmick. It's still flashing there today.

57

NBC and *Bonanza*

Capitol Records was becoming the number-one record company in the country, and every competitor was trying to lure Alan away, particularly RCA. The wooing started at the top with General David Sarnoff, who after meeting Alan developed a real appreciation for and friendship with him. Alan refused to uproot his family and move to New York, though, so he kept turning down RCA. But they didn't give up.

They sensed correctly that Alan was worried about remaining in the recording business because it was already dramatically changing, so in 1956 they offered him the role of senior vice president in charge of NBC Television on the West Coast. He accepted enthusiastically. Many years later, when I was cleaning out a file of Alan's papers, I found a copy of a telegram that Alan had sent when he was at NBC. It was to the producer of a new series that Alan was deeply involved in developing and enthusiastic about. The telegram read, "Suggested title—Bonanza."

I knew that he helped cast the series and hired Jay and Jay's partner Ray Evans to write the title song, which became a hit single. I showed Alan the telegram, and he looked at it a long time. He then began to tell me a shocking story.

He told me he enjoyed working in a new field and wanted to contribute something that was uniquely his.

General Sarnoff had appointed his eldest son, Bobby, as chairman of NBC Television, and Bobby hired Bob Kintner to be the president. Alan reported to Kintner, who, it turned out, was a deeply disturbed, insecure alcoholic and someone easily threatened by any real talent that might diminish his position. Alan by nature was a creator, and it didn't occur to him that anyone within his own company would want to stop him.

While developing *Bonanza,* he worked closely with the writer, director, and producer, even going with them on location, but when he got to Madison

Avenue to sell the project to advertisers, everyone turned it down. Alan could not understand this until one day he received a phone call from a friend at the William Morris Agency, who said, "Alan, Bob Kintner has sent a communication to the advertising community to never accept any project that Alan Livingston brings to them. It will be dead on arrival at NBC." Alan was shocked and went to General Sarnoff to explain why he must resign. There was no point in his remaining. From what I understand, the general truly appreciated who Alan was. He looked at Alan sadly and said, "Bobby's my son. He depends on Kintner. I cannot interfere. However, I will do something for you, Alan. I take your word for it that this is a worthwhile project, and I will personally see to it that NBC will own this series and will air a nine-episode season."

The rest is history. *Bonanza* became the most valuable property that NBC Television ever had, running for an astonishing fourteen years.

I was stunned by this story, but it didn't end there. Alan said that before he left, he made an appointment to see Bob Kintner. He walked into Kintner's office, sat down, and said, "Bob, why? What did I do that made you determined to never let me succeed?" Mr. Kintner exclaimed, stuttering, "W-w-w-what do you mean? W-w-w-what are you talking about?" Alan just got up and left. I've often wondered how Bob Kintner felt when *Bonanza* became such a glorious hit.

Years later, another one of Alan's creative contributions at NBC came to my attention. At the time, I was a board member of the Los Angeles public-radio and television station KCET and gave a dinner for fellow board members and major contributors. I stood up at dessert and welcomed everyone with a speech that, in my usual fashion, went on a bit long. Our close friends Ginny and Henry Mancini were there, and in the middle of my speech Hank began gesturing with his finger across his throat as if to say, "Cut! Stop talking!"

I said, "Hank, do you have something to say?"

"Yes!" He then stood up and said, "I have never taken the opportunity to thank Alan Livingston for changing the course of my career. When Alan was at NBC in charge of television, I was a struggling musician and was thrilled to be hired to write the theme song for the TV series *Peter Gunn*. Alan came from a very successful career in the record business and called RCA Records when he heard my song. I heard later that he insisted it was a hit single, and they were crazy not to release it. And guess what? They released it. It became a huge success, and my career took off. I am so happy that I can thank Alan with all of you here." I asked Alan later if this was true, and he said it was, but he had forgotten all about it.

As a final exclamation point, before Alan left NBC, he helped arrange for his brother and Ray Evans to write the theme song for *Mister Ed*. Jay wound up singing the song.

After leaving NBC, Alan spent several months without a job until one morning Glen Wallichs called him and said, "We need you, Alan. Please come back." Alan returned to Capitol in 1960, this time as president.

When I married Alan, he told me about going back to Capitol and hearing that Frank Sinatra was demanding a new deal. Frank wanted a separate company, of which he would own 50 percent, with Capitol releasing and distributing his records. Of course, Capitol refused because it would have to do this same thing for every other successful artist. Frank's response was, "You can't make me sing." That was nine months before Alan returned to Capitol.

Alan called Frank and said, "Frank, this is Alan, I'm back at Capitol." Frank said, "I know." Alan said, "Let's get together and see if we can work out your problems."

Frank responded, "Fuck you, and fuck Capitol Records! I'm going to see to it that that round building of yours will come toppling to the ground." Alan was stunned and thought, "Good God, this is the man I gave the opportunity and support to come back from obscurity. How could he talk to me that way?" All Alan could do was respond, "I'm sorry, Frank. I had no idea you felt like that," and he hung up.

Capitol could not make Frank sing, so Alan put him on suspension. It was a stalemate. Frank wanted desperately to have his own company, and Alan wanted more Sinatra records to make their Sinatra catalog as large as possible. Alan offered a compromise. He suggested that Frank make seven more albums, and Capitol would release him after that. It was agreed.

The albums were made in less than a year, and Frank started Reprise Records. The name was pronounced "Repreese," as in the musical term, but Frank made it known that it really was "Reprize," as in *reprisal*.

Because Frank's contract gave Capitol unlimited rights in perpetuity to all his master recordings, Alan went through all of Frank's songs, both released and unreleased, and put together a series of new albums, which he released one after another in addition to the seven new albums Frank had recorded before he left. Alan repackaged everything. For all the songs written by Cole Porter, Alan created a new album called *Sinatra Sings Cole Porter*. There were many masters that Capitol had never released, and they all were included in these new albums. The album that Frank found most irritating was a two-album set that Alan titled *The Best Years*. I think history has clearly shown that Frank's years at Capitol were indeed his best.

Alan then flooded the market with all the new albums, so when Reprise tried to get its recordings into the stores, it was told, "Sorry, we're loaded with Sinatra."

Frank's attorney threatened Alan and Capitol with multiple lawsuits, but Alan stood his ground. I remember he said, "More than one person in the industry said I was crazy and was apt to get my knees broken." When he told me about this, I thought, "Good God." I could only visualize a black limousine pulling up to our house to gun us all down. That never happened, and Alan's knees remained intact.

It's so interesting to me that this story continued to invade our life in such interesting ways.

58

An Ex-Girlfriend and an Ex-Wife

As Alan and I settled into our new life together, I started to learn more and more about my new husband. As it turned out, in addition to the first two marriages, Alan had faced other challenges in his personal life, and he gradually shared with me some of these painful and extraordinary stories.

His affair with the actress Inger Stevens started in a restaurant—Alan was having lunch with a fellow executive from Capitol at the Brown Derby, and the waiter brought him a note. It said, "I'm sitting across the room looking at you. This is my phone number . . . I would love to hear from you. Inger Stevens." Alan was single and lonely at the time and of course called her. They had an intense affair for close to a year before Alan began to understand and see Inger's deep inner problems. He felt guilty about taking all her time, knowing it could go nowhere, and began to end the relationship. She finally got the message, and they parted.

One evening while Alan and I were having our ritual martini together, he said, "I've been meaning to tell you something. It's actually a very sad story. Last week I came to my office after lunch, and my secretary said Inger Stevens was waiting for me. I joined her, and she said to me, 'Alan, I miss you. I know you're married, and that's OK. I just want to see you whenever it's possible.'"

I must have looked alarmed because Alan quickly added, "Nancy, I'm only telling you this story because, of course, I made it clear as gently as I could that that would never be possible."

About a year later, Inger died of an overdose of sleeping pills. It was never officially classified as suicide, but Alan was sure Inger wanted to die. His story of Inger was extremely tragic and reveals his honesty about himself and the people in his life. He told me this story not with the intent to try to prove to me how everybody couldn't live without him but with deep compassion for a lost soul. I could only reply, "Poor Inger."

205

But Inger wasn't the only past relationship that attempted to disrupt our new marriage. Alan had another shocking revelation about Betty Hutton, his second wife. A few years after Betty divorced her fourth husband, the jazz trumpeter Pete Candoli, she called Alan in his office at Capitol and said she missed him desperately and needed to see him. He explained that he was married and had a new baby boy (we'll get to that!). She responded by exclaiming, "That's wonderful! You know how great I am with children!" Poor Betty.

59

Judy Garland, Oscar Levant, and The 2000-Year-Old Man

O ur nightly cocktail hour was a great source of joy for Alan and me, and the conversations we had were very often opportunities to learn about my husband and not just about reemergences of his past romances.

Alan told me many stories about his encounters at work. One such story involved Judy Garland and a repeated set of uncomfortable circumstances that turned into an opportunity. Alan shared with me the multiple phone calls he received over the years from a drugged-out Judy, who would wail into the phone, "I'm a legend! I'm considered the greatest singer in America, why won't you record me?!" She would then add, "But I won't do it unless you guarantee me a million dollars!"

Each time, poor Alan tried as delicately as possible to turn her down. However, when he returned to Capitol in 1960, he received another one of those calls, and this time, because he was aware she was about to do a live concert at Carnegie Hall, he decided to gamble on taking his crew to New York to do a live recording of her performance.

This concert appearance on the night of April 23, 1961, has been called "the greatest night in show business history." Garland's live performances were big successes at the time, and Alan wanted to capture that energy on a record. It turned out to be a two-record disk album, and it became a legendary success, both critically and commercially.

The album was released on July 10, 1961. It was a huge best seller—remaining on the Billboard chart for seventy-three weeks, including thirteen weeks as number one—and was certified gold. It won four Grammy Awards, including Album of the Year (the first live-music album and the first album by a female performer to win the award), Best Female Vocal Performance,

Best Engineered Album, and Best Album Cover. The record has never been out of print. In 2003, it was one of fifty recordings chosen by the Library of Congress to be added to the National Recording Registry. It was an amazing success, and Judy was forever grateful to Alan.

An interesting aside to this story took place one afternoon when Alan announced we were going that evening to a taping of Judy's live TV show. Apparently, Judy wanted to see Alan and had asked him to come backstage after the performance. When we walked into her dressing room, there were Dean Martin, Frank Sinatra, and Mack "Killer" Gray, Dean's bodyguard. Dean shook hands with Alan, Judy gave him a hug and a kiss, and Frank turned his back on both of us. Mack said innocently, "Hey, Frank, you know Alan." Frank didn't move. That's the way it was for many years every time we bumped into Frank Sinatra.

Over another martini one night, Alan shared with me another shocking story about one of his experiences as senior vice president at NBC television.

He was in his office one day when he got a call from Oscar Levant, whom he did not know. Oscar had a local TV show that was way ahead of its time, dealing with subjects and interviews that would be tame by today's standards but at that time ranged from unthinkable to outrageous. Alan reminded me that in the early days of television the restrictions on broadcasting, both by the Federal Communications Commission and self-imposed by the networks, were bordering on ridiculous. For example, Alan had been instructed that he could never allow the word *pregnant* to be used on any shows. Also, a married couple could not be shown in the same bed together—remember, *The Dick Van Dyke Show* had twin beds!

Alan wasn't sure what Oscar Levant wanted to discuss at lunch, but he was an admirer of Oscar and happy to meet him. Oscar suggested a brand-new restaurant named La Scala, then on Santa Monica Boulevard. It was not yet open for lunch, but Oscar knew the chef and arranged it so they could talk quietly.

Alan met him there, parking his car on the street. When they sat down in a booth, they were the only people in the room. Oscar got the chef out to tell Alan of all the wonderful foods he was going to prepare. Poor Alan, who ate only a very light lunch, couldn't stop the chef. He ended up with a plate of Italian food that was well beyond his capacity. Oscar had nothing in front of him but a pot of coffee.

Oscar chain-smoked and drank cup after cup. This went on for more than an hour while they talked politics, current news, people, and various other subjects, but nothing about television. Finally, Alan said he had to get back to his office. There was no check, and Oscar said he'd walk Alan out to his car.

Alan said goodbye and got in. The window was down on the street side, and while Alan was in the driver's seat, Oscar leaned in and said he wanted to talk about a network show for himself. Truthful Alan said, "Oscar, your show is very controversial. The subjects you cover would never be acceptable by network standards."

Oscar got very flushed and leaned farther inside the window. He shouted, "I have more brains in my little finger than all you fucking network vice presidents put together." He was red in the face and sweating so profusely that Alan thought he might have a heart attack. Finally, Oscar sat down on the curb. Alan moved over to the passenger seat and looked down on him from the window. Oscar's head was in his hands, and his feet were under the car, so Alan could not drive away, even if he were prepared to.

At that point, a police car came along and saw this bizarre picture. It stopped, and the officer asked, "Is everything OK?" Alan replied, "Everything's fine, thank you." Finally, the policeman drove off, and Oscar got up and walked away without another word. Poor Alan drove off totally confused.

When he returned to his office, his secretary said, "Oscar Levant's on the phone." When Alan got on the phone, Oscar gave an abject apology that went on and on. Alan told him not to worry about it and said Oscar was probably right about the brains of the network vice presidents. He made a joke of it, and that was it.

After that, Oscar called him on many occasions, and they had lunches and dinners together. They became friends and enjoyed the relationship. Alan remembered telling him about how mixed up his personal life was and how depressed he was about it. Oscar said, "I'll tell you what I do when I'm depressed: I go outside and lie down on the sidewalk. It's great, Alan! If you feel uncomfortable about it, I'll come and lie down with you." Alan said that Oscar had a great mind, but it would invariably fall off the deep end. However, he confessed that today Oscar could probably have a very successful network show.

One other small thing I learned about Alan over martinis was that he recorded *The 2000-Year-Old Man* with Mel Brooks and Carl Reiner. No other record executive was interested in doing anything with the comedy routine, and no one at Capitol Records was enthusiastic about it, either. But Alan was determined, and, as usual, his instinct was right. The album became a cult classic that is quoted from and referred to even today.

60

Enlarging the Family and JFK

In October 1963, I discovered that I was pregnant. It surprisingly took a fair amount of time for this to happen, which puzzled me, but Alan and I were overjoyed, and I mysteriously did not even suffer my usual morning nausea. All the children as well as my mother had their own set of reactions. My mother was only fearful that this might take some attention away from her; Liza and Jenny also worried about sharing their mother with another sibling; Laurie and Peter, of course, were extremely concerned about how a new baby would affect their status and future in the family. None of us knew what the next months might bring.

It was about a month later when the world shifted in a way we could never have expected. Everyone was getting ready for the holidays, planning Thanksgiving and Christmas vacations. As Thanksgiving was getting closer, I knew I would have to create the dinner with all its trimmings, and I also had to prepare for Laurie's Christmas visit as well.

I think I was in a somewhat delicate place and found myself on the morning of Friday, November 22, taking to my bed with a runny nose and a small temperature. I remember I was taking a nap when the phone rang. It was Alan, calling from the office to tell me to turn on the television. The president had just been shot, and Alan had closed down the entire company for the rest of the day.

In the meantime, my other phone rang, and it was the John Thomas Dye School asking that we please pick up the children as soon as possible because it was also closing early. I called my friend Judy Balaban Franciosa, who shared a carpool with me, and explained that I was not feeling well, so was it possible for her to pick up the children from school?

During this conversation, I became extremely emotional and started cursing the conservative southern politicians with their right-wing agenda and their hatred for our Democratic president. Judy hesitated for a moment and suggested that we shouldn't jump to any conclusions. "Nancy, it could be anyone. It might even be someone like that young man who was protesting and went to Cuba and eventually to Russia—what was his name? Something like Osbourne or Os-something?"

I have never fully recovered from the shock over my friend's prescient intuition. Two hours later it was announced that the authorities were arresting Lee Harvey Oswald, who had gone to Cuba and Russia in protest of America.

Who can ever forget that weekend, those images? Jackie, Caroline, little John John, Robert, and Teddy . . . all of America weeping.

I don't remember Thanksgiving very well. Shock and grief permeated the air and stubbornly remained with all of us. It wasn't very exciting to think of Christmas, either, but we had to face up to it. Christmas Eve, of course, would be at our house with the children and my mother and brother, and a trip to Yosemite was planned for skiing, but a personal event changed everything again.

On December 23, I began to experience cramps, and tiny spots of blood appeared on my panties. I was put to bed, but by the next afternoon it was quite clear I was going to have a miscarriage.

Alan drove me to UCLA, hugged me, and left with my instructions on how to host the rest of the evening for the family. Although I was only three months pregnant, the labor pains were quite severe, and when they wheeled me into the operating room, I finally gave birth to a tiny fetus enclosed in a round ball of liquid.

I sat on the edge of the delivery table looking at it. The intern and I talked about what it might have been. The little figure inside the bubble of fluid bounced back and forth. It was the color of the inside of a young sapling branch and reminded me of the tiniest doll in a set of Chinese nested dolls that get smaller and smaller as you open each one. I turned to the intern and said, "It's Christmas Eve."

Alan came to the hospital to pick me up and take me home. It had been a hectic night, and he had not enjoyed being in charge. The children had loved their gifts and were excitingly planning their skiing adventure.

I'm not sure how I managed, but the next afternoon we piled into the car and drove to Yosemite. I stood at the bottom of the hills watching the children racing down. Alan hovered over me and reassured me but was extremely busy taking care of everybody. On the last night of our trip, he took me in his arms and held me and whispered, "The new year is coming."

You might think that after this miscarriage I would give up trying to have another child, but that never occurred to me. There were weekly meetings with our architect; we were building the nest, and I was determined there would be an egg in it ready to hatch. My doctor said that if I were serious about having a baby, it was extremely important for me to get pregnant as soon as possible after the miscarriage. Apparently, the fact that I had no morning sickness was a signal that none of my hormones had been in gear; now that my body had begun preparing for birth, those hormones were finally awakened, and I should move quickly. I was fortunate to know exactly when I was ovulating and planned my attack on my unsuspecting husband on a Sunday afternoon while the children and the housekeeper were attending a movie.

Poor Alan. My seduction was irresistible and worked out exactly as I planned. I remember lying on my stomach after he left the bed to be sure that my egg and his sperm were connecting. In fact, that evening we attended a large black-tie dinner party, and I remember sitting at our table, smiling to myself, and thinking, "I'm pregnant"—and I was.

The morning sickness arrived on schedule, and nothing made me more deliriously happy.

61

The Beatles

One day I got a phone call from Alan asking if he could come home for lunch because he wanted to play something for me. He never came home for lunch, so I was prepared to hear something amazing. He sat me down and said, "Nancy, I want you to listen to a group that I believe might very well change the direction of the music business. First there were the big bands in the '30s, then Frank in the '40s, of course Elvis in the '50s, and now this may be what comes next."

It's very hard for me to confess, but I have to admit that when I heard the song "I Want to Hold Your Hand" with the chorus "I wanna hold your haaaaaaaaaaaaaaaaaaaaaaaand," I responded by saying, "Alan, I'm sorry, but that's the worst thing I ever heard."

Alan was now the president of Capitol and no longer directly in charge of new artists, but he still attended the weekly meetings with the A&R (Artists and Repertoire) staff to hear what new talent they were considering. He kept asking Dave Dexter, a producer he had put in charge of screening new artists, about this young British group he'd been reading about in the trades. Dexter said, "Forget it, Alan. I listened to their records, and they're nothing. They're just a bunch of long-haired kids."

The Beatles were signed to EMI in England, Capitol Records' major stockholder. Capitol always listened to EMI artists but was not obligated to sign them, so it initially turned the Beatles down. EMI then approached CBS, RCA, and Decca, who also refused to sign them. They next tried smaller US labels, like A&M, which said no as well. Finally, in desperation EMI settled on Vee-Jay Records, a tiny Black-owned company that was on the verge of bankruptcy. Vee-Jay was glad to get a free album and so put out the first Beatles record. The album was a total flop, and Vee-Jay told EMI it was no longer interested in this band. EMI persisted and finally got Swan Records to release two singles, four sides. Swan was a small but good label in Philadelphia that had some hits. Nothing happened, and Swan gave up on the Beatles as well. The Beatles were dead in this country, and that would have been the end of it.

Just before Alan called me that day, he was sitting in his office when his secretary told him there was a Brian Epstein on the phone calling from London. Alan didn't know who he was but took the call.

"Mr. Livingston," Epstein said in his posh English accent, "I manage the Beatles, and I don't understand why you have not put out their records."

Alan replied, "Well, frankly, I've never heard them."

"Would you please listen and call me back?"

Alan said, "Of course," and sent his secretary down to Dexter's office to get some copies.

He later told me he didn't know how big the Beatles would be, but he heard something new and good. He also liked the way they looked and felt that their distinctive long hair with bangs and their narrow suits were an asset, not a liability. That's when he called me and, thank God, didn't accept my opinion. He called Brian Epstein back the minute he returned to his office and said, "We'll sign them."

Shrewdly, Brian replied, "Wait a minute, you have to spend at least $40,000 on promoting their first single." In the early 1960s, this was a lot of money to spend on a first record, but for whatever reason Alan agreed.

Alan later began to wonder about his $40,000 commitment. He wondered if Dexter, Capitol's producers, and all those other record companies could be right and he wrong. He knew he had made mistakes before, like the time he turned down "Rudolph the Red-Nosed Reindeer" with the response, "Are you kidding?" Nevertheless, he proceeded full steam ahead with the Beatles, exposing them visually with many photographs in their public-relations and ad campaigns. It didn't take long, nor did it take the full $40,000. The single "I Want to Hold Your Hand" exploded, and Capitol had to rush to get out the first album, *Meet the Beatles!*

In the meantime, Vee-Jay Records, with no license to do so, released its previously unsuccessful album, *Introducing . . . The Beatles*. By the time Capitol legally forced Vee-Jay to take it off the market, it had sold a million copies!

Ed Sullivan had wisely booked the Beatles on his TV variety show before any of this happened because of their success in England and because he saw them as a novelty English act to introduce. He now had major guest stars to promote.

Alan brought the Beatles to the United States and booked them at the Plaza Hotel in New York under their real names, John Lennon, Paul McCartney,

Ringo Starr, and George Harrison. That meant nothing to the Plaza. But when they checked in and word got out that the Beatles were there, the frenzy began. Fifty-Ninth Street and Fifth Avenue were jammed with kids; traffic was stopped in every direction; the hotel would admit no one unless they could show that they had a key and could prove they were staying there. It was absolute bedlam. The Plaza later warned Alan never to book "those kids" in the hotel again!

But the Plaza did arrange for Alan and his children, Laurie and Peter, to get into the hotel to visit the boys. John, Paul, George, and Ringo were in their suite with the radio on, sitting on the floor listening to a disc jockey play their records and comment on their success. Paul would occasionally stick his head out the window, and the crowd below would scream. Alan spent a great deal of time talking with Brian, who was very bright, and Alan saw quickly how much the Beatles owed Brian for his unceasing efforts on their behalf. Alan left with a favorable impression of them all, and his children had a great story to tell their friends.

Capitol was delighted with the Beatles' success and couldn't get the first album pressed and distributed fast enough. Much as it would be nice to have the windfall business, Alan knew it would not be wise to flood the market with Beatles product, so he was careful to plan releases with proper timing. That strategy paid off, and the Beatles remained the top artists in the business year after year. Alan felt that this was made possible by John and Paul's talent. With the help of the Beach Boys, Sinatra, Nat Cole, and now the Beatles, Capitol became the number-one record company in the business in the 1960s.

Many years later, I found a description that Alan wrote about the Beatles in his memoirs:

They were indeed the biggest thing I have witnessed in the music business over three generations of teenagers. Personally, they were each different in their own way. Paul was gracious and outgoing. I enjoyed my relationship with him. John, I never fully understood. He was in a world of his own, and I never knew for sure whether he was for real or whether it was an act for the public—probably the former. George was totally withdrawn, at least on the surface. Ringo was just a plain, happy-go-lucky good guy, and easy to be with.

62

The Beatles in My Mother's Garden

One of the new challenges in my new marriage was learning how to entertain not just for the pleasure of sharing a party with my friends but for political or business purposes. In other words, it was my new role as a partner with my husband to further his corporate career.

I also had never had the experience of planning an event for a fund-raising group. I had no idea that this would be one of the most daunting challenges of my future life.

Because of Alan's son, Peter, the Hemophilia Society and its fund-raising organization had been keeping after Alan to plan events to raise money. Alan turned them over to me! And so I had my first taste of working for a non-profit group. It's all about money; however, you won't raise any unless you come up with a very enticing event.

Of course, I knew the Beatles would be a fantastic draw; the question was what would make them happy and willing to participate. I also knew this had to be a private affair, and every guest had to be someone we knew. I think I came up with a brilliant idea, if I do say so myself.

At the time, Alan and I were still living in a very small house that did not lend itself to any major social or business gatherings, but my mother had a large home with a beautiful garden on almost an acre in Brentwood Park, entirely enclosed by greenery. I asked her if she would be willing to host the Beatles in an afternoon event with our friends and their children. We would serve lemonade and cookies, and the children would go through a receiving line to meet the Beatles.

My mother said she would love to host them, and as she walked into her garden, she said, "I have the perfect spot to put four stools, one for each of the boys. We will put them under the Deodar tree."

We reassured the Beatles that they did not have to perform, and we would invite only our friends with their children and charge $100 for each

217

adult and $25 for each child, all proceeds going to the Hemophilia Society. Something about this invitation intrigued them, and they did not feel used but seemed happy to do this for Alan and his hemophiliac son, Peter.

My challenge was what to wear. I was seven and a half months pregnant, so my options were limited. Since it was the end of summer, I chose my best maternity gown—a pale-blue sleeveless silk sheath with ample space for my large tummy. My hair was quite blond, so I wore pale-beige leather pumps to match and accessorized with simple pearl earrings, my Schlumberger wedding ring with its diamond crosses, and my beloved pearl-and-diamond engagement ring.

The people who attended this party have never forgotten every moment of that afternoon. Even the Beatles talked about it years later. In fact, Paul discussed the party on *Jimmy Kimmel Live!* in September 2013.

We alerted the police, roped off the house, and had the riot squad hidden in the garage. The event was not publicized, but of course with so many invitees word got out. Alan was deluged with requests, but we finally had to cut off the list at the maximum the police felt they could handle.

Of course, Alan had to arrange getting the Beatles there and called his usual limo service, feeling obliged to tell them who they were transporting. They turned him down—they didn't want to risk getting their limo damaged by "crazy kids." He called every limo service in town, but not one was willing to handle the job. He called Brinks armored cars, told them of his problem, and asked if they would transport the group. They had to call their home office in Denver and came back with a negative response.

Finally, Alan went back to his regular limo service again and said he would pay for any damage to their car. "It isn't only that, Mr. Livingston," was the answer. "It's the loss of business if the car is laid up in the body shop." Alan asked, "What's the average fee you get per day per car?" They told him, and he sent them a letter guaranteeing not only damages but loss of use of the car.

They finally agreed, and the Beatles were delivered to my mother's home with no mishap. The riot squad never was called out of the garage, but there were a couple of close calls. The police told us later that in one area the rope almost gave way to the surging crowd of kids. My mother's next-door neighbor called, said he had a gun, and warned us that he would shoot anyone who put a foot through the hedge into his garden. Thank God it all stayed under control.

We invited Hedda Hopper, the Hollywood columnist for the *Los Angeles Times,* who stayed with my mother on the front porch watching this spectacle with a certain amount of disbelief. She was concerned that the women with high heels were puncturing my mother's beautifully manicured lawn. My mother responded by saying, "Oh, no, Miss Hopper—that only helps to aerate the soil."

The children arrived through the front gate and barely glanced at the lemonade and cookies. They were shaking with emotion, and the bravest took the first steps to the receiving line. I greeted them and introduced them one by one to each Beatle. Alan was waiting at the end of the line to thank them for coming.

Of course, we had photographers (not too many), who took pictures of each child saying hello to his or her heroes. These pictures are still exhibited all over the world and are prominent in people's homes today.

Our friend Dominick Dunne had a cherished picture in his New York townhouse of his beloved daughter, Dominique, curtseying as she said hello to Paul. Another little girl started to cry uncontrollably as she murmured, "I love you, Paul." My daughter Liza was in love with Ringo and had tears in her eyes when she said hello. If Paul stamped out a cigarette on the ground, there was a mad scramble to get it as a souvenir.

As the afternoon progressed, the helicopters arrived, circling our garden and the Beatles. When the chaos reached a crescendo, the guards said it was time for them to leave.

Alan arranged to have the photographs displayed in the lobby of Capitol Records the next week so the families could order prints. There was a picture of me attending to one of the emotional children on the front page of the *Los Angeles Times* the next day. And, most importantly, we raised good money for the Hemophilia Society as Capitol picked up all the expenses. Brian Epstein personally wrote a check for $10,000.

At the end of the twentieth century, the *Los Angeles Times* published a beautiful book of the history of a hundred years in Los Angeles. Alan and I were stunned to see the picture of the Beatles with the two of us in my mother's garden. The caption read, "The most celebrated event in 1964."

A footnote: At the time of the party, Barbara Rush was married to Warren Cowan, one of the most successful and powerful publicity agents in town—every one of his clients was a star. Barbara was a friend of mine, and we of course invited her, Warren, and their daughter, Claudia, to attend the event.

Warren immediately called Alan and asked if he could invite some of his clients. Alan said yes, "send me a list and their addresses, and we will send them a private invitation." It became apparent many years later that Claudia always felt that her father had been responsible for the party and its success. In fact, she wrote an article that was printed in *Los Angeles Magazine,* showing many pictures of that afternoon with the Beatles and taking full family responsibility for the party's creation. At the time, I was upset with her need to take credit—it always astonishes me how unimportant the truth can become when it stands in the way of advertising oneself. Today, I simply want to set the record straight.

63

Christopher

At midnight of Thursday, November 12, 1964, I lay beside Alan and began to feel my whole torso begin to shake.

Alan immediately got up and dressed, wrapped me in my robe, and drove me to UCLA. We arrived at the emergency entrance, where the staff put me on a gurney and rolled me through the doors into the delivery room. Alan walked beside me, squeezed my hand, and left when he was told to please wait in the adjacent waiting room—within an hour and a half, our child was born.

Alan and I would have been happy with either a boy or a girl, but I was hoping and praying that I would have a son and that I could give Alan a son as well. In those days, the sex of the fetus could not be determined while the baby was still in the womb, so you simply had to wait and see. When the doctor said to me, "It's a boy," I reached out for my infant son and took him in my arms.

When the nurse went to get Alan, he asked whether it was a boy or girl. She said she was not allowed to answer that. When Alan walked down the hallway toward me as I lay on the gurney holding our child, he said to the nurse, "You don't have to tell me it's a boy—I can tell by the expression on my wife's face."

One of the staff was standing next to me with a clipboard. He asked for the name of our new son. Alan said, "Christopher Livingston." And I said, "No, Christopher Alan Livingston." I think Alan was close to tears.

There is no way that I can capture in words the joy and peace and fulfillment of this time with my little boy and my wonderful husband. It was six in the morning; Alan kissed me and went home to tell Liza and Jenny about their brother and to call Laurie and Peter, my mother and brother, and the rest of his family. I think he went to the office for a brief time and came back to the hospital about four in the afternoon. The baby was in a crib next to my bed. Alan washed his hands and walked over to pick up the baby. The sound of his words and his voice still ring in my memory. As he tucked our baby boy in his arms, he simply said, "I like this boy."

For the first four months of Christopher's life, I was moving us into our new home on Alpine Drive. My New York apartment furniture had arrived along with the paintings, porcelain, silver, lamps, books, pots and pans, and just about everything one needs in one's household.

Alan and I had great fun picking out which paintings would be hung in each room, deciding where to put all the furniture, and creating a wonderful nursery for Christopher and his nanny. Liza and Jenny had their own rooms with a connecting bath, and Alan and I had a master suite with our own dressing rooms and bath. What a luxury after Camden Drive! We loved our home, and at least once a week for the rest of our lives we talked about how much we enjoyed living in our house.

64

Another Beatles Party

Of course, our new home put an extra pressure on me: I had no excuse not to entertain for Alan's business interests.

In August 1965, we decided to give a cocktail party for the Beatles. We invited everyone in Hollywood, from Gene Kelly to Rock Hudson, Jack Benny, Hayley Mills, Natalie Wood, Tony Bennett, Nick Dunne, the heads of the studios, you-name-it. My vision for this party was that it would be a successful blend of the most talented people in Hollywood getting to know the newest, most revolutionary artists in the music world. The fascination with the Beatles was amazing, and the band had only begun their journey of creating a legend—everyone who was invited came.

Other than that, however, nothing about this party came together as planned.

The first challenge came the afternoon of the event. I had an appointment at UCLA with my gynecologist, who said that he was concerned that I might have the beginning of a cancerous spot on my cervix. He took a biopsy and said that he would let me know the results as soon as possible. The timing of news like this is never good, but that day was the worst possible day.

The seeds of another problem were brewing that afternoon as well, albeit one with less potentially dire consequences. I received a call after my doctor's appointment from Ruth Berle, possibly one of the more ambitious wives of celebrity husbands, in her case Milton. She explained that she understood that no press was invited or allowed to this party; however, her current house guest was Gail Sheehy, a renowned writer, particularly for *Life* magazine. Could she please bring her?

I hesitantly said yes and reminded her to tell Ms. Sheehy that she could not write about the party. . . . We'll get back to this.

Regardless of the scary news from the doctor, I had to forge ahead. There's the old adage in the theater, "The show must go on," and, after all, I was throwing a party for the Beatles. That meant focusing on the realities of the evening, and one of them, although much less important than my health, was what I was going to wear.

Thankfully, it had been many months since I had given birth to Christopher, and as a small consolation prize for the already challenging day, I was finally able to fit into one of my treasured outfits from New York: a sleeveless floor-length sheath made of exquisite Japanese silk in the most seductive, beautiful colors. I dug into my jewelry box and accompanied my ensemble with pearl-and-diamond earrings and a pearl bracelet and ring.

As I look back, one of the only relatively happy moments of that evening was when I stood before the mirror and felt pleased about how I looked.

Before the guests arrived, I went to check on Christopher. He was standing in his crib demanding attention, particularly needful this day because everyone was so preoccupied with everything else going on around him. His nurse, Suzanne, was understandably focusing on *her* wardrobe, nervously relishing the responsibility of bringing Chris into the party. I had to leave Chris alone as it was getting time to start receiving the guests.

The Beatles arrived around 4:30 p.m., and my pulse was accelerating—I would guess to about 120. Paul was the first through the door and, as usual, was a gracious and charming guest.

Ringo was next and equally charming and extremely accessible. John followed Ringo, barely mumbled hello, and immediately stood in a corner and talked to no one.

Even in my hysterical state, I seemed to recall that there were *four* Beatles. Who was missing? Oh my God, George! Where was he? Paul explained to me that he decided not to come. "Oh, dear God!"

Of course, the house looked beautiful filled with my garden roses. The buffet table was laden with fabulous hors d'oeuvres, and I had a wonderful pianist with the explicit instructions to play only the standards, nothing that competed with today's music or the Beatles.

By this time, John had left the living room and was standing alone on the patio overlooking the pool. I followed him out and gently took his arm, moving him over to meet Gene Kelly. He pulled his arm away so sharply that I almost lost my balance and shouted at me, "Please leave me alone!" I said, "I'm sorry; of course I won't bother you."

Things were not going quite the way I had hoped.

My friend Gene Kelly observed this, obviously concerned for me, and walked over to John to tell him about what a wonderful artist he was and how much he admired his music. I think Gene Kelly was the only movie star who could possibly break through John's rude, angry barrier. In fact, John was one of the last to leave the party.

While this was happening, I heard someone singing, and it sounded not only familiar but wonderful. I walked into the living room, and there was Tony Bennett standing at the piano crooning softly and seductively some of America's most beautiful songs. I honestly felt that if Tony Bennett felt comfortable in this strange atmosphere, the party had to be somewhat of a success.

But we were just getting started.

When I went to get Christopher, I noticed that Suzanne, his nanny, seemed quite nervous, but I didn't think much of it at the time. Everyone was feeling nervous to some degree. I asked Suzanne to pick up Christopher, and, as she had hoped, she was granted the opportunity to take him into the living room to meet the guests. As we entered, I could see her eyes seemed unusually glazed over as she took in the celebrity status of the room. Suzanne managed to get through meeting many of the stars, including the Beatles, and Christopher remained safely tucked in her arms, until . . . the one celebrity Suzanne had not met yet just so happened to be standing next to her, and when she turned away from Paul McCartney, she bumped right into Rock Hudson.

Suzanne, looking dazed, began to teeter. She was so overwhelmed by the proximity of her movie star idol that she turned white and started to tumble with Chris in her arms. She was fainting!

I grabbed Chris, several people took Suzanne by the arm, and we helped her back to the nursery. She immediately lay down on her bed, and I put Chris in his crib, who started to cry. I tried to console him and promised I would be back. Chris would have none of it, and his relentless wails could be heard as I closed the door behind me. . . . "Oh God," I thought, "this night is turning into a disaster!"

But nothing prepared me for what happened a week later!

Of course, there were multiple phone calls, all expressing their joy at attending the event and sharing their genuine gratefulness for having been invited. Gene Kelly called me the next morning, asked if I was alright, and said he had had a very interesting conversation with John. My friend Nick Dunne told every one of his Hollywood friends about what they had missed by not being there. Nick couldn't help himself: he just had to make it clear that he was one of the guests; it was a sign of his status.

The best news was that when my biopsy results came in, they were negative. Thank God! All of that worrying was now behind me.

Alan felt that he had met an important obligation to the Beatles. And George mentioned to Alan the next time they were together that he was so sorry he had missed the party.

All of this was very nice, but I was not prepared for the article in *Life* magazine that Gail Sheehy wrote. She, of course, could not resist reminding the world that she had been to this party and could comment on it with superiority. Even though she began the article, "Despite a charming hostess . . . , " she followed with, "This party didn't quite come off."

Her point was that it's impossible to mix superstars with super superstars, and she was so sorry the party wasn't more successful.

I truly felt terrible, but the good-health news made Gail's article a mere footnote to the evening.

Several months later Alan and I attended a dinner party at the Paul Ziffrons in Malibu, and Alan was seated next to Gail. She was extremely uncomfortable and awkwardly tried to apologize. Alan had such grace and, without accepting the apology one way or another, simply changed the subject. I would have poured my drink over her head.

65

Russia

The Beatles were a godsend for Alan, but he was still looking for an acquisition that could give Capitol a larger base of catalog sales (as opposed to having to develop a new hit artist year after year). There was endless pressure on Alan to keep Capitol in the black, and I think it was at about this time he had his first bout with pneumonia. I was extremely concerned for him and realized that the constant pressure was taking its toll. Alan knew that the large base of classical artists under contract with CBS and RCA served those labels very well, and classical music could be a potential solution for the catalog problem at Capitol. But, unfortunately, there was no way Alan could compete with the other labels. How in the world could he develop a large classical catalog without unacceptable cost and without orchestras, conductors, or soloists, all of which were already controlled by RCA and CBS?

Again, Alan's genius for solving problems rose to the surface. RCA and CBS were releasing Russian recordings of the violinist David Oistrakh, the pianists Emil Gilels and Sviatoslav Richter, as well as other top musicians. They competed extremely successfully in the market, particularly on CBS. Recording arrangements were made one at a time, but Alan realized that the Russians were not making exclusive deals with either company.

He managed to contact a man who had been dealing with the Russians on other matters and through him made contact with the right people in Moscow. Remember, this was the Russia of the 1960s, not of today. He arranged a meeting, taking an interpreter, his chief legal counsel, and me. I will never forget this trip.

It was November 1965, and after reading the weather reports from Moscow, I knew that I would have to find a way to stay warm. I decided to take my mink coat even though I knew that the Communist government might brand me an evil capitalist. We flew from Los Angeles to Stockholm, which is the first time I ever saw Sweden. We had a seven-hour layover before our flight to Moscow, so we drove into Stockholm to a room in the Grand Hotel to rest and refresh ourselves. As we drove through the countryside, I thought about how much Sweden reminded me of northern Wisconsin and understood why my ancestors chose to live there when they immigrated; it reminded them of home.

We flew from Sweden to Moscow on a Russian airline, which was completely different from American Airlines. The interior of the plane was sparse, and the snack was inedible. The government also had us fill out multiple pages of information. One of the things that startled me was that I was asked to write a detailed description of every piece of jewelry I was traveling with. Alan told me that I would have to show the jewelry when I left the country to prove that they were mine.

Gray is the color that comes to my mind when I think of this trip. It was cold, damp; the earth was covered with slate-colored snow; the trees were bare; the houses looked worn and lonely. I couldn't imagine living in this bleak environment. The only relief was the incredible skyline of domes of gold, mixed with beautiful colors, on exotic buildings that emerged in the middle of Moscow, reflecting a glorious past.

We stayed at the Metropole Hotel. It was across the street from the home of the Bolshoi Theater. As I walked up the stairs, I tripped on a block of wood that was wedged in a hole on the marble step. As we entered the lobby, the overwhelming odor of wet plaster mixed with the faint smell of cooking cabbage greeted me. My stomach still turns when I think of it.

Alan's American contact told us to be very careful of what we said in our suite because it was certainly bugged, and someone was taping our every word, possibly even photographing us. Alan and I were very complimentary of our hosts, the "wonderful Communist government," and we somehow managed to be celibate as well. We were not interested in being stars in a Russian porno film!

We ate mostly cabbage soup and stayed away from the meat. Alan remembered Moscow as having the most depressing atmosphere he had ever experienced. As he later wrote, "Nancy is movie-star beautiful, with her blond hair and good figure. The Russian women were poorly dressed and overweight. Our walking down the street was a sight for them to behold. They made an attempt not to stare, but their furtive looks and nudging were clear."

While Alan was in negotiations with the government, I was escorted around Moscow by government representatives. I particularly wanted to visit the Pushkin Museum, housed in a palace built by Emperor Nikolas II and members of the royal family. For me, it told the story of the past in juxtaposition with the present.

As I entered the first room, there on the walls were portraits of the royal family and their friends painted by famous European portrait artists. I was struck by how handsome the men were and how beautiful the women looked. There was a refinement and elegance about them, and I wondered what terrible things had happened to these Russians in the ensuing years. The people I saw on the streets of Moscow bore no resemblance to any of the individuals portrayed in the paintings. I thought perhaps even their genes and DNA had disappeared. There was a long line of visitors to the museum, all poorly dressed in thin wool coats and thick leather boots, their cheeks bright red from the cold. I wanted to wrap my mink coat around them all. I was touched by their deep interest and reverent attention to what they were looking at.

As we slowly moved on, we finally came to the European modernists, the most glorious examples of this period I had ever seen. At this time, there were not even photographs of these paintings existing outside of Russia, though the world would eventually see them much, much later. They were dated from the end of the nineteenth century to 1917, where they abruptly stopped. The people in the portraits I had just viewed had purchased these paintings for their homes and had bought only the finest.

There was a wall of startlingly beautiful Picassos from the Blue Period; they gave me an electric shock to look at them. The early Cezannes and the more contemporary Kandinskys were unbelievable; the red fish in a bowl on a pink tablecloth by Matisse was unforgettable; but perhaps the most awesome were the huge portraits of the South Pacific natives by Paul Gauguin. At this time, these paintings had never left Russia and could be seen only by the Russian people and the few privileged visitors like me.

My escorts stayed about ten to twelve feet away from me but watched my every move and interaction with people at the museum. A gentleman in tattered clothes approached me and said in French, "Do you speak French?" I stammered with my high school French something like, "No comprende," and in English said, "I am so sorry." I gestured to the paintings and added, "J'aime!" When I turned back to him, he was gone, and my delegation had suddenly surrounded me! I'm not sure who this stranger was, but I imagined that because he spoke French so fluently, he was a survivor from the past. It is well known that the Russian aristocracy spoke French. I wonder what happened to him.

In the meantime, Alan was in deep negotiations with the government in the Metropole Hotel conference room. Alan, his attorney, and his interpreter sat across from six Russians, including their interpreter, at a long table.

Alan told me that within half an hour he was ready to give up and go home. Negotiations were difficult enough in one's own country using one's own language, but the Russians did not even understand the meaning of the words *copyright* or *music license fees*. Alan was surprised to learn that the Russians paid their artists no royalties and no license fees for the music. The major artists, of course, worked for the government on some compensation basis.

After a while, Alan somehow became accustomed to the translation process and its delays, and things began to move along. He spent four days sitting at that table listening to them repeat their standard response: "It is contrary to the policy of the minister of culture." Finally, Alan reached a point when he stood up and said, "I don't want to talk to you any longer. I am the president of my company, and I can make final decisions on all matters right here. Bring in your minister of culture!"

What a reaction. Their spokesman let go: "OK, OK, you can have it!"—in English, not waiting for the translator! He could understand Alan the whole time, and the minister routine was just that, a negotiating ploy with no basis in truth.

On the last day of negotiations, the two parties got to the issue of exclusivity, which Alan insisted on having. He was told, "The Russian government can give exclusivity to no one." It was without question a dead end. But my brilliant husband did it again. He said, "I don't want exclusivity on your artists. I just want to be your only distributor of records in the United States."

"Oh," they quickly replied, "that's OK." That subtle change of language accomplished the same thing for Capitol and got around the problem. Or, as Alan said, "Maybe they just don't understand what they are giving me." In any event, a deal memo was signed, followed by a celebration lunch with a lot of caviar spread on rye bread, with no lemon or onion or chopped egg white, and too much vodka. Alan requested at least lemon for his caviar, and their answer was "no lemon." But when the tea came, it was served with lemon. We both couldn't wait to get out of Russia.

One year later, after all the agreements were signed, Capitol Records put out a routine press release. Alan immediately received a call from someone at the *New York Times* who clearly doubted the facts. The reporter said that Columbia Records at CBS told him that Capitol couldn't possibly have exclusive rights because Columbia had been releasing Russian product for years and hadn't received any notice that this business relationship would be ending. Finally, at the *Times'* request, Alan read the portion of the contract related to exclusivity. The result was a major full-page story titled "American Makes a Record Catch in Moscow." It featured a picture of Alan.

Moscow had excellent recording equipment but didn't have anyone who knew how to make the best use of it. Alan sent over a Capitol engineer, and the result was extremely high-quality tapes. Capitol released the top Russian classical artists on the Melodiya/Angel label to immediate success in the classical record business, as Alan had wanted, with no financial investment and a modest royalty. We even had the pleasure of having David Oistrakh in our home for dinner; not speaking Russian, we had to converse through our friend the cellist Gregor Piatigorsky, who had joined us. At Oistrakh's request, Alan gave him some Beatles records, which he wanted to hear. Alan did the same for Jascha Heifetz, who called Alan a few days later to say he didn't understand their music at all. Oistrakh never called—I'm sure his reaction was the same.

66

Share

With all the distractions of getting married, starting a new family, and adjusting to being the wife and hostess of an entertainment executive, it suddenly dawned on me that I needed to find an outlet just for myself here in Los Angeles.

Friendships had always been important to me, and my long hours working in the studio as an in-demand actress were no longer a hurdle toward this end.

Judy Balaban had from the beginning been a wonderful friend, but she was wrapped up in her new marriage to Tony Franciosa, and they were the center of a social group that Alan and I didn't fully relate to.

Sally Goodman became a close friend. She was married to George Goodman, an intellectually gifted writer (the author of best-selling books on economics under the pseudonym "Adam Smith"), and came from a well-known family in Texas. Like me, she knew and had spent time with prominent people all over the world and shared my more sophisticated overview. She also had her first child a few months before I had Christopher, so we could talk about breastfeeding! Unfortunately, a few years into my time in LA, Sally left California to live in Princeton, New Jersey, leaving another void.

I was still trying to find my way in Los Angeles when Judy Balaban put my name up for a very famous Los Angeles charity group called Share. I was surprised to be accepted into the organization and attended my first meeting with a certain amount of trepidation. I didn't know any of the members or fully grasp how the group functioned or even what it supported. It turned out that all of the women had some connection to the entertainment industry. Their husbands were actors, producers, songwriters, and performers. Some of the members I remember were Dean Martin's wife, Jean; Sammy Davis Jr.'s wife, Altovise; Steve McQueen's wife, Neile; Sammy Cahn's wife, Gloria; Milton Berle's wife, Ruth; Jack Benny's daughter, Joan; singer Jo Stafford; and the actresses Janet Leigh and Barbara Rush. They raised money producing one event annually: a take-off on a Broadway revue.

I thought becoming a member would be a good way to meet new people and get involved in something worthwhile in Los Angeles. The Share Show was one of the social events of the year. It took place at the Santa Monica Civic Center, a well-located venue with a large stage, a huge empty space in the center of the auditorium, and a built-in semibalcony in the back. The Share uniform was a cowgirl outfit, boots and all, and every guest was invited to dress in Western garb. Most celebrities in the entertainment industry attended this party, and many of them participated onstage as they all felt completely comfortable surrounded by their peers—no one was asking for an autograph!

It didn't take me long to realize that my career as a performer would not help me stand out in this venue and that the Share Show was a very competitive event not especially well suited to my abilities.

A description of the annual show might help you understand why. The big evening started in the lobby with cocktails and an auction. A sit-down dinner in the Civic Center auditorium followed, and the evening culminated with a stage production. The large orchestra in the pit was conducted by Henry Mancini (his wife, Ginny, was a member), and volunteer performers such as Sammy Davis Jr., Frank Sinatra, Dean Martin, and Milton Berle would start the evening's entertainment. The celebrity appearances were followed by a lavish dance production involving all of the Share members, and every member was expected to participate whether she could dance or not.

The highlight for all the members was to be chosen to dance in the "Middle Number." The ego competition to be a part of this exclusive group was riveting. Please understand that I had just had my name on the marquee of Radio City Music Hall in New York City for *Son of Flubber,* the sequel to *The Absent-Minded Professor,* and a picture of me with the Beatles had recently been published on the front page of the *Los Angeles Times,* but because I had two left feet, I had little chance of impressing the professional choreographers hired to put on the show. My lack of dancing ability was the only quality that defined my status in the new group. Not only was I never chosen to be in the "Middle Number," but I was always put in the back row of the opening number.

I quickly found that it was hard to stay motivated to participate (there were twelve weeks of rehearsals!). The show's glitz and glam and the members' competition for stage time seemed to have become the organization's dominant focus, and the funds we raised for charity somehow took a back seat to the drama surrounding the "Middle Number."

It took some time for me even to find out who the organization raised money for, but eventually I learned that the proceeds raised by Share went to the Exceptional Children's Foundation, an institution devoted to young people with learning disabilities. Astonishingly, I later discovered that none of the members had ever even visited this facility or truly understood what its specific function was.

After several years of my dancing in the back row and hosting some meetings at my house, Share fortuitously decided that it might have more use for me decorating its next party than performing in its annual show. It wasn't much of a job—choosing tablecloths, flowers, and lobby décor and decorating the auditorium—but it opened a door for me to find a way to contribute something of value in a way I could have never expected.

I went to a very talented florist and invited him to come to the dining space with me and discuss all the possibilities. The ceiling was very high and covered with round openings for lights or other objects. I wanted to create the illusion of a lower ceiling, so he suggested dropping long ropes covered with flowers and balloons from the holes. Every rope ended at the same level, giving the impression of a lower ceiling. We covered the slanting seats in the back, which were always empty and dark, with large letters spelling SHARE in tiny lightbulbs.

My next problem was the lobby.

It was clear to me that most of the guests attending the Share Show had no idea what they were donating their money to. All they cared about was being at one of the most glamorous evenings in Los Angeles.

I decided to approach the event from a different angle and went to visit the Exceptional Children's Foundation. I wanted to see for myself just what we were supporting. I called and made an appointment and was directed to a large building in Jefferson Park. I asked the staff member who greeted me if there was an art department. She became very animated and said that they had a thriving art program and an extremely gifted teacher. I asked if I could visit and found myself in the most beautiful room.

The ceiling was high, and at the top of the walls hung magnificent posters of some of the most famous paintings in the world by Picasso, Miro, Gauguin, Kandinsky, Matisse, and others. Beneath these posters were the students' paintings, which had obviously been inspired by the great art surrounding them. The art teacher, Wilma James, explained to me that people who have learning disabilities can often possess great artistic talent. I was stunned and inspired and asked if I could take some of the students' paintings to be framed and exhibited in the lobby of our event.

I took several of these paintings to the next rehearsal and asked members if they would go to their picture framers and ask them to frame some of the paintings as a donation. The members looked at me at a little funny but agreed. I took about twenty paintings to seven or eight framers used by members and found a perfect place in the lobby to hang them. I then took a large piece of cardboard and had professionally printed at the top, "The Exceptional Children's Foundation Artists." Beneath that, I wrote a description of the foundation's art program with a quote from Wilma James: "The unique ability to create a work of art is within us all."

I figured the guests and Share members could now look at this exhibit and have a greater understanding of what they were giving their money to. As it turned out, something even better occurred, something I hadn't expected. They loved the art so much that they bought every single painting. In fact, this art show became not only a topic of conversation but one of the most valuable and successful parts of the Share evening from that point on. Over the years, when I have been given responsibility and a leadership role, I have discovered and been amazed by the creativity that can be awakened inside when one is asked to take charge.

And then something miraculous happened. Believe it or not, I finally had a great opportunity to have a solo moment on stage in one of the shows. It was a year Share did a take-off on the Ziegfeld Follies. Candice Bergen's mother, Frances; a brand-new member, Mrs. Boyer, who was related to Max Factor; and I were put in Ziegfeld Girl costumes, which included a huge headdress that looked like an upside-down chandelier. The number consisted of the orchestra and singers singing a song as the three of us crossed the stage. In the middle of the song, I was to leave my position in the center of the girls and wiggle down to the microphone to sing the line "and we ain't kiddin'!" We rehearsed this three-minute number for twelve weeks.

The big night came, and we started to cross the stage. Frances Bergen leaned her head toward me, and, to our horror, her headdress became entangled with mine. I pulled myself away from her but in the process somehow managed to ensnare my headdress with Mrs. Boyer's. Now the three of us were hopelessly locked together and had to move in the same direction or fall down. The audience began to howl with laughter and cheers.

My solo moment to run down to the microphone was about to happen, but I couldn't break free. I was determined. God damn it, I had rehearsed for three months, and I was not going to miss my solo! I violently shook my head and freed myself, sending Frances stumbling offstage to the left and Mrs. Boyer flying to the right, and I just made it to the microphone in time to triumphantly sing my line "and we ain't kidding." The audience went wild with applause, stamping their feet and screaming, "Bravo!"

I exited the stage, and within two minutes Gene Kelly and Gower Champion came rushing backstage to embrace me. "You were fantastic!" said Gene. "I have never seen anything onstage quite like it!" Gower said, "Nancy, if I had my dancers rehearse your number for six months, it would never have come close to what we just witnessed."

Meanwhile, the "Middle Number" ladies were getting ready to make their appearance onstage. The loudspeaker in their dressing room allowed them to hear the show so they could time their entrance, but when they heard the audience reaction to my solo, Neile McQueen commented, "Well, I thought Nancy was rather cute in rehearsal, but I didn't think she was *that* good!"

Frances Bergen sent me flowers the next morning with a note begging me to forgive her for ruining my solo. Mrs. Boyer had left the theater immediately after our routine and resigned from Share the next day. I called them and explained that we were the hit of the evening and would never be forgotten. We would go down in history as having created one of the all-time greatest Share performances.

Share eventually created a world of friendships for me in my early years in LA and helped me get my life started in California. Two particular friendships I formed were with Felisa Vanoff and Shirley Turteltaub.

Felisa Vanoff was a former dancer, tall and beautiful, with an exquisite posture that gave her a regal air. She had grown up in a small town in western Pennsylvania, and we shared a midwestern sensibility. Felisa was very smart, which was a pleasure for me. Her husband, Nick, was half a head shorter than she was and had also been a dancer. Without a formal education of any kind, Nick had become one of the most powerful executives and innovators of early television, producing TV specials with Perry Como and Bing Crosby as well as *The Tonight Show* with Steve Allen, winning five Emmy Awards in the process.

Shirley Turteltaub was a very smart and talented woman who shared my moral values. She was married to Saul Turteltaub, a prominent comedy writer for television, perhaps best known for his later work on the series *Sanford and Son.*

Unfortunately, my time with Share did not end well. Several years later, I attended a meeting where one of the women made a speech that offended me. She was addressing how to get recognition and to secure the best table at the party, something that she accomplished every year by giving an incredibly large personal donation. At that moment, I decided I was leaving the organization.

I had thought about leaving Share before this point, especially after a rehearsal, which seemed to me to be an exercise in primitive ego building—people trying to prove that they were more important than the next person. I could not face feeling diminished yet again after a meeting or a rehearsal. The woman's speech that day was the final straw.

That afternoon I wrote a letter offering my resignation. I was as gracious as I possibly could be, thanking everyone for a wonderful experience and simply stating that it was time for me to open a space for someone new to join. For many years, Shirley Turteltaub kept asking me what the real reason was for my leaving. I never told her.

67

Jennifer Jones

I want to share another very special friendship I made in my early years in LA.

I had met Jennifer Jones Selznick once long before I married Alan Livingston. It was one August evening during the chaotic summer of 1957 when Alan Lerner told me he was going to leave me. At a small gathering at Veronique and Gregory Peck's Brentwood home, Jennifer had sat quietly next to her husband, David Selznick, and even in the midst of my turmoil she impressed me with her poise and exquisite deep-red silk dress.

But it wasn't until ten years later that I saw Jennifer again. It was after the death of her husband and her later suicide attempt in 1967. She didn't inherit a great deal of money from the Selznick estate, and it was clear that she was struggling and in an extremely fragile state. She was leasing a small cottage on La Costa Beach in Malibu and was bravely attempting to put the pieces of her life back together.

Trying to explain Jennifer is a challenge. Every morning of her life until the day she died, her makeup artist and hairdresser arrived at her home to make her "movie star perfect." She understood her psychological illness and saw her psychiatrist every afternoon, five days a week. I never saw her when she was not impeccably dressed, and even her humble surroundings at the beach house were always in the most exquisite taste.

More than anything, her ability to be a sincere friend amazed me. Her own psychological suffering was apparent, but she was able to control it and reach out to connect with others.

It was apparent to me that what Jennifer needed more than anything was a strong and powerful partner. It was not surprising that she had left her first husband, Robert Walker—who had a history of deep psychological issues compounded by his drinking—for industry titan David O. Selznick. In the early 1970s, I was happy to be instrumental in introducing her to multimillionaire art patron Norton Simon, who fell madly in love with her, married her, and gave her the protection she craved.

Soon after they married, they bought a large house on Carbon Beach in Malibu and filled it with treasures from his magnificent art collection. Jennifer was a wonderful hostess, and everyone in Los Angeles was always thrilled to be invited to one of Norton and Jennifer's incredible parties.

Norton was an interesting man who had created a museum with art ranging from the old masters to contemporary twentieth-century artworks. The Norton Simon Museum in Pasadena is considered one of the great museums in the world, which is astounding when one realizes that every single piece in it was chosen by one person. When Norton and Jennifer came to Alan's and my house, Norton would stare at a few of the paintings in our modest collection for at least ten minutes each. I once asked him, "Norton, how do you distinguish a very good painting from a great work of art?" His answer was, "You look at it, and you look and you look and you look . . . ," repeating "and you look" at least twenty-five times.

Both Norton and Jennifer took great delight in creating a board of directors for the museum, and of course they wanted celebrities. Tom Brokaw, who lived in Los Angeles at the time, joined the board and remains a member to this day. Jennifer told me that they needed a prominent person from Pasadena to join and asked if I had any suggestions. Several weeks later I put together a small dinner party, inviting John Van de Kamp and his wife, Andrea. The Van de Kamps were one of the founding families of Pasadena, and John had been district attorney for Los Angeles and attorney general for the state of California. A week after my dinner party, John was a Norton Simon Museum board member and remained a member until the day he died.

As perfect as Norton and Jennifer's marriage was, it had a major problem, for Jennifer in particular. She had a daughter, Mary Jennifer Selznick, who not only had been royally spoiled but also struggled with mental-health issues and drug addiction. Because Norton had a son with the same issues who ultimately committed suicide, he felt that he knew best how to deal with this challenging situation. He insisted that Jennifer stop coddling her daughter and set limits on her behavior. Mary Jennifer was not allowed to live with them, and she was given an adequate but small amount of money for her living expenses. In other words, she was not to be indulged any longer.

On Tuesday, May 11, 1976, two days after Mother's Day, Mary Jennifer, this sad and tortured twenty-one-year-old girl, jumped out the window of the top floor of the highest building in Westwood. Danny Selznick, her half-brother, told me that he was asked to pick up her personal items at the coroner's office. There were shoes, a few broken pieces of jewelry, and a small handbag. Inside the bag were a few dollar bills and a card that read, "Happy Mother's Day."

Shortly after this tragic event, I remember receiving a call from Jennifer asking me to join her for lunch at a restaurant at the end of Sunset Boulevard with a view of the Pacific Ocean. She didn't want to pour her heart out to me; she just wanted the comfort of being with a friend who could help her maintain control.

A number of years later, we took a long walk on the beach in front of her home at twilight. Images of the horizon were changing with the setting sun; she tried to explain to me how these images frightened her and how difficult it was for her to stay in the present. She said, "There is always a danger that I will go into a different space and not be able to come back."

In 1993, Norton died, and Jennifer sold the house at the beach. She remained the head of the museum and took this role seriously and professionally. She moved into a small house in Brentwood, where all of her friends continued to gather at her elegant parties, still surrounded by breathtaking art from the museum. Several years later, it became clear that Jennifer was experiencing signs of early dementia. Soon she was no longer able to live alone, and her son, Robert Walker Jr., took her to his home in the Malibu colony. By this time, she did not recognize any of us.

I cannot finish my story of Jennifer Jones-Selznick-Simon without remembering how gloriously generous a friend she was. The morning after every party that Jennifer attended at my home, I received fifty roses in every color in a large crystal bowl.

68

The Band

Around the time when I was first getting to know Jennifer in the early 1960s, my new husband's career was picking up even more steam. The success of the Beatles could easily have been a flash in the pan with changing trends, but it turned out the Beatles were not only prolific songwriters but also progressive artists, constantly evolving not just in their music but in their look as well. They literally came to define that era of music. Alan had many big follow-up signings, but he was always feeling pressured to find new talent in a very competitive environment.

One evening during our cocktail hour, he said he was flying to San Francisco the next afternoon to hear and meet a group that had been the backup musicians for Bob Dylan. They wanted to have their own identity and were interested in signing a record deal. The head of Capitol Records' talent department thought they were quite good but was hesitant to sign them. Alan had a feeling that they might be unique; he liked their work with Dylan but needed to hear them in person. He planned to spend the night and return the next morning.

That night I received a phone call from Alan around midnight. The group was terrific, and he had agreed to sign them. There was only one issue: what name to give them. They were adamant that they didn't want anything outlandish or gimmicky. They explained they were just members of a band. Of course, my brilliant husband said, "I think we should simply call you 'the Band.'" They were thrilled, but I said, "You're kidding, Alan! You're just going to call them 'the Band'?" He was quiet for a moment and then said, "Nancy, I love you, and I'm going to say goodnight. See you in the morning."

After my unfortunate reaction to "I Want to Hold Your Hand," I should have known better to keep my mouth shut on all things related to pop music.

69

A Miracle

The beauty and majesty of the Pacific Ocean have always been a great source of pleasure for me living in Los Angeles. While Alan's career was moving upward, we decided one summer to lease a house on the beach in Malibu from August 1 through Labor Day. It began a tradition of spending every August on the ocean that lasted for many years. Each year we were in a different house, principally in the Malibu Colony or sometimes on Carbon Beach. In 1967, we rented a small, cozy cottage in the Colony and took all the children, including our three-year-old Christopher. I remember taking long walks on the beach alone and pondering the mystery of being on this planet; I remember Alan joining us between five and six in the evening and the simple joy of being together; I remember going to sleep with the rhythm of the ocean lulling us into peaceful dreams.

On Sunday nights, we invited friends to join us for a family barbecue. On one particular night, we invited Gordon and Judy Davidson. Gordon was the artistic director for the Mark Taper Forum and the Ahmanson Theater at the Los Angeles Music Center. They arrived a little late, as dusk was descending, but Judy insisted on taking a short walk on the beach with me before dinner. We started walking north, and the fog began to surround us. It was not too long before we saw a single person coming toward us, a woman who looked vaguely familiar.

I asked Judy, "Who is that?"

She answered, "Nancy, don't you know who that is? . . . It's Micheline Lerner."

Everything stopped. I turned to Judy and said, "What day is this?"

She said, "It's Sunday, August 27th."

"What year is it, Judy?"

"It's 1967."

I gasped. "Judy! Turn around. Look at our house lit up with the sounds of children laughing. Alan, my fabulous husband, is waiting for me to return. Liza and Jenny feel protected and loved, and they have a new brother."

I'm sure Judy thought I had lost my mind, but I explained to her about the night that Alan Lerner told me he was going to marry Micheline. I had gone out on the balcony at the beach, and as the fog enveloped me, I asked the heavens, "Where will we all be ten years from tonight?" That was August 27, 1957.

"Judy," I said, "this is where we all are ten years later!!!"

70

The End of an Era

As blissful as this time of our life was, there was also a new development happening with Alan that caught us off guard and threatened our security and happiness. One night I was awakened by Alan's coughing so violently that I was afraid he would stop breathing. The next day he was diagnosed with pneumonia. Antibiotics cured him, until eight months later it happened again. But why? He was in excellent health and succeeding in everything he was doing at Capitol Records.

What I didn't fully see or appreciate was the physical and emotional toll his work was taking on him. Also, he had a new wife, two new stepchildren, a new son, and his own children, who were desperate to have their father in their lives. Alan was a sensitive, creative man with a powerful sense of responsibility. EMI chairman Sir Joseph Lockwood had said to him, "All you have to do is just create a group like the Beatles every other year or so." Alan knew how ridiculous this statement was, but that nevertheless seemed to be the expectation.

Alan also had the burden of financing our new life as well as taking care of Peter, who would have lifelong health expenses. It is hard to imagine, but at that time the salaries of people who were as successful as Alan were considerably modest, somewhere in the six figures. In the same position today, Alan's salary would be many millions of dollars a year.

Having graduated from the Wharton School of the University of Pennsylvania, Alan understood the importance of accumulating wealth during his prime. He maneuvered EMI to take a portion of its ownership of Capitol and put it on the New York Stock Exchange, and then he cleverly found a way to participate by owning a certain number of shares that could be cashed in only when he left Capitol.

In 1968, he found it more difficult to deal with EMI's unrealistic demands and decided he must resign. Actually, he was thrilled to be able to leave Capitol and finally have a more than adequate nest egg. I was frantic and felt the timing was too soon. He was just turning fifty, and the stock could only go up with everything he had done for Capitol. In addition to the Beatles, the Beach Boys, Frank Sinatra, the Band, and Nat Cole, Alan had also signed Bobby Darin, the Kingston Trio, Steve Miller, Glen Campbell, and, just before he left the company, Pink Floyd.

I knew that Alan faced an uncertain professional future, and even though he was so highly regarded, finding a new position in which he could use all of his gifts would be daunting. Years later, he acknowledged to me that he had left Capitol too soon, even though he never stopped creating amazing successes.

71

Mediarts and Don McLean

Alan was offered the presidency of RCA Records soon after leaving Capitol in 1968, but that would have meant leaving Los Angeles and uprooting our entire family to New York City, something he was not about to do, so he turned down the offer.

His first project after leaving Capitol was to form a new company called Mediarts, a combined film and record company. He took on two partners, very successful agents from England, Richard Gregson and Gareth Wigan.

Richard had recently married Natalie Wood, and Alan gave him an office at their new company headquarters in Los Angeles. Gareth worked in London. Each partner put in a nominal amount of money, and Alan dealt with Wall Street to fully finance the company. They completed a private placement in advance of going public.

Richard Gregson proceeded to produce *Down Hill Racer* with Robert Redford for Paramount under the Mediarts banner, and Gareth produced *Unman, Wittering, and Zigo* in London, also with a Paramount release. For the record business, Alan first signed and produced a series of Dory Previn records that developed a strong following and had profitable sales. Dory had just been through a messy divorce with her husband, conductor Andre Previn, which was followed by Andre's public affair and marriage to Mia Farrow.

Dory was a brilliant and fascinating woman, which her lyrics certainly reflected. I got to know her a little bit, and she shared with me that she had struggled with schizophrenia since she was a little girl. Her song "With My Daddy in the Attic" tells of a true experience with her mentally unstable father. She told me that she had always struggled to stay within the boundaries of reality, and when she heard about Andre and Mia, she had gotten on an airplane to confront him in New York and then removed all her clothes as the plane took off. The plane turned around, and when it landed, someone came to escort her off the flight.

The second artist Alan signed was Don McLean, who had been turned down by virtually every record label in existence—by his count, thirty-four in all. Don had sent Alan a cold demo record, and Alan was so impressed he asked Don to come to Los Angeles from New York. Don had no money, so Alan sent him a plane ticket and put him up at a local motel. It's hard to imagine any other prominent entertainment executive doing this for an artist who had been so thoroughly rejected.

McLean arrived at Alan's office with his guitar hung over his shoulder, wearing blue jeans, and in bare feet! He sat down and played song after song. Alan put him under contract immediately and released his first album, *Tapestry*, which contained the wonderful song "And I Love You So," which sold quite well. As a matter of fact, "And I Love You So" later became a top-ten single hit with Perry Como, which Mediarts recorded and had the publishing rights to.

The next McLean album Mediarts produced became number one in the country. I remember Alan bringing it home to play for me and saying, "Nancy, this song will define the second half of the twentieth century and will be played forever." It was "American Pie."

72

EST

In the 1970s, as Alan continued his success in the record industry, I was going through some changes, too. My friends Felisa Vanoff and Fay Harbach told me they had signed up to take a two-weekend class in something called EST (pronounced "est"). I had no idea what EST was about, but Laurie Livingston, who had been so difficult to deal with for so many years, had taken this course in San Francisco and had become a different person. She even changed her name from "Laurie" to "Laura," a recognition that she had finally grown up. It was like a miracle had taken place inside of her—so I was intrigued.

I decided to commit to two consecutive weekends and found myself with Fay and Felisa entering a hall somewhere in Santa Monica with fold-up chairs, a stage, and a large group of young men directing us to our seats with a strange and very deliberate attitude of authority. I felt as if we were back in elementary school and expected to behave according to their instructions. Fay was immediately uncomfortable and said she had to go to the bathroom and would be right back. She was not the only one. There were people lining up behind her, also trying to escape. Every single one of them was challenged: "You just arrived. Are you sure you really need the restroom?" And it didn't stop there. Half of those people ultimately came back to their seats, and I was relieved that the other half were allowed to leave the hall. It was obvious to me that the people who returned to their seats were facing the fact that they really didn't have to go but couldn't deal with feeling as though they were being treated like children or prisoners.

That was just the beginning. I wasn't surprised that at the lunch break Fay Harbach left the group and never returned. Felisa and I stuck it out for both weekends, and we were never quite the same again!

I am writing about an experience that happened many years ago, and I want to convey as precisely as possible why I am so grateful that I took this course. It was as if I were beginning a new chapter of discovery that followed exactly where I had left off with Diana Kemeny.

I remember that by the second day of the EST training, I found myself following the leaders' instructions with ease. I was able to close my eyes and be led to images of my mother and father. My mother emerged in her red-velvet evening gown; I was standing next to her watching her comb her dark hair and thinking how beautiful she looked. She always communicated to me how serious and intellectual she was, but what I suddenly realized in this vision is that she was actually a "party girl." She wanted to have fun and for some reason would not allow herself to acknowledge that. I finally had some understanding of why she so deeply resented all the fun I had.

I saw my father and started to examine his beautiful hands. In my mind, I looked up from his body to his face and saw the pores on his cheeks. I started to weep. I forgave both of them for the unnecessary pain that human beings inflict on each other—even their children, even me—and felt only a compelling love and appreciation for them.

The second weekend was conducted by the founder of EST, Werner Erhard himself (EST stands for "Erhard Seminars Training"). I was impressed with his use of language and articulation. He was going in a certain direction and encouraged all of us to stick with him and stay on his path. On the last day, he wheeled out a large rectangular blackboard and with a piece of chalk drew a line from left to right, dividing the blackboard into top and bottom halves. He explained that all of us exist in the bottom half, which he referred to as the "Zone of Survival."

What was the essence of survival? Being right about everything, never acknowledging that one might be wrong about even little things. In fact, Erhard said some people will commit suicide to prove that they are right. Their goodbye note might say, "I told you I was desperate, and you didn't believe me. Now you will know that I was right and you were wrong."

He then talked about saints and about great teachers like Jesus, Moses, and Buddha. He said that even they barely touched the middle line on the blackboard, but if a tiny part of a person surmounts the middle line, that person will start their journey to sainthood. If any human being actually reaches the top of the blackboard, that person no longer needs to come back to this world. I think both Felisa and I understood that there was an opening for us possibly to leave the Zone of Survival and start making our way on the long journey up to the middle line.

Years later, facing some particularly daunting challenges, I remembered one of the more powerful aspects of what I learned in EST: that we create everything—our triumphs and successes as well as our failures and defeats. We can even accomplish something as mundane as finding a parking space by simply visualizing a spot opening at exactly the moment we need it. This way of looking at things helped me understand how powerful one's leadership can be.

I remember also writing speeches and carefully crossing out the words *I* and *me* and changing them to *you*: "Have *you* ever felt this?" or "Have *you* ever questioned this?" In other words, what I was communicating was never about me—it was about the people I was addressing. There is nothing more powerful than making everything about "them"! Even Hitler never used the word *I*, always *we!* What a tragedy that he used this power to cause such horror and destruction in the world.

It is true that people became addicted to EST and took all the available courses for graduates. They were called "est-holes." I confess—I was one of them. In fact, I insisted that my son, Chris, who was then about eleven, take the children's weekend course. He held it against me for years; whenever he had an argument with me, he would remind me that I made him take this "horrible course."

It was years later, when he was in his early thirties, that he finally said to me, "Mom, probably the best thing you ever did for me was insist that I take EST."

I had another experience with a graduate EST weekend that demonstrates how powerful the EST experience was. Werner Erhard conducted the seminar and asked us to try and identify something in the deepest place inside of us that we kept concealed. The original experience could have been so damaging that it was now buried in our memory but still affected our daily life and behavior.

The morning after this speech I thought about a compulsive behavior I had that was filled with fear and anxiety, but I couldn't remember where it came from. Every day, after my bath, I dried myself carefully, avoiding touching my breasts. I was afraid I would find that something terrible was happening inside them, and I didn't want to know what it was.

As I washed myself in the tub that morning, I closed my eyes and thought about this and took my hands and put them over my breasts. I asked out loud, "What am I afraid of?" Suddenly, a memory came back to me that made me sit up and shriek.

I remembered when I was in sixth grade and all the other little girls were developing small breasts. I sadly remained almost flat-chested. One day I went into my father's bedroom, opened his handkerchief drawer, and took out two of the largest I could find. I went back to my room, crumpled them up, and stuffed them underneath my undershirt. I then put on my dress and went to school. This became a daily routine that I of course kept totally hidden.

One night I was getting undressed, and our housekeeper walked in the room as I pulled my dress over my head. She shouted, "What is that?!," as she looked at my underwear filled with handkerchiefs. I ran into my closet and closed the door, put on my nightgown, and went to bed. I knew she would share this discovery with my mother, and I also knew that nothing would enrage my mother more.

The next morning I had a dilemma. Would I go to school without the handkerchiefs? How could I? Everyone would notice. So I put them under my undershirt and went to school. At that time, I came home for lunch every day, and that day I walked through the back door, through the kitchen, into the hallway, and heard my mother's voice at the top of the stairs, "Nancy! Come up here immediately!" I knew she had been told.

I slowly walked up the stairs, where she met me and demanded that I go into her room and take off my dress. Of course, there were the handkerchiefs. She looked at me and said, "Now we know all about you!," and walked out of the room.

This memory not only opened my eyes to a great sadness I carried around inside me from when I was a little girl who just wanted to grow up like the rest of the little girls but also helped me understand my mother's issues with me in a way I had not fully allowed myself to acknowledge. Her greatest fear was that I would someday be her competition.

The miracle of EST took away my fear of undressing, putting on my nightgown, putting on my brassiere, washing myself, including my breasts, and allowing my husband to touch me—and I forgive my mother.

73

On Board at the Music Center

My journey into the LA performing-arts scene started long before the 1970s. In December 1964, a few weeks after Christopher was born, Alan came home and said we were going to attend the opening of the new Los Angeles Music Center. He explained that he was on the board of the new center and that Capitol Records was a founding donor, so we were expected to attend. It was a black-tie event with the Los Angeles Philharmonic performing and an evening that would change my life.

I remember walking across the spacious plaza and entering the Dorothy Chandler Pavilion lobby, which was glittering with brightly lit crystal chandeliers and filled with some of the most prominent people in Los Angeles, or certainly that's how they viewed themselves. That might be unfair—many of these people had actually helped create the Music Center, which was one of the most important cultural institutions in the city.

Alan and I walked up the stairs and entered the Founders' Circle, which was a low balcony facing the stage in a beautiful pale-wood-paneled hall. We were seated in the third-row center, and I remember asking Alan, "Who is that woman against the wall in the first row that everyone seems so excited to be talking to?"

Alan explained that she was Mrs. Norman Chandler—Dorothy, but her nickname was "Buff." The Chandler family owned and published the *Los Angeles Times* and were among the earliest prominent members of Los Angeles society. Buff had two children, a daughter, Mia, and the light of her life, a son, Otis, who had recently taken over the *Times* as its publisher.

It was Buff alone who was inspired to create the Los Angeles Performing Arts Center, better known as the Music Center. Alan said she was a fascinating woman whose reputation coupled with her unabashed tenacity made it very difficult to ever turn down one of her requests. In fact, her letters were famous for demanding contributions to the institution, and if she felt a dona-tion wasn't adequate, she would send back the check and insist that the amount be increased. That's power!

Mrs. Chandler also understood how divided the society arts community of Los Angeles was. There was the Pasadena group, the Hancock Park group where she lived, and the West Side. The West Side was dominated by enter-tainment-industry families and was predominantly Jewish. The Pasadena and Hancock Park groups intermingled comfortably, but you rarely saw any of them on the West Side.

This was entirely different from my experience in New York City, which was much more sophisticated and inclusive. Mrs. Chandler understood that she must engage with both the corporate and creative powers of the enter-tainment world, and from that world she chose Lew Wasserman, Gregory Peck, Bob Hope, Kirk Douglas, and Alan Livingston. She was a genius.

The Los Angeles Philharmonic began to assemble on the stage, and its new conductor, Zubin Mehta, marched out, stepped on the conductor's plat-form, and started to conduct "The Star-Spangled Banner." It was a magnifi-cent moment for everyone. When it was finished, the audience clapped and cheered, and Zubin turned to us and said, "Yes, we think the acoustics are wonderful, too!" Alan said that Jascha Heifetz would be playing the Beethoven concerto and added, "Nancy, he is the greatest violinist of this century. You are going to hear something rare and special."

It is hard for me to explain just how special this evening was. I realized immediately that the Music Center would be a very precious part of my new life. Alan and I became immediate subscribers to the symphony and attended the theatrical performances at the Ahmanson Theater as often as possible. I felt that I had come home.

In 1976, five years after releasing the album *American Pie,* Alan had left the record industry and had started an investment-capital group managing not just his own money but other people's as well. Even with the success of *Amer-ican Pie,* Alan had been worried about paying his debts and paying back his investors, so he had sold Mediarts to United Artists Records. He knew it was too soon to do so but admitted to me, "I have always been too conservative with other people's money."

Alan also decided it was time to leave the Music Center board to focus on his next endeavor. He explained to Buff Chandler that he no longer had the time and said, "I'll give you Nancy."

I had no experience working in fund-raising and was a little intimidated by the prospect of working with Buff, but Alan was right; this would be a good project for me. Soon after, I received an invitation to join the Blue Ribbon 400 of the Los Angeles Music Center.

Mrs. Chandler had created the Blue Ribbon to completely fund the two resident companies that currently resided at the center: the symphony and the Ahmanson Theatre group. She needed $400,000 a year, so her goal was to have each of four hundred women pledge $1,000 a year to in order to accomplish her objective. She gathered a circle of ladies from some of the most prominent families in Los Angeles. Mrs. Walter Annenberg, Mrs. Peter Bing, Mrs. Kirk Douglas, Mrs. Hal Wallis, and Mrs. Gregory Peck are just a sample of the women she chose to help her create this organization.

Mrs. Chandler started by inviting everyone to be board members and divided the group into honorary presidents, presidents, and vice presidents. After the number of women became greater than sixty, she stopped automatically making each new entrant a board member.

She also designed a process of how one became a Blue Ribbon member. Membership was by invitation only. The invitee was nominated by two existing members and voted on by the board. That person was sent a letter stating that she was now on the waiting list to become a member. Several months later, the nominee would receive an invitation to join, handwritten by Mrs. Chandler, which always made that person feel extremely special and fortunate to be included. In my forty years of being a member, I have never experienced any nominee who did not ultimately accept an invitation to become a member of Blue Ribbon. It was a slow dance, brilliantly choreographed.

Although Mrs. Chandler put herself on the list of honorary presidents, it was clear that she was the chairman of the group. The working leader of the group was the executive president, Helen Wolford, whom Mrs. Chandler appointed, of course. Helen remained in this position for ten years, until her husband retired, and they moved to Hawaii.

Nothing fascinated me more than a Blue Ribbon board meeting. It began with Helen Wolford welcoming everyone, which was followed by a ten-minute speech glorifying Mrs. Dorothy Chandler's many special qualities. Mrs. Chandler accepted these speeches with a slight smile. Several announcements would follow about the events planned for the coming months—the

Children's Festival, for instance, or tea parties for Mrs. Nixon and Mrs. Ford, an interview with Paul Newman and his wife, Joanne Woodward, were typical. Each meeting ended with a discussion of the new nominees for membership and a vote.

I sat for three years with all the other vice presidents (this position held a three-year term), and I assumed that I would then leave the board. But, to my surprise, I received a letter inviting me for an additional three-year term as a president. I had no idea how these decisions were made, but I noticed that some of my fellow vice presidents disappeared from the board. The process was mysterious to me, but I accepted my new term and was ready to listen to three more years of Helen Wolford telling us how wonderful Mrs. Chandler was.

But something more was in store for me, something I didn't see coming.

74

A New Challenge

It was around this time that a new family challenge presented itself. Alan's son Peter, who certainly faced enough problems as a hemophiliac, was beginning to show symptoms of bipolar disorder. To suffer growing depression is bad enough, but to begin a manic phase of this terrible disease is possibly the most challenging tragedy that any family can endure.

Peter would slowly but relentlessly start to feel optimistic, which would escalate to levels of unrealistic elation. There were credit-card buying sprees that he could not possibly afford, plane trips to Hawaii and back, rambling phone conversations, and demands for money. Ultimately, he wound up being put in prison in Miami. Alan flew there to meet with the judge and arranged for Peter's release, committing him to a local mental hospital.

Peter stayed in the facility for about two weeks and then very cleverly found a way to escape and continue his manic behavior. There were phone calls in the middle of the night; some of them began to be threatening, which really scared me.

During this trying time, Alan accepted a major position at 20th Century-Fox. He was made executive vice president of the company as well as group president of several different divisions, including the record company, Deluxe Labs, and eventually the television department.

Obviously, Alan was well suited for the record division and put his efforts into recording albums with Barry White and Stephanie Mills and even put out an album of other artists singing Beatles songs, including Elton John performing "Lucy in the Sky with Diamonds." When *Star Wars* was produced and became a cultural phenomenon, Alan immediately signed the actor Roscoe Lee Browne to narrate a two-disk rendition of *The Story of Star Wars*. It was brilliantly produced, with John Williams's score interspersed throughout the narrative, and the double album went gold.

Deluxe Labs was another interesting story during Alan's tenure with Fox. At the time Alan was given the responsibility of overseeing Deluxe, it was a very minor competitor to Technicolor. Alan immediately deduced that the company's management was to blame and realized if Deluxe were to succeed, he needed to make some changes. Rather than relieve the top brass and simply move people up within the company, he felt that new management from an entirely different source was in order. He did his homework and cleverly went to every small lab in the country until he found a truly gifted president of a lab in New Jersey, a man by the name of Bud Stone. Alan hired Bud without the Fox board's enthusiasm (the last thing the board members wanted was for Alan to be a success and show them up in any capacity!), but Alan did it anyway. He convinced Bud to bring his family to southern California and take over Deluxe. It didn't take more than a year for Deluxe to turn a corner, and within two years it became the number-one technical lab in the world. I wanted to send my condolences to all the other executives.

Alan Ladd Jr. was particularly watchful of Alan and his growing presence at Fox. He insisted that Alan have nothing to do with the Fox movie division and was extremely concerned when Alan took over television at Fox. I honestly don't think that Alan enjoyed this environment, but, true to his nature, he worked as hard and as creatively as he knew how.

Alan had a beautiful office right next to the president of Fox, Dennis Stanfill, and as the years went by, I was again reminded of how difficult it is for a person to deal with complex relationships, jealousies, threats to other people's weaknesses or ambitions—the fears that lie just below the surface of survival.

I realize today that Alan was a far more evolved human being and man than most, and sometimes it made him more vulnerable to other people's insecurities. He was at Fox to create new ideas and projects and of course succeed, but, more than anything, creating for him was part of his enjoyment of living. It is so sad to me that most people will try to stop someone like Alan from truly succeeding.

Assimilating to again being an executive's wife was difficult for me. I did everything to support my husband and tried to enjoy his new role. As I look back, though, I realize that even the dinner parties I gave were strangely resented and became a challenge to people's egos. Just walking into the beautiful environment that Alan and I had created, filled with art and treasures as well as warmth and welcoming, seemed to challenge the other executives and their wives. I have one memory that I find extraordinary.

Alan and I were invited to a large black-tie party that Dennis and Terry Stanfill were giving on a stage at the lot. It was to be covered by much press—in particular *Women's Wear Daily*, which happened to be an extremely important paper at that time. It documented who was important and who was well dressed and emphasized in particular the jewelry the ladies were wearing.

I had in my closet a strapless, long, white organza dress with appliquéd pastel flowers cascading down the front. I wore it with a pearl necklace, pearl-and-diamond earrings, and a white, ruffled, organza shawl around my shoulders. I had not worn this dress in ten years but chose it for this occasion because it was so special and quite spectacular.

When I went into Chris's room to say goodnight before we left, even Chris, who was about twelve, got up from his desk and said, "Mom, wow! You look beautiful."

When I arrived with Alan at the canopy that led us into the stage, all the photographers rushed toward me, in particular the ones from *Women's Wear Daily*. They made me stand for at least ten minutes while they took endless photographs. When I entered the party, the reaction was quite similar to Chris's.

I'm sure you're wondering why I am telling you this story. Am I being egocentric and self-centered? Perhaps! But that is not the reason.

The next day I received a phone call from *Women's Wear Daily*, saying, "We have the most beautiful, full-length picture of you in that spectacular dress and are planning to put it on the front page of our next issue." I thanked them and waited anxiously for the mail to deliver the magazine.

When it came, I was not on the front page. In fact, I was nowhere on any page or even mentioned. I wondered what happened. Weeks later, the original caller from *Women's Wear Daily* got in touch with me and explained that Mrs. Stanfill had killed the picture. She had told them that I was not the reason for the party, that I was only one of the guests and should not be highlighted.

It makes me so sad that this kind of reaction has haunted me most of my life. Strangely enough, even today. Perhaps when I'm one hundred, it will end! I hope so.

75

Grace Kelly and the
Heimlich Maneuver

One of the most interesting and rewarding aspects of Alan's term at Fox was attending the board meeting events with Princess Grace Kelly of Monaco, who was a board member.

Grace had started her career at Paramount and was not only one of the most beautiful women in the world but also a truly dedicated and gifted actress. She won an Academy Award in 1955 for her performance with Bing Crosby in *The Country Girl*. She had an elegance and poise that were in part a result of her upper-middle-class family background in Philadelphia. We shared that similarity; however, she chose a different path. She wanted to be and became a really important actress. In 1955, I had already been married five years to Alan Jay Lerner, had given up my career, had two little girls, and was listening to the creation of *My Fair Lady*.

I remember being surprised and somewhat saddened when I saw Grace in the late 1970s. Clearly, she had let herself go. She was a little overweight, had given up her contact lenses for a rather thick pair of glasses, and even with the influence of the French fashion world next-door to her in Monaco, she somehow never put herself together with the taste and instinct of a beautiful woman—I never understood why she married Prince Rainier. At the time she married him, she was already a "princess."

I think the highlight of Alan's tenure at Fox was when everyone on the board was invited to the palace in Monaco for its year-end meeting. Fox had just released the very distinguished movie *The Turning Point* with Anne Bancroft and Shirley MacLaine, and Grace thought it should premiere in Monaco. What a good idea!

There were luncheons, a black-tie dinner in the palace, and then the black-tie premiere and dinner the following night. Planning my wardrobe for this trip took time and all my ingenuity; I have never been as studious and thoughtful about what I was going to wear. Two black-tie outfits—two luncheons to dress up for—I needed comfortable shoes for museum viewings: it was all an overwhelming challenge.

However, the real drama occurred when we arrived in Paris, and my luggage got lost! I remember flying from New York to Paris, which was not as challenging as flying all the way to Paris from Los Angeles, so I was able to put myself together with a little more style, thank God! I remember arriving in a two-piece, pale-blue, wool skirt and top, with a fluffy, deeper-blue wool coat that I purchased from Neiman Marcus for just this trip. I had to wear this outfit for a day and a half. Thank God my luggage finally arrived in time for me to put on my evening gown for the palace dinner.

I arrived wearing a sleeveless, long, silk sheath in a soft topaz beige, topaz-and-diamond earrings, and a beautiful full flower in shades of coral and pink on one of my shoulders; everything blended with the color of my hair. I was prepared for my entrance, but I was not prepared for the drama of this evening.

Grace and Rainier were gracious hosts and conducted a very warm and informal cocktail hour before dinner. I remember Grace wore her glasses, but her hair had been done perfectly.

Sometime during the predinner gathering I found myself standing in a circle with some of the Fox lawyers and their wives, and the conversation somehow turned to people having dinner and someone choking. David Handleman, who was second in command of the legal department at Fox, started to tell us a story about how his best friend was having dinner with his wife and two children when he began to choke. He frantically kept pulling at the top of his chest, and they thought he was having a heart attack. They called 911, but, of course, by the time the paramedics arrived, he was unconscious and could not be revived. David said he was so heartbroken by this unfortunate tragedy that he took special Red Cross lessons to learn the Heimlich maneuver and on the blackboard in his kitchen put explicit instructions of what to do in case someone in the family choked when he wasn't there. I left the group when someone tapped me on the shoulder and said that Herb Ross, the director of *The Turning Point* and an old friend, wanted to say hello to me.

When we entered the dining room, there were numbered tables with our names on them. Alan was seated across the room from me. I was seated with Arthur Laurents, the writer of *The Turning Point*, and, coincidentally, David Handleman was seated across from me at the same table.

Arthur was a small man, talented, gay, and somewhat arrogant, with an obvious ambivalent attitude toward women, or so it seemed to me. I tried to be as friendly and solicitous as I could, but after a while I turned to the gentleman on my left.

I cannot remember what we talked about, but the conversation was quite animated and suddenly interrupted by Arthur poking the top of my right arm with urgency. I turned to him and saw him leaning forward and pulling at the top of his lapels and bowtie. His mouth was open, and he was turning red. Startled, I said, "Arthur, are you in trouble?" He nodded desperately. It suddenly dawned on me what was happening. I said, "Arthur, are you choking?" He nodded even more vehemently. I panicked and stood up in the middle of the palace dining room and shouted to David across the table from me, "David, now!!"

David looked at me oddly, as if to ask, "What is the crazy woman doing, shouting my name in the middle of the most glamorous evening of my life?" I became even more animated and almost screamed, "He's choking!!!"

Suddenly, David got what I was saying and with great dignity pushed his chair back, walked around the table, picked up little Arthur, turned him away from the table to face me, and pulled his diaphragm back to his spine. Of course, the salmon, which was mixed with a heavy cream sauce, came spewing out of Arthur's mouth, down the front of my dress; tiny pieces thrust into my flower, spilled onto my chair, and covered the floor in front of me. Arthur's own chair remained immaculate. His clean napkin was waiting. He simply turned to David and said thank you, sat down, and started talking to the woman next to him.

He never said thank you or apologized or even looked at me, but that was not my concern at the moment. Thankfully, three waiters and a waitress came to my aid, took me to the side of the room, cleaned the front of my dress, took my flower away for it to be cleaned, mopped the floor, gave me a new chair and napkin, and helped me take my seat.

I was shaking and turned my head slightly to the left. I saw Herb Ross looking at me and whispering, "Is everything alright?" I shook my head. Herb didn't have the bravery to get up and come to me. He was too intimidated by his royal surroundings.

After dinner, Alan came, put his arms around me, and said he was reassured when he saw me resume my seat. The most comforting moment for me was when the waiters brought back my clean flower. Grace did come over after dinner and asked if I was alright. She said no one had ever choked in this dining room before and thanked me for knowing what to do. The only person who never thanked me was Arthur Laurents.

I cannot finish this story without sharing the sadness I felt for the choice Grace Kelly made the day she decided to marry Prince Rainier. My friend Judy Balaban, who was close to her, told me that Grace was truly very much in love with Rainier.

But I don't believe she had any idea what it would be like to live in the isolation and loneliness of this small piece of geography called Monaco, surrounded by borders that weren't easy to cross, especially when you were the princess. Also, this culture completely accepted and condoned the multiple affairs the prince was rumored to be having, which took place even in the palace.

The news that Grace had had a stroke while driving her daughter on the mountain road near the palace and had rolled her car down the ravine, killing her but sparing her daughter (thank God), made me saddest of all—but the incident didn't surprise me. I don't know what more she had to live for in this prison environment.

76

Natalie Wood

Natalie Wood was another person I had the good fortune of meeting during my time married to Alan Livingston. We became friends when she was married to Richard Gregson, who was working with Alan at Mediarts. I liked Natalie very much and stayed close with her long after their divorce, and we remained friends through her remarriage to Robert Wagner, better known to us as RJ (Natalie had been married to Robert Wagner prior to her marriage to Richard Gregson but then went back to Robert after her marriage to Richard ended). About a month before she died, we were invited to a large party at RJ and Natalie's house.

I will never forget waking on the morning of November 29, 1981, turning on the news, and hearing of her body being found in the bay of Catalina Island. Natalie was only forty-three years old, a talented, decent woman whose life had been distorted and destroyed by a career that started at much too early an age. I was recently asked to write my description of Natalie for a friend who was writing a book about her life. This is what I wrote:

I always felt that there was a missing part to her—a gap. She didn't see the big picture. I attributed that to the fact that she was a child actress; therefore, there was a development factor that was missing. Richard Gregson was one of Alan's partners at Mediarts, and he was impossible. He was a Hollywood type playing the game, but he was not the real deal. I never understood why she married him. Natalie was not stupid—she got it eventually. She had a narrow point of view—was locked into a narrow space—she had been pinched into that small space by being a star her whole life. Her view didn't show the full landscape, which is one of the tragedies of being a movie star, especially beginning as a child star.

When I knew her during the sixties and early seventies, I always felt she was very cordial, but not intimate. She was warm, and she invited us to her home and made herself very accessible to us—there was a very genuine quality to her—but we could never have been close friends. I admired her going back to R.J., and I admire him taking her back. The hardest thing to do is say, "I was wrong."

As an actress she was very gifted. If you see her in West Side Story, *she was wonderful, very believable. She understood how to perform in a musical, even without singing or having had any stage experience. Not just anyone would be able to pull that off.*

I remember when details emerged about Natalie's death. The whole episode shocked and saddened me. It was revealed that a lot of alcohol had been consumed, and I think there was a confrontation of some kind. Even though she was afraid of water and couldn't swim, she drank a lot and wanted to escape. I think what happened is that she tried to get into the small boat that was attached at the bottom of the ladder of their yacht. Apparently, the bottom step was slippery, and she fell into the water. Other yachts heard a voice screaming, "Help!," but they couldn't distinguish where it was coming from. I know that Christopher Walken was with Natalie and RJ, and there had been some kind of dispute—I don't know what it was, but to me it represents the deterioration of a marriage—of a life. Her death was tragic.

77

My Mother

The most compelling and sad circumstance that Alan had to deal with during his time with Fox was the acceleration of Peter's manic behavior. I don't know how he dealt with Peter calling the Fox switchboard and leaving bizarre messages for "Alan Livingston."

It was around this time that I encountered some difficult developments involving my own family.

I never forgot my mother's birthday. She was born on February 12— Abraham Lincoln's birthday—in the year 1900. On February 12, whatever year it was, that was how old my mother was. By the late seventies, she was having increasing health issues.

When my father died in 1963, only a year after Alan Livingston and I were married, my mother turned to me to be the anchor in her life. This responsibility was daunting, but nothing was more terrifying than when she had her first heart attack. She survived but needed to move into my house or a nursing home to recuperate. I was literally paralyzed and insisted she be put into a recuperating facility. The thought of my mother moving into my home was something I could not accept, but, of course, eventually I had to. My mother was spirited, independent, demanding, anxious, musically gifted, one of the best-read women of her time—and she was extremely difficult. Her saving grace when she moved in was being with her beloved grandson, Chris. They spent time together, and she introduced him to a section of literature he had not explored. This was a blessing.

Of course, during her stay my mother read every book in my library that she had not yet investigated. She also read the *Saturday Review of Literature* religiously and insisted that I get her a copy of *Sophie's Choice*. I will never forget that when she came to a passage in the book that refers to a biography written by a German psychologist who had examined the psychosis of Hitler, she said, "Nancy, I read that book a number of years ago, and I think you can get it at the Brentwood Library if you're interested."

My mother never bought a book; she read all the reviews, went to the Brentwood Library, and asked the librarians to please order whatever it was she wanted to read, which they did. Over the years, the library grew its collection by several hundred books, all ordered by Evelyn Olson.

Sometime after she had started to recover from her heart attack, we somehow got her back in her home. She gracefully moved into the guest house and gave the main house to my brother, David, and his family. She loved his children and was a great grandmother to them all. Shortly after New Year's Day in 1979, she had her second heart attack. She went into intensive care at UCLA and died a week later. I was at her side every day and planned a funeral for her at her beloved Unitarian Church in Santa Monica. David arranged, in her memory, to have her name engraved on a plaque at Brentwood Library (that plaque hangs there today). Her ashes were buried with my father's in a small cemetery in Santa Monica called Woodlawn. If you recall, David and I were born and grew up in a house on Woodlawn Court in Milwaukee, Wisconsin.

I didn't have time for tears until several weeks after her service. I walked past a tree filled with beautiful white blossoms. I remember stopping and starting to weep.

Evelyn Olson took such joy in the beauty of this amazing world. She was conscious of every flower in her garden and every miracle that life offers us, and she had great concern for others, especially the vulnerable. Whatever issues I had with her, she had done all she could to give me the best life she knew how to give and saw enough potential in me to send me to one of the best midwestern high schools in the country, which changed my life forever. It made my future success possible and gave me the confidence to step into a much wider world.

I thank her for being my mother.

78

A New Path for Alan Livingston

D espite the tragic loss of my mother, life, as it always does, kept moving on.

Peter, who had been spiraling out of control for several years, finally came crashing down, landing in a profound depression so deep and dark that he spent the next six months on his mother's couch.

Of course, Alan came to the rescue, as he always did, and arranged for Peter to have the medical and psychological help he needed. Peter slowly came back and started to embrace Buddhism, which was intellectually challenging and spiritually healing. He wanted to go to Boulder, Colorado, to attend Naropa University and the Tibetan temple there. Alan found him a job and a place to live in a special home for homeless young boys, where Peter helped to cook and keep house as well as care for the children.

Alan also found Peter a doctor who specialized in bipolar disorder, who immediately put him on lithium, which proved to be extremely helpful. Peter began to be himself—what a blessing for us all, especially Alan.

But in concurrence with decisively good news came some bad news. Things at 20th Century-Fox were changing. In 1981, the company was suddenly and unceremoniously sold to a group of entrepreneurial corporate vultures. The new power players wanted every head of every department fired except Dennis Stanfill, who was allowed to stay an extra nine or ten months.

It was extremely hard for Alan, a truly devoted and outstanding executive, to be asked to leave. Even as a longtime member of the entertainment industry and the former wife of a writer, I wasn't prepared for the ugliness of the corporate world. I don't know why I was so surprised. All I had to do was read the daily paper and see what everyone in the world was doing to each other.

I know that Alan worked hard to make a real contribution to 20th Century-Fox despite the vicious politics and the conflicts of power and ego that existed in such a large corporation. It seemed that no one there wanted Alan to become more powerful than they were, and it was a constant struggle for him to accomplish his goals while navigating his way through that maze of self-serving agendas. Dennis Stanfill had looked to Alan to transform the record company, but the record industry had changed. Alan's taste and judgment were on such a high level, but the industry was interested only in the lowest level. The one contribution Alan knew he could make was to reorganize the company and use everyone's gifts to their best advantage. In fact, the president of the Grammy's, Neil Portnow, who worked with Alan at Fox, never forgot how Alan's guidance and knowledge accelerated his own career.

Fortunately, the change at Fox happened in the late fall, and we already had made plans to go to Sun Valley, Idaho, our favorite Christmas holiday journey. When Alan brought his suitcase into the front hall, I noticed that he was also bringing his typewriter. It didn't take long after we arrived for him to set up a cozy, quiet space in our condominium, and twice a day, before skiing and after his bath, he sat at that instrument and typed as fast as any secretary I've ever heard.

I finally asked him, "Alan, what are you writing?" He answered, "I'm writing a novel for young adults. It's a story I know so well. It's about a gifted and wounded young person, the kind of artist I've had the pleasure to work with. It's about growing up in the Midwest and being misunderstood. It's about the triumph of talent when it's recognized. It's also about the isolation when that talent becomes so vulnerable. I hope it will reach, teach, and touch young people with dreams." I asked if he had a title. He answered, "*Ronnie Finkelhof, Superstar.*"

Believe it or not, this book was immediately picked up by Random House and then optioned by the Zanuck/Brown Company, which had produced *Jaws* and *The Sting*. The company paid $250,000 to own this property. Unfortunately, they never found a screenwriter to capture the book's magic, and so the film was never made. I defy any young boy or girl of twelve to eighty-five not to be captured by the compelling truth and power of this book.

The day before we left Sun Valley, a registered letter arrived from the office of Dennis Stanfill at 20th Century-Fox. It contained a short letter from Dennis thanking Alan for his contribution to the company and a cashier's check for $100,000—a lot of money at that time.

79

An Escape

A lan had also become quite skilled in investing over the years. He had always done his homework and chose the best investment firms for our money. He also helped these firms by bringing in many of his colleagues and friends. He decided to focus on investing full-time at this point in his life, and it soon became clear to him that he would be spending much more time in New York, so he came to me with the suggestion that we buy an apartment in the city.

My mother had died, Liza was living in New York, Jenny had graduated from Berkeley and was offered a job in New York, Christopher wanted to go to college somewhere in the East, and I still had many friends living there. New York seemed like a wonderful place for a second home, and the thought of picking up my life in Manhattan again felt welcoming.

We were extremely lucky and found the perfect apartment at the Ritz Tower on Park Avenue between Fifty-Seventh and Fifty-Eighth Street, virtually in the heart of the city. It had a large living room with a dining area, a tiny kitchen and bar, two bedrooms, two bathrooms, and a daily maid service that supplied all the clean linens, towels, bathroom rugs, tissues, soap—it was like moving into a hotel. The building even had room service!

Buying a condominium apartment in New York is an experience all its own. There is a process. You have to turn over all of your financial information, and in the case of the Ritz Tower you also needed four letters of recommendation.

We asked New York Republican senator Jack Javitz, writer Theodore H. White (best known for his *Making of the President* books), California Democratic senator John Tunney, and, to top it off, Sharman Douglas, whose father had been the ambassador to England, where she had become one of Princess Margaret's best friends.

We were given an appointment to sit down with the building's board and answer all of their questions. At the end of this interview, the gentleman sitting next to me turned to me and quietly said, "We have never received such impressive letters of recommendation. I have only one question. . . . Mrs. Livingston, why do *you* want to live with *us?*" This was clearly a man with a wonderful sense of humor!

We asked Liza, who was now a successful New York decorator, to transform the apartment, particularly for Alan's taste; everything had to be in shades of beige. In fact, we even bought beautiful bleached-pine antique furniture. Alan and I were also traveling around the world at that time and visiting the most prominent art museums, so we bought the most incredible posters to hang on the walls. Of course, when Jenny accepted a job in New York, she moved into the second bedroom for a year until she married.

When Christopher went to Connecticut College and to New York University Graduate School, he made the second bedroom his home as well. And Peter, who was now a thriving literary agent in Toronto, used the apartment as his New York address. I'm not sure what our family would have done without apartment 13-D at 465 Park Avenue.

80

New York Life Again

It was wonderful to be part of New York City again. I began getting excited each time we flew in for a landing at JFK. Sometimes we had a car waiting, and sometimes we just took a cab, but what I loved best was reaching the Triborough Bridge (now renamed the Robert F. Kennedy Bridge) and seeing the city emerge in all of its grandeur. I was excited about the prospect of exploring again, the theater, the museums, the incredible restaurants, as well as seeing old friends, being with my kids, and walking up Fifty-Seventh Street with the anticipation of reaching Bergdorf Goodman! I loved it all.

Of course, it was great to spend time again with Sally Goodman and her interesting husband, George, and to resume my friendship with Hannah Pakula, director Alan Pakula's wife, who had become a veteran New Yorker after growing up in Los Angeles.

However, the most interesting friendship I resumed was with Kitty Hart. Her husband, Moss Hart, had directed *My Fair Lady,* and so Alan Lerner, Kitty, Moss, and I had become close friends. Moss went on to direct *Camelot* in 1960, and then it became somewhat awkward for me to see them because they were spending time with Alan and Micheline. I got the distinct feeling that Micheline never became a close friend of Kitty's, but I didn't intrude because I didn't want to hurt the professional relationship between Alan and Moss.

Moss died of a heart attack one year after *Camelot* opened on Broadway. In 1962, I moved to Los Angeles to be with my new husband, but now that we had bought an apartment in New York these many years later, I felt comfortable getting in touch with Kitty again, and she seemed thrilled to resume our friendship. As a matter of fact, I remember she gave a beautiful dinner party for Alan and me in her New York apartment, inviting all of the most prominent New Yorkers at the time.

I also remember her giving me a luncheon and seeing Happy Rockefeller after Nelson's death and scandal. She was subdued and sad. Her dreams of glory had been robbed; however, she was still Mrs. Rockefeller. Isn't it amazing how life can turn around and bite you after you thought you had finally become victorious?

But the most fascinating get-togethers were the lunches and dinners that Kitty and I had alone toward the end of her life because we were totally honest with each other in looking back and examining our past.

She told me a story that she said she had never shared with anyone. It's true that Moss had a sexual-identity issue. Years before he met Kitty, it was rumored that he was gay. He didn't want to be gay and spent most of his life visiting his psychiatrist, who assisted him in taking a different path. But it was Kitty's need to be Mrs. Moss Hart that changed the situation. She seduced him in a manner that he couldn't resist. He was eternally grateful, and they had two beautiful children, a son and a daughter to give him the most joy.

Kitty was an extremely smart woman with a big heart and a great deal of love to share. The story she told me haunts me even today. Apparently, Moss came home one day and said that he unfortunately could not attend a dinner for the theater elites that was important to both of them. He had promised to go to New Haven to help a new playwright work out some problems with his new production. He said to Kitty that he had bought two seats and had asked his psychiatrist to take her to the dinner. Of course, she said that was fine.

The psychiatrist picked her up on a rainy night—they attended the dinner, and when he brought her home, he said that he had left his umbrella in her private vestibule by mistake. She, of course, invited him to join her in the elevator and go up to her apartment to retrieve his umbrella. When the elevator doors closed behind them, he gently led her into the living room but then suddenly grabbed her and desperately tried to pull off her clothes with such force that he ripped an entire sleeve from her blouse. She rescued herself as gently and resolutely as she could, corralled him to the elevator, and shoved him in when it opened.

She didn't have to tell me why this happened. It was clear that Moss had talked about his physical relationship with Kitty, which had turned on this poor doctor and given him an obsessive sexual longing to experience what he was hearing about every day.

Very quietly, Kitty almost whispered to me, "I never told Moss or anyone else about that night." She told me Moss never stopped his appointments.

Kitty Hart was eighteen years older than I, with a lifetime of experience that I couldn't even imagine. Her father and mother were of German Jewish heritage, her father dying when she was ten years old. Her life then was taken over by a mother obsessed with breaking into the gentile society. She took Kitty to Europe, where she hoped she could marry her off to European royalty. Kitty was put into an exclusive boarding school in Lausanne, Switzerland, and went on to the Sorbonne and the London School of Economics. She also studied acting in London at the Royal Academy of Dramatic Art.

She came back to New York and appeared in several musicals. She made movies in the mid-1930s and early 1940s, and she tried desperately to make George Gershwin marry her. She married Moss Hart in 1946 and had two children. She was gracious, elegant, smart, and worldly; she certainly knew more about the world and how it worked than I did. She had the art of being a successful, prominent woman down to a science, but her wisdom was what intrigued me and kept my affection for her until the day she died.

There is one evening I will never forget. Kitty was a close friend of Pamela Harriman, who was then the ambassador to France. Pamela always had a mystery and intrigue for me. I saw her for the first time when she was still Pamela Churchill, recently divorced from the British prime minister's son, Randolph. She had begun dating Leland Hayward, the prominent New York agent. Everyone in New York was talking about this new couple, and I was so intrigued to finally meet her.

One evening when Alan and I were in New York, I was in a large group, and there she was. I was astounded to find her somewhat plump, and although she had a beautiful English complexion, she was not overwhelmingly attractive. She had married Leland Hayward in 1960, and after he died in 1971, she had married the famous Averell Harriman, the former governor of New York from the prominent New York family. She was now the ambassador to France. Who was this woman, and what was there about her that was so intriguing? In particular, I wanted to know why these men had become so enamored with her. I knew Kitty could unravel this mystery, and she did.

I remember sitting in a chair across from Kitty in her apartment living room. She was in the middle of the sofa, propped up with some elegant needlepoint pillows. When I asked her what it was that made Pamela so compelling to all these men, she smiled slightly and said, "She listens. She looks at you and listens with such interest and intensity, it's as if she has never heard what you are saying ever before, and it's the most fascinating thing that she could possibly hear at that moment. She is not aware of anyone or anything else happening in the room. It is only the person that she keeps listening to that matters." Kitty paused and said, "Nancy, the ability to truly listen is an art and one of the most powerful attributes anyone can possibly possess."

81

An Unexpected Offer from Blue Ribbon

During Alan's years at Fox, my experience working with the Blue Ribbon 400 of the Los Angeles Music Center had been an interesting one, but I couldn't have foreseen where this special chapter in my life would lead me.

Around the time we were buying the apartment in New York, things were heating up in Los Angeles. Helen Wolford was leaving California, and Mrs. Chandler chose Mrs. Harry Wetzel, Maggie, to be the new executive president of Blue Ribbon.

I was delighted because Maggie and I had become friends. She was smart and down-to-earth, with none of the typical affectations of the "Los Angeles elite." She also was one of the few women who called Mrs. Chandler "Buff."

Her husband was a prominent corporate citizen and had one of the most successful wineries in Napa Valley. I wasn't surprised when she began to put Blue Ribbon on a new footing. Because she welcomed the contributions and ideas of everyone on the board, I found myself expressing strong opinions about future events and the future of the organization.

About two and a half years after Maggie began her reign, she invited me to have lunch in Venice (California) to visit some of the art galleries we both were interested in exploring. We had great fun, but it became obvious to me that she had something more than art on her mind. She talked about restructuring Blue Ribbon and insisted that the executive president should have a term of only three years. She then absolutely shocked me when she said, "Nancy, my term will end in June, and Buff and I have decided that you should be the next executive president!"

I was flabbergasted. It had never occurred to me to be the president of anything, much less the president of the major support group of the major performing-arts institution of Los Angeles. I knew how to walk onstage and take charge, I was never at a loss for words, I knew how to plan a party—but to be an executive? To be responsible for raising more than $400,000 a year? To have some of the most distinguished women in Los Angeles accept me as their leader? The whole idea was appalling.

Maggie was insistent and said that she and Mrs. Chandler were confident I could do the job. I then suggested that she should stay one more year, and I could be her assistant, carefully watching and learning the job from her. She closed her eyes and almost whispered with such emotion, "Nancy, I simply cannot stay one more year!" I answered quietly, "Maggie, give me a few days. I will go home and discuss this with Alan."

The first thing Alan said was, "Nancy, that's not you." When I asked Liza and Jenny, their response was, "Mom, that's not you!!!" I then thought, "What *is* me?" Please remember that I was born in 1928, when young women weren't expected to be leaders of anything. We had only recently been allowed to vote. Being a successful woman was defined by being married to the right man and selecting the most beautiful silver service. And yet I felt this position with Blue Ribbon was an important challenge at the right time of my life. I thought I might be able to pull it off and do a good job.

And then I had an epiphany. I called Maggie and said that I would take on this assignment with the condition that she become the chairman, with her name over mine on the stationery. I could then freely ask for her advice and counsel, and all the members would see that her name came first, making them more willing to accept me. This structure has remained with Blue Ribbon to this day.

I will never forget the afternoon Maggie Wetzel announced that she and Mrs. Chandler had decided to appoint Nancy Livingston as the new executive president of Blue Ribbon. They then asked for a vote of support from the board, which was unanimous. (The members didn't dare challenge Mrs. Chandler's decision!)

After the meeting, we gathered in the living room of Harriet Deutsch's house in Beverly Hills, and a small group of us joined Mrs. Chandler around a coffee table as we were being served white wine or iced tea. Helen Wolford, Terry Stanfill, and Harriet Deutsch called Mrs. Chandler "Mrs. C," but somewhere in the middle of the conversation Mrs. Chandler turned to me and in an emphatically authoritative voice said, "Nancy, from now on I want *you* to call me 'Buff.'" I whispered, "Thank you, Bu—Bu—Buff," and quickly changed the subject. None of these women ever treated me quite the same again.

No one understands the challenge that I faced. I realized my first step was to sit down with myself and examine what Blue Ribbon was missing that I alone could bring to it. Having been a performer, I knew that if I delivered the goods, I did not have to worry about my reviews; they would automatically be positive.

I realized that we all had attended too many teas for too many celebrities and that we were losing the importance and beauty of what the Music Center stood for: the magnificence of the performing arts. Having spent a lifetime in the theater watching great works being written and performed, I understood the mystery and the fascinating power of the creative process, and I wanted to put together an event that would bring Blue Ribbon members into that realm.

What might be the elements of such an event? What would I call it? It occurred to me that I was thinking about the extraordinary process of what happens before the curtain goes up—beginning with the idea, followed by the writing, the direction, the performing, the set and costume design—all the ingredients that come together to make a work of art. I thought about using the title "Behind the Curtain," but I hated the ungraceful word *behind*. I turned to my brilliant husband for help, but he was at JFK Airport about to fly to an investment meeting in London and had called just to say he loved me and would call again when he arrived. I said, "You can't hang up! I need you! Please give me another title for 'Behind the Curtain!'" He replied, "Nancy, it's 'The *Other Side* of the Curtain.'" I was thrilled and said "I love you and goodbye" as quickly as I could.

My presidency started in the fall of 1983, and my first challenge was to create an event that would investigate the artistic efforts on the "other side of the curtain." My professional background also gave me the understanding that having a star appear at my first event would set a high standard that everyone could look forward to. I knew Beverly Sills was bringing the New York City Opera Company to the Dorothy Chandler Pavilion for an eight-week series of its operas—among them was one of my favorites, *La bohème*.

I had never met Miss Sills, but I knew many people who had, and because I was spending so much time in New York, it was easy for me to arrange a meeting. She was cordial but cool and listened intently to my goal, which was to stage an event at the Mark Taper Forum at eleven o'clock in the morning, followed by a luncheon in her honor in the Grand Hall of the Pavilion. One of Sills's gifted young singers would begin the program with an aria from *La bohème*, and then Beverly would sit for an intense interview about her company, her goals, her own career, and how she had excelled at them all.

After my pitch, she sat for many moments just looking at me. I couldn't tell if she was enthusiastic about this project. Much of my future leadership as the new president of Blue Ribbon depended on her saying yes. I held my breath until she finally said, "Nancy, I will do this under one condition. I will allow only one person in Los Angeles to interview me, and that is the Pulitzer Prize–winning music critic of the *Los Angeles Times,* Martin Bernheimer."

You might think I would have been thrilled at that point, but I knew Martin Bernheimer was possibly the most self-centered, egotistical, difficult man in Los Angeles. He took his title "critic" extremely seriously and literally. He always wanted you to know that if he had played that violin or conducted that orchestra, the performance would have been far superior. I have always found that most successful critics feel that their role in life is to "criticize." At that moment, I wondered if he would even be willing to participate. Of course, I thanked Miss Sills and said I would let her know about Mr. Bernheimer's availability as soon as I arrived in Los Angeles.

Flying home, I constructed a plan to "get" Mr. Bernheimer. I knew the only way was to seduce him—tell him how much I admired, respected, and adored him, thus stretching the limit of my acting abilities.

With the help of Otis Chandler, I reached Mr. Bernheimer directly, and after I made my well-rehearsed request, he immediately said yes! However, he had one caveat—that the *Los Angeles Times* be invited to cover the event. Little did Mr. Bernheimer or I know that Beverly Sills was out to nail him. He was totally unprepared.

When I left Beverly the message that Mr. Bernheimer had said yes, she immediately called back, and together we planned the event. The Mark Taper stage was the perfect venue for the performance and interview to take place, with its intimate proximity to the audience. I ordered a piano for the singer and placed on center stage two chairs with a table between them and two glasses of water. All Blue Ribbon members received an invitation with a provocative picture of a hand pulling back a stage curtain and a description of what the planned events were designed to do. I was amazed at the response. Out of 400 members, 350 signed up. Of course, my next problem was what to wear!

This event would be my debut as the new president of Blue Ribbon, and I was expected to walk onstage, welcome everyone, and introduce Beverly, Martin, and the young opera singer. I chose a two-piece dress in beige wool. The skirt was gathered and full, and the long-sleeved bodice hugged my still tiny torso. Pearls, of course, went around my neck, and on my feet were suede high-heeled pumps in a deeper beige.

Poor Martin Bernheimer.

Beverly cleverly, intellectually, and above all theatrically skewered Martin, and the audience ate it up. She described to him the amount of talent, detail, and hard work that makes an opera company a success, only to have it so cavalierly dismissed by a writer whose own ego wants to be on display. The crowd also learned something valuable about creating art and how vulnerable the artist is to criticism. I think as unprepared as Martin was for this attack, he graciously accepted it. Thank God!

We all went to lunch, and even Martin joined us. That evening, as Alan and I had our martinis together, I had such a good time telling him what a success the day had been. Later that night, when Alan walked out of his dressing room in his pajamas and I walked out of my dressing room in my nightgown, he took me in his arms and whispered in my ear, "Congratulations."

82

Changing Traditions

One of the annual events that Mrs. Chandler created was something called the Children's Festival. Every spring, Blue Ribbon invited fifth-grade children from all of the public schools in Los Angeles County to visit the Music Center. It was an inspired idea to expose students to the performing arts and make them aware of our special institution. The schools responded, and when I was president, at least thirty-six thousand children attended.

My problem with this program was that all performances took place outdoors on the plaza with the children seated on bleachers. It was too much like going to Disneyland or the circus. As the new president, I was determined to change this tradition and bring the kids into the theater to witness a performance onstage.

Bill Severns, head of the operating company, had an office in the Dorothy Chandler Pavilion. I called and made an appointment and marched into his office at four o'clock one afternoon with my heart pounding. I came prepared to make my case and started by saying that I had a history of starring in three plays on Broadway and reminded him that I had been married to a librettist who had created some of the most brilliant musicals in the history of the twentieth century. My husband, Alan Livingston, had recorded some of the greatest orchestras in the world, and our passion for the performing arts was a giant part of our life. How could I bring thirty-six thousand children to the Music Center and then isolate them on the plaza? How could I let Blue Ribbon spend $75,000 to bring every fifth grader to the Music Center without letting them inside our great hall to experience a live performance?

He looked at me for a long time, and I tried desperately not to show my anxiety. He then said, "Nancy, what timeframe are we talking about?" I replied, "March or April. And we must, of course, avoid the Easter holidays." He was silent again, then asked, "Nancy, who are you considering or have you approached to perform on our stage?" I answered a little too eagerly that I had talked to Bob Joffrey, founder of the Joffrey Ballet—which was then a resident company of the Music Center—about bringing his dancers in to create a special children's program.

Bill picked up the phone and asked his assistant to please bring in the Chandler Theater schedule for March and April. A young man came in, sat next to Bill, and explained what had already been planned for the theater. They talked between each other about various openings, and finally Bill looked at me and said, "You can have the Dorothy Chandler hall and stage for these four days, Tuesday through Friday in the middle of March." . . . I couldn't wait for my martini with Alan to tell him of my triumph.

The first thing our fifth graders learned was the etiquette of entering a theater. There were no popcorn-and-soda stands but rather glittering chandeliers and a grand staircase; they responded with an immediate hush. They were ushered to their seats in the orchestra and up the stairs to the Founders Circle and up the second flight of stairs to the balconies. Most of them had never seen a concert hall with wood paneling and elegant crystal lighting. They chattered until suddenly the lights of the hall began to slowly dim and the stage lit up. They all understood that it was time to stop their chatter and focus their attention on the giant curtains that were slowly beginning to rise to the accompaniment of grand symphonic music.

The first images they saw were ballet slippers dancing to the music, then as the curtain rose higher, they began to see knees, torsos, and faces against a glorious backdrop. Between each ballet number, Bob Joffrey would come to the center of the stage and explain the story of what the dancers were portraying. The applause was deafening, and the children were transfixed, returning home with memories they would never forget.

The Music Center's education department sent each class a description and history of what they were going to see as well as a record of the music they were going to dance to in the plaza following the performance. They also were given a letter from Mrs. Chandler thanking them for coming and welcoming their families to visit the Music Center. The Blue Ribbon volunteers were absolutely thrilled to be a part of this triumphant event, . . . and, once again, I couldn't wait for my martini with Alan.

The Children's Festival has never again taken place in the plaza since that performance.

One of the most valuable results of my friendship with Bob Joffrey was an event he created for the "Other Side of the Curtain" series. It took place at eleven o'clock in the morning on the Dorothy Chandler Pavilion stage and was followed by a luncheon in Bob and Helen Wolford's (Blue Ribbon's first executive president) honor in the Grand Hall. His dancers performed six pas de deux. Before each began, he explained to the audience the period in which it was choreographed, the story it portrayed, who the composer was, and the special skills that the dancers needed. One pas de deux demanded the tallest dancers with the greatest athletic ability, which he described in such a way that our audience looked at ballet from a completely fresh view from then on. He was brilliant, the dancers were extraordinary, and the audience was entranced.

Before and after lunch, the line at the ticket booth extended down the steps and into the plaza, which had never happened for any previous ballet performance.

The luncheon that followed was another challenge for me. I knew the audience would be excited by what they had just witnessed and would be eager to express their appreciation. They would also be thrilled to have Helen Wolford visit a Blue Ribbon event for the first time in several years. I decided to try something new. As dessert was being served, I whispered to Bob and Helen not to stand up during my speech. I then walked to the microphone and asked people in the room to please stand if this was the first "Other Side of the Curtain" event they had attended. I told them to remain standing. I then asked those people who had never been to a ballet to please stand. After several more questions, including if this performance was one of the most special Blue Ribbon events we had ever had, everyone was standing except for Bob Joffrey and Helen Wolford. I then asked everyone standing to please show Helen and Bob their deepest appreciation, and the room exploded with applause and cheers. I think Helen and Bob were very touched.

In the third year of my presidency, I hosted an "Other Side of the Curtain" event with the Los Angeles Philharmonic and at the same time was also costarring in an hour-long weekly television series produced by Leonard Goldberg. The show was called *Paper Dolls,* and I played the wife of the main character, played by Lloyd Bridges, and the entire Bridges family became great friends of ours. I was thankful it was a large ensemble cast, so I didn't work on the show every day.

The show wasn't picked up for the following season, but it didn't matter to me, anyway, because my character was killed in a plane crash in the twelfth episode! I had a large group of friends in Blue Ribbon, and some of them remain my closest friends today; however, there was a certain group that seemed delighted when they heard of my plane crash. As far as they were concerned, I had been applauded more than enough.

83

Four Weddings and Two Funerals

Things seemed to be going smoothly at this point in our lives. Alan's son Peter was doing quite well. He had fallen in love with a lovely young woman named Patty who came from an interesting family in Nova Scotia, Canada. She was a serious Buddhist, studying medicine at Boulder University. She adored Peter, and they married. Alan bought them a house, and they had a beautiful baby boy named Alex (for Alexander the Great).

They eventually moved to Toronto, where Peter became a successful writer's agent, handling many prominent Canadian authors, and Patty became a very successful anesthesiologist. All seemed to be going extremely well until the moment Peter felt he didn't need his bipolar medication any longer. He stopped taking it, and slowly the symptoms began to return. Thank God his doctor explained to him that he would spiral again and crash again—it was inevitable. For Peter, the thought of returning to the depths of the depression he had once experienced was too frightening, so he went back on the medication immediately.

Also at this time, Laura found the man she wanted to marry, Gary Gibson. Alan and I gave a dinner for all the visiting families at our home the night before the wedding, which took place in our garden the next day.

Liza also met the man of her dreams, Porter Bibb, who just so happened to be the first publisher of *Rolling Stone* magazine. They were married by a justice of the peace in New York City and celebrated with a small luncheon at Orsini's. Two weeks later Alan and I gave them a large celebration at our home in Beverly Hills. Liza soon gave birth to my beautiful first granddaughter, Zoe.

Jenny met a young man while she was staying in our Park Avenue apartment, and Alan and I gave her and Carlyle Fraser another lavish wedding at our home. Everything seemed to be on track . . . for the moment, anyway.

Before I even had a chance to start planning Jenny's wedding, Alan insisted that he had to be in New York for a week on business. I don't remember whose party we were invited to, but I do remember bumping into some of my old New York friends, who were surprised to see me. Drew Heinz was one of them, and she said to me, "You used to be Nancy Lerner! I have something to tell you. I know that Alan Lerner is married, but I also know that he is pursuing the daughter of a friend of mine in London." I was amazed to hear that Number Nine was waiting in the wings.

Of course, Alan Lerner was invited to Jenny's wedding. In fact, the invitation said:

Alan and Nancy Livingston
and
Alan Jay Lerner
Invite you to attend the wedding
Of their daughter Jenny
and
Carlyle Fraser.

Alan Livingston and I took care of all the expenses for the wedding, and Alan Lerner wanted very much to come with his new wife (Number Eight), Liz. They had been living in London, and when he called me to say he was coming, he added seductively, "We are staying at the Bel Air Hotel—you remember the Bel Air Hotel, don't you, Nancy?" Shortly after that phone call, he was diagnosed with advanced lung cancer and was admitted to Sloan-Kettering Hospital in New York for treatment.

Susan Lerner was now living in Los Angeles with her second husband, Dr. Olch, and was very much a part of our family life. Unfortunately, she too was diagnosed with cancer (of the uterus) and was destined not to live much longer. Thank God she was able to come to Jenny's wedding.

It was soon after the wedding that Susan's cancer progressed so dramatically that her husband took her to New York to consult a specialist, who put her immediately in Sloan-Kettering as well.

Alan Jay apparently couldn't face Susan's impending death and refused to visit her. But her desperation to see her father was so overwhelming that one day she persuaded the nurses to put her in a wheelchair with all of her intravenous paraphernalia attached, and she burst into Alan's room. They sobbed uncontrollably in each other's arms, and shortly thereafter she was taken back to California to die.

Liza, Jenny, and Michael saw their father every day and watched him slowly become more fragile. Alan Jay's wife, Liz, flew to Miami for a week as she could no longer handle the situation. The girls called me every day, not only for the purpose of keeping me informed but for me to give them my loving support.

One morning they told me that when they had arrived at the hospital, they had been met by the intern in charge of Alan. He told them that he was scheduled to take Alan to the basement for another X-ray and another probing exam. He said that Alan was about to die, but the doctor simply could not tell his famous patient the truth, so these exams were nothing but further torture. He asked Liza and Jenny if they would give him permission to tell Alan that he was canceling all tests because they were worthless; he wanted Alan to know the truth. Liza and Jenny gave the intern permission to talk to their father. They waited for about fifteen minutes before the intern came to them and said, "Your father knows now and wants to see you."

They described Alan as extremely quiet—subdued—whispering a request for the girls to get a bottle of champagne, which they did. They poured glasses for themselves and him, and he toasted a thank-you for his life and for them. That night Liz arrived from Miami and lay down on the bed next to Alan's. His last words were, "I hope you will be alright." It occurred to me that this might have been the first time he ever expressed his concern for someone other than himself.

My phone rang at about 6:00 a.m. the next day, and Liza said, "Mom, he's gone." About half an hour later, I got up and wrote them the letter that starts this book.

Three weeks later, a memorial highlighting Alan's work took place at the Shubert Theater in New York. I remember Julie Andrews, Leonard Bernstein, and Arthur Schlesinger Jr. were just a few of the notable people who took part in this tribute. Something in me wanted to be there because I had shared so much of his creative life and had borne two of his children.

But I was never invited. Susan, of course, wanted very much to be there as well but was too ill to travel. We decided that I would come to her home at one o'clock, when the tribute started. We then would wait for the phone call from Liza and Jenny to tell us all about it, and we could reminisce together.

As I was getting ready to leave to be with her, the phone rang. It was Susan, who could barely speak but managed to whisper, "Nancy, don't come. David is taking me to the hospital immediately." She died that night.

As a postscript, when Liza and Jenny did call, they said that Billy Harbach, who produced the tribute, asked them, "Where is your mother? This was her life too."

84

LA Politics

The most baffling difference between Alan Livingston and me was that I, of course, was a staunch Democrat, and Alan defined himself as a loyal Republican. I would like to think that I had a great deal of influence on Alan; I honestly thought I could persuade him to be on my side. God knows I tried, but it wasn't easy. I insisted that we get the *New York Times* every day, and I quoted it every morning at breakfast. Alan did not subscribe to the *Wall Street Journal,* but he certainly didn't read the *Times,* either. However, he did read *Time* magazine thoroughly to keep informed of world events.

When Jimmy Carter became president in 1976, I did my best to convince Alan of Carter's very special qualities and integrity. In 1980, I insisted that we watch the Carter–Reagan debates and thought I persuaded Alan that Carter should remain president. But to no avail.

Election day arrived, and it was clear that I was going to vote for Carter and Alan was going to vote for Reagan. At 8:45 that morning, Alan was about to leave for his office and asked me to walk him to the front door. He took me in his arms and said gently, "Honey, I am very late for an appointment. We both know we're going to cancel each other's vote, so why don't we make a pact? Let's both promise not to vote at all."

I looked at him and said, "OK. Go to your appointment. I won't vote."

The best part of this agreement was a long, passionate embrace. He whispered, "Thank you," and walked out the door.

At about four o'clock that afternoon, I was in my car listening to the radio as the returns from the East were being announced and the exit polls were coming in from the Midwest. It was obvious that Reagan was going to win by a large majority. I had no intention of voting until that moment and thought, "Dammit, Alan's going to get his candidate, so I might as well at least deliver one more vote to President Carter."

I drove to Coldwater Park, where we usually voted, and walked to the table to sign in. The poll worker opened the book to my name, Nancy O. Livingston. The name listed directly above mine was "Alan W. Livingston." I started to sign my name when I realized there was a signature above mine. It was Alan's! And in his own handwriting next to his signature was the time of his vote—9:50 a.m. Ten minutes after we made our pact!!

That night as we sat with our martinis, I looked him straight in the eye and said, "Alan, you broke our agreement. You voted."

Alan replied with a slight, self-conscious smile, "So did you."

"Yes," I said, "but at least I waited until four in the afternoon."

On that day I had no idea that Alan's and my life would become very involved with Ronald and Nancy Reagan and the famous "Kitchen Cabinet," a group comprising their closest California friends. Most surprisingly, our association with them would include several visits to the White House.

Felisa Vanoff, my old friend from Share, and her husband, Nick, had become two of Alan's and my closest friends in California. They invited us several times to be their guests in Washington, DC, to attend the Kennedy Center Honors weekend, which Nick had created, to honor and pay yearly tribute to the greatest American artists.

Saturday night involved being a guest at a small dinner for the honorees at the State Department. On Sunday evening, there was a black-tie cocktail reception at the White House hosted by the Reagans for the honorees, their guests, and distinguished members of the Washington elite. On those trips to Washington, Alan and I chatted with Nancy and Ronnie, bringing them up to date on all the latest Los Angeles gossip. We would then go to the Kennedy Center to watch the awards ceremony and to attend a lavish supper party afterward.

It was around this time that I persuaded Felisa to join Blue Ribbon, which was a natural fit for her interest in and knowledge of the performing arts. However, she was extremely competitive with me, which always surprised me and took me off guard. Being president of Blue Ribbon was a very high-profile position in Los Angeles at that time. The society columnists Jody Jacobs and Mary Lou Loper mentioned me in their *Los Angeles Times* social columns every other week.

I found out many years later that Felisa had told several of our mutual friends how she could accomplish what I was doing much more superbly. I think she was probably right, but she wasn't the one taking on the responsibility.

The last time we were invited to the Kennedy Center Honors, Alan Jay Lerner (this was before his passing) and Frederick Loewe were among the honorees. We accepted, but I told Felisa that we should probably not attend the small State Department dinner; I did not want to put Alan and his new wife (Number Eight) in an awkward position. But we all saw each other at the White House, and I was very pleased that Liza and Jenny had been invited for that weekend as well.

Every single member of the Kitchen Cabinet in Los Angeles was a Blue Ribbon member. Their devotion to the Reagans was somewhat nauseating; however, they were very powerful and showed up in Jody Jacobs's column every other week. It was apparent to me that my next big Blue Ribbon event should be a luncheon honoring the First Lady. But how could I make it a very special event as well as one that highlighted our devotion to the performing arts?

I had a teacher in high school who said something once that I have never forgotten: "If you want to make someone happy, give them a problem to solve." I think it's one of the most valuable lessons I have ever learned, and I continue to use it into my old age. It certainly helped me in creating an event for Mrs. Reagan.

85

Nancy and Ronnie

When I was involved in Share, I had met and become friends with Edye Rugolo, whose husband, Pete, was a major Hollywood composer. She was now head of development of the Los Angeles Young Musicians Foundation, which supported musically gifted children, some starting at four and five years old! I had attended many of their concerts and was amazed at their talent.

I called Edye and asked if it was possible to put together a small chamber group—a pianist, a violinist, a cellist, and possibly a bass player—to perform at Mrs. Reagan's luncheon. She was very enthusiastic and said that the ten-year-old pianist was a composer as well, and perhaps he could write a piece in Mrs. Reagan's honor.

I knew I was onto something special and started to make a plan. I asked each "cabinet" member to be on my honorary committee and asked Buff Chandler and Maggie Wetzel to stand with me and Mrs. Reagan at the top of the stairs in the Grand Hall. This receiving line seemed to dazzle all of our members, and we were off to a great start.

I put all of the "cabinet" at the main table with Mrs. Reagan and Mrs. Chandler and put myself at the number two table. In front of the hall was a platform with a grand piano and three small chairs with three miniature music stands. Edye and the children were seated in the far corner and stayed as inconspicuous as possible.

At dessert, I walked to the microphone on the platform, welcomed everyone, and introduced the honorary committee members by name. The glow of self-importance from this table emanated throughout the room. I then introduced the children, "our future solo artists at the Music Center." They took their places, and I announced their first Mozart piece.

If you closed your eyes, it would be hard to distinguish this music from that played by the most professional adult chamber music performers. When you opened your eyes, you couldn't believe you were watching children from seven to eleven years old.

After their first and second pieces, I came to the microphone again and introduced the young boy who was playing the piano. I said that he had written a special composition dedicated to Mrs. Reagan and that he would like her to please come and sit beside him. The audience was entranced.

It was then that I realized how difficult and awkward it was for Nancy Reagan to be charming and gracious. She did not have the ability to react spontaneously and so retreated in her "thank you" speech by talking about Mr. Blue Eyes (Frank Sinatra), who had just attended an event at the White House. It was odd hearing about Frank Sinatra at this moment—it had no relation to anything that had just taken place.

Alan's and my friends Harriet and Ardie Deutsch had become part of the Kitchen Cabinet. When I first met the Deutsches, they were Democrats; in fact, Ardie had helped John Tunney raise money for his Senate campaign in California.

However, being a part of the Reagans' intimate circle was so seductive that they became enthusiastic Republicans almost overnight and attended White House events regularly.

On the evening of the Blue Ribbon luncheon, the Deutsches gave a dinner party for Nancy. Alan and I were not invited, but I heard that Ardie got up to make a toast to Nancy and said, "Isn't it interesting that it takes a liberal Democrat like Nancy Livingston to give the best party Nancy has had in our town in a long time?" Thank you, Ardie!

Obviously, Nancy had been very impressed because a week later I received a phone call from the White House asking me how to get in touch with the Young Musicians Foundation. The Reagans were eager to have the children come and entertain at one of their events, and the White House representative said to me, "Mrs. Livingston, perhaps we could persuade you to come too?" . . . I was never invited.

Three years later, in 1988, after I had finished my tenure as president of Blue Ribbon, Ronald Reagan's two terms in the White House were over, and the Reagans came back to Los Angeles. The entire city was salivating at the prospect of having Ronnie and Nancy in their community once more. A perfect example of the clamor over their return occurred one morning when I called

Ray Stark, a corporate entertainment and social leader in the city. When asked by his secretary who was calling, I answered, "Nancy Livingston." Apparently, all Ray heard was "Nancy," and when he picked up the phone, he was so obsequiously glad to hear from me that I slowly realized he thought—and certainly hoped—that I was somebody far more interesting!

I quietly said, "Ray, who do you think I am?"

He answered breathlessly, "You're Nancy Reagan, of course!"

I paused and said very quietly, "I'm so sorry, Ray. It's Nancy Livingston."

"Oh," he replied in a disappointed voice.

About six months after the Reagans returned to California, my friend Joanne Kozberg, who was then the president of Blue Ribbon, asked if she could consult with me about creating a Blue Ribbon event for Nancy Reagan. She had already reserved the Mark Taper Forum for one morning and wanted to do an interview and luncheon with Nancy but was uncertain about how to put the whole thing together. She thought that she could be the moderator and have three Blue Ribbon members, including me, join her and ask questions.

Having gone through my one experience with Nancy as a guest of honor, I had to tell Joanne that I felt that this event could be a disaster; she needed something more. My problem-solving mechanism took over, and I said, "This will work only if we get Ronnie himself involved, and that won't be easy." Thank God I understood an actor's mentality and knew that I had to write a script in which he could play a part. I felt we could engage his theatrical sensibility by surprising the audience as well as Nancy.

I wrote a script:

The audience arrives facing the set of the play that is running at this time. In the middle of the stage are three chairs in a row for the members of Blue Ribbon who will be asking questions, and on stage right are two armchairs with a table in the middle for Joanne and Nancy R. Joanne introduces the panel, and we take our places. She then introduces Nancy R. with a summary of her accomplishments as First Lady and asks the panel to please begin their questions.

After the first three or four questions, I, Nancy Livingston, politely interrupt them with this dialogue: "Excuse me for interrupting, Joanne, but I have a burning question that I must ask

Nancy." Joanne turns to me expectantly, and I say, "Nancy, I want to ask you about all the pictures that we have seen of you and the president together. In each one, you look at him with such adoration that I have always wondered: Is it possible that you truly feel that emotion every time you look at him?"

Ronald Reagan's famous voice is heard over the loudspeaker from backstage. He says, "Nancy, before you answer that question, I would like a word with you."

The door on the set opens, and the president walks out, surprising not only the audience but Nancy as well.

Joanne said, "That's brilliant, but how are we going to make it happen?" I said, "We'll send the script to Ronnie with a timetable of a car picking him up and delivering him to the back of the theater, where he will be met by the stage manager and directed to a microphone behind the set. The moment he is in place, the stage manager will walk to the back of the theater and signal to me that he is there and ready. I will then interrupt you with my question."

Joanne said, "But, Nancy, how are we going to get this script to the president and persuade him to do this?" I said, "We'll ask Marion Jorgenson, one of the Reagans' closest friends, to take it to Ronnie personally with the secret that it is a surprise for his wife, and I think his sense of fun"—which was one of his more outstanding qualities—"might compel him to go for it."

And he did . . . with the understanding that no one must know anything about this other than Marion, the stage manager, Joanne, and me.

Can you imagine how I felt when I saw the stage manager signal to me that everything was ready, the president at the microphone waiting for his cue. Trembling, I then spoke my lines and almost fainted when I heard the voice of the former president of the United States recite my dialogue perfectly! It was weird.

He walked onstage, and not only did the audience practically fall out of their seats, but Nancy was obviously in complete shock as well! She was dumbstruck and could barely stammer, "But-but-but we had breakfast together, and you didn't say a word about this!"

The president took Nancy's hand and walked to center stage, looked at the audience, and said, "When this lady leaves the room . . . I miss her!" Everyone swooned. There were no more questions. We all simply went to lunch, and Joanne and I knew we had triumphed.

That night Alan and I had our martini as usual, and he asked, "Well, tell me . . . how did it go?" I said, "Before I tell you, I have a question—Alan, if I left the room, would you miss me?" He looked at me strangely and replied, "Well, you're coming back aren't you?" I could only imagine all the Blue Ribbon members across all of Los Angeles asking their husbands, "If I left the room, would you miss me?"

Alan and I were invited to many parties for the Reagans after their return to Los Angeles. As thrilled as everyone was to be with the Reagans, I was surprised that I was always the one left talking to Ronnie. He loved telling stories, and he loved an audience, but his friends had heard the same stories repeated again and again. They gave him a warm greeting and then left me alone with him, making their getaway as quickly as possible.

I must have heard one particular story about building a fence at the Reagans' ranch about ten times. I think my gift for reacting as if I were hearing the story for the first time was one of the reasons Alan and I were always included at their parties. I also knew that Ronald Reagan was approaching a very, very sad ending.

86

Twenty-Fifth Anniversary Chairman

When I finished my tenure as president of Blue Ribbon, it was my responsibility to choose my successor. William Kieschnick, the chief executive of Arco at that time, was on the Music Center board, and his lovely wife, Keith, was on the Blue Ribbon board. She was an obvious candidate and accepted the presidency with gracious enthusiasm. I became the chairman of the Blue Ribbon board, and even though it was time for me to leave the Music Center board, I was asked to remain.

Because 1989 was the twenty-fifth anniversary of this institution, a chairman was needed to plan the celebration. Fortunately, or unfortunately, the board asked me to take on this responsibility. I had no idea then that I would find myself in the center of one of the most traumatic, challenging, and life-altering experiences I have ever been through. Where do I begin?

While I was president of Blue Ribbon, the president and chief operating officer of the Music Center was a charming man named Michael Newton. His office was down the hall from my Blue Ribbon office, and one of the pleasures of being there was my time spent with him. He was in charge of raising money for all of the resident companies, and Blue Ribbon was his major funder. In fact, he came into my office one day and said, "Nancy, I need you to raise your dues from $1,000 a year to $1,500 a year, and I want you to add one hundred members." I'm not exactly sure how I managed that, but I created a space for it to happen.

Down the hall from me was a volunteer (also a Blue Ribbon member) who had started a very profitable yearly public fund-raiser called "The Mercado," which took place in the Music Center plaza. There was something relentlessly ambitious about her, and I felt strongly that I should not trust her. She was after something that I did not quite understand, but it had something to do with accumulating power and creating an image of wealth and importance.

Actually, she was not rich but wanted everyone to believe she was. She was also Jewish but went out of her way to deny it. Her name was Mrs. Thomas Wachtell . . . Esther.

I will never forget the day Michael walked into my office and said how grateful he was to Esther for the amount of money she was able to raise from her event. He said, "I think I've made her feel very good today. I have arranged with our board to honor her by adding her name to the $100,000 Benefactor category."

To this day, she has never acknowledged that she never actually wrote a check to the Music Center. It did not surprise me that when Michael took a medical leave and sadly succumbed to the AIDS virus, Esther Wachtell became the Music Center's new chief operating officer.

It was quite clear to me that Esther was not really in favor of my chairing the twenty-fifth anniversary event. However, I was in need of a new challenge, and I strongly felt that I could do something special for this institution with which my life had become so intertwined. In fact, I was determined to create a unique twenty-fifth anniversary celebration.

My first step was to choose two powerful cochairs who would protect me from any attempts Esther might make to thwart me. I selected Lod Cook, who was then the chairman of Arco, the largest corporation in Los Angeles with a national presence. Lod was on the Music Center board and was fascinated with my movie career; he was particularly interested in stories about Bill Holden and John Wayne. ("What were they really like, Nancy?") My choice for the second cochair was Dan Frost, the husband of Mia Chandler, Buff's daughter and Otis's sister. Dan was also on the Music Center board and was one of the most prominent lawyers in Los Angeles.

I also needed a working partner, someone professional, smart, and, above all, not in need of having her ego polished and buffed every day. Debbie Telefson was a fellow Blue Ribbon member who obviously possessed all of these qualities and more. I asked her to be the coordinating chairman of the twenty-fifth anniversary celebration; she accepted enthusiastically, and we worked in our little office together daily for a year and a half. I could not have accomplished this overwhelming challenge without her.

For the anniversary, Esther said she wanted an elaborate coffee table book detailing the Music Center's history, with beautiful pictures on high-quality paper and a stunning cover. I needed another chairman to work exclusively on the book, someone who had journalistic experience and access to the Chandler family and history. I made an appointment with Dan Frost to discuss the person I thought would be perfect: Bettina Chandler, Otis's new wife who was also on the staff of the *Los Angeles Times*. I was confident and proud of my inspired choice and announced my decision to Dan.

His reaction was shocking and opened a Pandora's box I didn't even know existed. The minute I said Bettina's name, Dan jumped from his chair and shouted at me, "You can't do that! We're trying to get rid of him!!!"

I was paralyzed and speechless. What did he mean? Were they trying to get rid of Otis Chandler, the publisher of the *Los Angeles Times* who had taken a small-town newspaper and was raising its stature to one of the most important newspapers in the country?

What I didn't realize was that certain members of the Chandler family were extremely conservative and felt that Otis was destroying their legacy by allowing his editorial page to express a much too liberal point of view. They were large stockholders of the newspaper and had the power to force him out. I had stumbled upon a plot that I wish I hadn't discovered, and this was just the beginning of the drama that would enfold me well into the future.

Dan then promised that he would give me someone for the book who worked at the *Times*. The next day he called and said that he had arranged for Angela Rinaldi to be my chairman. She turned out to be the most professional and effective person I could have hoped for. She suggested that we ask Nancy Zaslavsky, who was a graphic artist with her own small office in Venice, to take on the task of putting the book together. Her job included gathering historic photos of Los Angeles and the construction of the Music Center as well as finding and putting together images of the famous stage productions that had taken place there over the past twenty-five years. Angela further contributed by persuading Mark Swed to write the text for the book. Still, I knew that the book was only one part of what I had to accomplish.

I started with this question: "What is something that has never been done with the anniversary of a major institution, something that could also attract more revenue?"

Believe it or not, I thought it would be so provocative to hire the controversial new artist Christo to wrap the Music Center buildings in his canvas-and-rope designs but decided that would not be practical. That thought, though, led me to the possibility of asking one of the most distinguished abstract expressionist artists in our city to create an original lithograph dedicated to the Music Center's twenty-fifth year.

I went to my friend the contemporary-art collector Marcia Weisman (Norton Simon's sister) and asked if she could help me. She was very enthusiastic and immediately suggested Sam Francis. She called him the next day, and within three days I had his commitment.

My scheme was to charge $5,000 per couple, which would include two tickets to the performance and gala, the book, and a limited-edition signed lithograph by Sam Francis. I also persuaded Gemini to volunteer the printing and Art Services to supply 250 frames. But I couldn't stop there. I wanted something even more special for this event.

I went to Ernest Fleischmann, the managing director of the symphony, to help me initiate a performing-arts award from our institution, something completely original that had never been done before. We came up with something brilliant, if I do say so myself. It started with the recognition that we were the youngest performing-arts institution in the country. What if we asked twentieth-century artists to choose an emerging twenty-first-century artist who they felt was the future of their respective area of expertise in music, theater, and dance? Ernest insisted that, along with the recognition, a generous amount of money be awarded, and he suggested $25,000 to each young recipient. I felt strongly that there should not only be a certificate but also a piece of sculpture, very much like an Oscar.

Our plan was to ask each managing director—Gordon Davidson, head of theater arts; Ernest Fleischmann, head of the symphony; and Bob Joffrey, head of his ballet company—to choose one distinguished artist in his field. Then together with that established artist, each would choose the up-and-coming artist of the twenty-first century. Ernest chose Zubin Mehta, Gordon chose Hal Prince, and Bob chose New York City prima ballerina Suzanne Farrell. The first recipients of the Dorothy B. Chandler Performing Arts Awards were the seventeen-year-old violinist Midori; the writer, director, and puppet designer Julie Taymor; and the choreographer Charles Moulton.

I had two major hurdles to conquer before I could move forward with these awards: Who would guarantee $75,000 a year for the three awards in perpetuity, and who could I get to design and cast three sculptures a year, also in perpetuity?

I had a meeting with Mike Ovitz, who was on the Music Center board at that time, to discuss the possibility of asking David Geffen for this contribution. It might have been the most awkward conversation I ever had with anyone. Mike was not going to personally benefit from this plan, so he killed the suggestion in the rudest manner.

I then discussed with Dan Frost the possibility of asking Armand Hammer to contribute the financing. Dan said, "Nancy, this whole thing will become the Hammer Awards, and the Chandler association with the Music Center will be completely lost." Thank God I had asked Dan to be one of my partners because he immediately said, "This should be the Dorothy B. Chandler Performing Arts Award. I will go to the family and see if I can't make this happen." And he did.

My next assignment was to ask my friend, the celebrated Los Angeles sculptor Robert Graham, to create an original piece of sculpture for the award and to preserve a mold that could be used well into the future. I will never forget driving to his studio and planning the most original proposal I could think of to seduce him. Having been married to an artist like Alan Lerner, thankfully I understood the creative process extremely well.

When I sat down with Bob, I told him about Alan Lerner's struggle to write a lyric about love that mirrored as closely as possible his understanding of that emotion. His inner picture was magnificently perfect, but translating that perfection into a song lyric never quite captured the depth of what he felt. Therefore, he had to write about it over and over again. I then looked at Bob and said, "I think your multiple sculptures of the female torso represent your need to match your inner picture of the perfect female body."

He looked at me, and I realized that no one had ever articulated this to him before—perhaps he had not even thought of it himself. He said, "Nancy, what do you want me to do for you?" I told him, and after looking away for about thirty seconds, he turned back to me and said, "I'll do it." I had never felt quite so triumphant or persuasive, and I sincerely admired and loved him for his generosity.

My next challenge was to appoint somebody to produce an event in the Dorothy Chandler Pavilion before the gala supper party that would introduce the new awards and showcase each awardee. Who could do that better than the man who created the Kennedy Center Honors, my dear friend Nick Vanoff? Believe it or not, he said yes! I had one more empty space in my giant puzzle: How could I honor and highlight the original founders who had helped Buff Chandler make the Music Center a reality?

I decided I had to have a separate event in which each of the founders would share a memory of his or her participation in creating the center, and I knew it had to have a quality of theatrical excitement. I made a list, including the board of supervisors, the head of each resident company, and the most prominent founders still living.

I did not want people to come to the microphone and make a speech, so I decided that I would sprinkle each of our special guests around the Grand

Hall and personally ask each to stand and speak from their table. I reviewed their histories, wrote to each of them a suggested theme of what he or she might talk about, and made it clear that they must not speak for more than three minutes. For instance, I asked Betsy Bloomingdale to tell us what her reaction was when she walked into the Founders Circle and looked at the theater for the first time; I asked Bob Ahmanson to reminisce about his first conversation with Mrs. Chandler; I asked Esther Wachtell to describe the enormous success and uniqueness of the "buck bag" fund-raising drive; And, of course, I asked Otis Chandler, the final speaker, to please share with us memories of his mother's inspiration to build the Music Center. I then asked Zubin Mehta to be master of ceremonies.

This event was called the Founders Luncheon, and everyone came, including Alan, who sat next to me at the head table. I had three volunteers with hand-held microphones, a script, and a seating chart.

At dessert, I got up, welcomed everyone, and introduced Zubin, who started with his own tribute to Buff Chandler and then introduced each special guest. As the attention moved from one part of the room to the next, there was a hushed focus on what everyone said, particularly because each story was so personal. By the time Otis stood, he was emotionally ready to give a heartfelt tribute to his mother and to everyone in the room. I was shocked that it all worked so well and could not wait for my martini with Alan.

Alan was quiet that evening but smiled every time the phone rang, knowing that it would be another "Congratulations!" for me. He didn't mind the phone ringing straight through dinner, and when we finally went to bed, he took me in his arms and whispered, "You were wonderful today. Go to sleep, darling."

The next morning when I woke up, Alan was sitting up in bed. He said, "You're awake," and leaned over me and whispered, "I have something to tell you." I knew something must be horribly wrong. He said, "Peter is in the hospital in Toronto with an advanced case of AIDS and isn't expected to live more than six months."

I started to scream through my tears. He grabbed me and held me so tight I almost couldn't breathe. I said, "When did you find out?"

He answered, "Two days ago."

I shouted, "Why didn't you tell me?"

He said through his tears, "I didn't want to take away the joy of your victory."

The tragedy of what was happening to Peter was also happening to every hemophiliac born before 1984. In the 1970s, factor VIII and IX concentrates were developed that hemophiliacs could inject directly into their veins to give themselves normal clotting for up to forty-eight hours. This injection liberated these children and young men, who could suddenly ride a bicycle, play tennis, run, jump, and not be in danger of internal bleeding. Peter was very wary of using this treatment too often, but he couldn't resist and injected himself at least once a month. Unfortunately, the blood used for the concentrates came from a pool of more than 100 million donors, and because this was early in the AIDS epidemic, it was inevitable that someone with HIV positive blood was a donor. More than 93 percent of those who injected themselves before the year 1984 became infected, some passing it on to their wives and newborn children, unaware that they were carriers. The company that produced the concentrates never pasteurized the blood because that would, of course, reduce its profits. However, a suit was filed five years later, and every parent received $100,000 in a settlement.

Fortunately for all of us, Peter didn't leave this world in six months but, thankfully, lived for almost another two years. He and Patty and their little boy, Alex, moved into a very comfortable home in Halifax, Nova Scotia. Patty's mother and father were wonderful overseers, and there was a strong Buddhist community there to help support the family emotionally.

I'm not sure how Alan and I were able to continue with this incredible tragedy in our lives. Unfortunately, I had taken on a serious responsibility at the Music Center and felt obligated to carry on.

I went back to my desk and hammered out the most detailed and fulsome events schedule for the twenty-fifth anniversary celebrations. You would think that I would have had support for this daunting project, but instead I was thwarted and schemed against at every turn. Incredible . . . but true.

One day Esther called me into her office and said, "Nancy, this book you are creating is going to be much too expensive. The $5,000 donor category won't cover it." I went back to my cubbyhole down the hall and wondered how I could raise extra money.

I thought, "Wouldn't it be wonderful to ask every professional photographer in the city to take a special portrait of those donors willing to contribute an extra $5,000?" Each picture would be designed by the contributor—they might want a single or group portrait taken in their home, in their garden, at the Music Center plaza, on the beach, or whatever setting they could imagine. Tiffany & Co. had already committed to giving a silver bookmark shaped into a treble clef symbol for the gala; perhaps I could persuade it to donate a silver frame for each portrait as well.

These photographs would be printed in the back of the book, accompanied by a personal statement of how each donor felt about the Music Center. This back section would thank them for making this historic commemorative book possible and would give us a $10,000 category. To my astonishment, the photographers and Tiffany said yes!

There was one contribution to the twenty-fifth anniversary celebration that I cannot take credit for. Music Center board member David Murdoch wanted to be a part of the celebration while serving his own needs as well. He was opening a new resort on the remote Hawaiian island of Lanai and asked if we were interested in forming a $25,000 category that would include a free flight to his resort for a three-day weekend, all expenses paid. Esther seemed pleased at the possibility of more revenue, but her attitude toward me and Debbie remained remote, slightly hostile, and mysterious.

I always knew that there would be a gala celebration and asked the most talented party planner in the United States, Pat Ryan, to build a tent on the empty lot across from the Music Center (now the site of the Walt Disney Concert Hall). She was a Blue Ribbon member and one of the most professional, straightforward, and lovely human beings I have ever had the pleasure of knowing and working with.

I also planned a major announcement in the Grand Hall for all the members of the local and national press. The Music Center press department delivered an impressive group. I invited the supervisors, the heads of all the boards, the artistic directors of all the resident companies, and the entire twenty-fifth anniversary committee to a morning press announcement.

Esther, my cochairs, and I were on the platform with a microphone, and we all spoke. I started by very carefully describing all the events to come. I introduced Nick Vanoff in the audience and explained that he would produce the theater event preceding the gala, which would consist of a ceremony introducing our twenty-first-century artist awardees followed by performances from each. I truly think that I was very articulate in describing our celebration and felt very satisfied when I sat down to listen to Esther's remarks.

Esther did not refer to the twenty-fifth anniversary but went on and on about the importance of the partnership with the operating company, a topic that seemed out of context and baffling.

Immediately following our remarks, the press stayed to ask questions of all of us. I remember Esther sitting with Judith Michaelson, the reporter from the *Los Angeles Times,* for what seemed to me a very long time. I purposely (and stupidly) kept my distance from them. To my astonishment, the article published on the front page of the Calendar section of the *Los Angeles Times* didn't mention my name until the last sentence on page 3. It read, "Nancy Livingston will be the dinner chair."

The next day Esther walked into my office and exclaimed how excited she was about the article in the *Times,* which, of course, talked only about her. I remember asking her to leave because I was filled with emotion and terrified that I might burst into tears.

It was only years later that I put some of the pieces together; Judith Michelson called me to assist her in writing an article about Joanne Kozberg, who was going to be the new president of the Music Center. I was very articulate as well as supportive. Two days later, Joanne told me that she talked to Judith, who said, "I had a long conversation with Nancy Livingston. I had no idea she was so smart!"

That's how clever Esther was in promoting herself and denigrating anyone she thought might take credit away from her. She had apparently told the reporter that she had allowed me to speak about the twenty-fifth anniversary events publicly but that I was really only responsible for the tablecloths and floral arrangements.

I realize after all these many years that my careful use of "we" instead of "I" in my announcement speech fit perfectly into Esther's need to take full credit. Because I didn't make it clear that the plans for this event all originated with me, it was easy for her to claim that I was merely the spokesperson.

It took me a little while to regain my endemic enthusiasm after this setback, but the job was so enormous that I simply had to keep going.

I had all the commitments in place—it was now time to create the original mailing describing the events and the categories to choose from ($2,000 for two seats to the performance and the gala and the twenty-fifth anniversary book; $5,000 would also include a signed original framed lithograph by Sam Francis; $10,000 would include the original photograph published in the book; and $25,000 would combine everything plus the three-day adventure in Hawaii).

I will never forget the moment the post office picked up the large envelopes being sent to every person who had ever participated with the Music Center. I couldn't sleep for the next three nights. What if nobody responded? It even occurred to me that this was what Esther was probably hoping for.

I don't remember how many days went by, but one morning Debbie and I walked into our little office, and there on our desk was a stack of envelopes. We trembled as we opened them and pulled out checks for $5,000 . . . $10,000 . . . $25,000, and, to our amazement, only a handful for just $2,000!

I scooped them up and ran down the hall to Jim Black, the chief financial officer for the Music Center, who very somberly accepted them with not even a speck of enthusiasm. His lack of reaction surprised me until I learned much later that he was complicit in all of Esther's schemes. Every day more and more checks arrived, and I couldn't wait for my meetings with Dan Frost and Lod Cook.

My first appointment was with Dan. I came into his office smiling, sat down, and proudly announced that the money was pouring in—we were a success! He looked at me for a long time and then quietly said, "Nancy, are you sure?"

I answered, "What do you mean 'am I sure'? Do you want me to make a list of the names and the amounts?"

He stared at me again and said solemnly, "Nancy, are you sure you're not exaggerating the amount of responses?"

I was stunned . . . confused . . . bewildered . . . and then slowly it dawned on me. "Dan, Esther was here, wasn't she?"

He said, "Yes."

"She told you that she's worried the money's not coming in."

"Yes."

"Why would she do that? Dan, I'm going back to the office to confront her."

Whereupon Dan stood up and shouted at me, "You will do no such thing!" He walked to his door and lashed out vehemently, "You are not putting me in the middle of this! You will not leave this room until you swear not to repeat this conversation."

Shaken, I reassured Dan that I would not confront Esther or repeat the conversation. Once Dan felt secure that I wouldn't betray him, he moved away from the door and said he looked forward to our next meeting.

This was one of my first experiences with the cowardice beneath the surface of the self-important male. Their egos were much more fragile than I ever realized, and this was not to be my last taste of such a display of male insecurity.

I got into my car and went back to the Music Center, walked down the hall, and knocked on Esther's door. "Oh Nancy, come in," she said. I sat down and told her that I had just had a meeting with Dan and reported to him that we seemed to be getting a wonderful response to our mailing. I then smiled and said with a slight chuckle, "You know what was so amazing, Esther, it seemed as if he didn't believe me!" Not wanting to betray Dan, I quickly looked at my watch and said I had to run to an appointment.

That night over my martini with Alan, he seemed as surprised as I was at Dan's response. It was clear to him, however, that Esther had to degrade me at every turn, and he assumed it was just her insatiable need for recognition that drove her to keep tearing me down. What we didn't realize was that Esther was motivated by something even larger than her gigantic ego.

Back at the Music Center, the undermining continued. Esther seemed desperate to prove that everything I was doing was a failure. There was nothing I could do but keep going. I next worked with Nancy Zaslavsky, the graphic artist who was putting the book together. She had accumulated incredible photos, which included historic images of Bunker Hill and Los Angeles before the Music Center was built as well as stills from the most spectacular productions that had taken place over the years. Mark Swed didn't delineate any chapters in the book's text, so I simply sat down and organized the chapters, giving each one a title. When Nancy and I selected final images to accompany the text, I became excited by the prospect of how special this book might be.

Esther later received the book's final proof sheets before they were sent to Japan for printing. Little did I know that she would use this book as a weapon to undermine me further. She took the book into her office and closed the door. I heard nothing for several days.

One evening, as I was leaving my office, Megan Reed, the staff member who was assigned to help Debbie and me, seemed to be nervous. When I asked her why she hadn't gone home, she said that Esther had requested her to stay for a private meeting with her after I left. I asked Megan if she knew what the meeting was about, and, to my surprise, she told me that the foreword of the book was signed by the chairman of the Music Center's board, Joe Pinola; the board's president, Esther Wachtell; and the three cochairs of the anniversary celebration, Lod Cook, Daniel Frost, and me. The names had been printed in alphabetical order, and so, of course, Esther Wachtell was last. Esther would not accept being at the bottom of the list, Megan said, and she needed her help to find a solution.

I immediately told Megan, "There is a very simple way to solve this. On the left side of the page list 'Joe Pinola, Chairman' and underneath 'Esther Wachtell, President.' And then, Megan, on the right side of the page list the three cochairs with Lod at the top, Dan in the middle, and me at the bottom." Of course, I thought to myself, I will be exactly where Esther wants me. Megan looked so relieved that her coloring visibly changed. She thanked me profusely and went down the hall to Esther's office. Wait until Alan hears about this, I thought!

Soon after that, Esther decided to seize complete control of the book and started to eliminate some of the most dazzling landscape photos that Nancy and I had selected, replacing them with images of children participating in the Children's Festival on the plaza. My book was beginning to look more like a brochure than a history book. Esther also told everybody who would listen that the book was filled with too many pictures of me and had a very "elitist" quality that she deemed "destructive to the Music Center."

One of the major events we planned as part of the celebration was a black-tie dinner party at the Huntington Museum in Pasadena. I chose this evening to announce the impending awards and introduce the twentieth-century artists who had assisted in choosing the award recipients.

There were three Blue Ribbon members, also board members of the Huntington Museum, chairing the dinner. Esther went to each of these three dinner chairs and said that I was not to be any part of the evening's celebration, nor was I to be consulted on any aspect of the evening's ceremony, and my name was not to be mentioned.

I will never forget how seriously Lois Erburu took these instructions—she treated me as if I were a hired hand and only allowed me to bring the small Bob Graham sculptures to Zubin Mehta, Hal Prince, and Suzanne Farrell to present to the award recipients. I felt like a stagehand until I rose from my chair and walked across the stage to Zubin, and the entire room burst into applause without my saying a word. The same thing happened when I walked up to Suzanne Farrell and my friend Hal Prince. Sorry, Esther.

When I look back, the roadblocks that cropped up in front of me seemed almost impenetrable. Nick Vanoff, who was scheduled to produce the program onstage before the gala, had a severe heart attack and couldn't continue as producer. He said he was turning the production over to Gary Pudney, a nice person but certainly not the talent Nick was. I honestly feel that as a professional who had been involved in the most successful theatrical productions for years, I could have been helpful had I been included in putting the production together, but Esther insisted that no one was to consult me about anything. I was being isolated—slowly but persistently. Yet somehow I kept going.

Pat Ryan quietly worked with me on every detail of the gala, below Esther's radar. I put together a stellar gala committee that Esther would not dare tamper with, and Pat used every ounce of her genius to create the most beautiful tent for eight hundred people. Patrons left the pavilion after the stage presentation and were greeted on First Street by a large group of mounted police officers. Across the street, the tent was highlighted with the most incredible fireworks, illuminating all of downtown Los Angeles behind it. I insisted that we have a large mirror ball twirling at the top of the center of the tent, circulating glittering stars across the four-foot-high centerpieces on the tables. A small chamber music orchestra donated by the Los Angeles Philharmonic played a charming selection of classical standards. Standing inside the entrance were two rows of waiters with trays of champagne, white wine, and sparkling water; and, of course, there was a handsome bar for anyone who wanted something stronger. The first course is still being talked about today. It was taken from a book that I've had for many years titled *Pasta*, which contains the most enticing recipes. It was a warm, buttery nest of angel hair sprinkled with drops of lemon juice and lemon zest, and in the center was a large scoop of fresh caviar!

I recently had a conversation with Pat about an experience she had with Esther and Jim Black when I wasn't present. She told me that she had handed Esther the plans and estimates for the tent, the rentals, dinner, and so on, and Esther looked at her and said, "Who authorized all of this?" It was a breathtaking question. As Esther started to examine the estimates, she demanded, "Who negotiated these deals?" Jim Black sat next to Esther with his arms folded in alliance.

The truth is that several weeks earlier the director of major gifts to the Music Center, April Riddle, had received a phone call from Wolfgang K. Flöttl asking if there was a distinguished project that he could endow with his name. April was friendly and sympathetic to me; she understood the torture Esther was putting me through, so she immediately suggested that Mr. Flöttl underwrite the gala, and they agreed on the sum of $250,000, which would completely cover the expenses of the evening.

At this point, KCET, the Los Angeles public-television station at that time, on whose board I had sat for eight years, came to me and said it would like to televise the awards presentation in the Dorothy Chandler Pavilion. Bill Kobin, the station's president, called me to discuss this and made it clear that to execute the filming we had to give KCET $40,000. Bill emphasized that this was the station's policy for all nonprofit organizations. I explained to him that we were a nonprofit arts center that couldn't possibly afford such a fee. He thought about it for a few days and called me back to say that for the first time in the station's history it would waive the fee.

After this conversation, I bumped into Esther in the hall and told her what I had just negotiated. She looked at me a long time and almost whispered, mostly to herself, "You were the only one who could do this job." It was weird.

The night of the performance and gala finally came. Because the front-row center of the Founders' Circle had an uneven number of seats, I volunteered to sit alone at the end of this section with Alan seated behind me. But nothing prepared me for Gary Pudney's recognition of the twenty-fifth anniversary committee, he acknowledged everyone's name but mine. At the very end of his speech, he said, "Nancy Livingston is the dinner chair."

The reviews for the evening published in the *Los Angeles Times* the next morning were absolutely wonderful. I awakened early, had my coffee, and drove to the Music Center. I was one of the first to arrive. I went into my office and completely cleared everything from my desk and drawers. I carefully placed my driver's pass to the building's parking lot in the center of the desk along with the key to my office. I left a note for Megan thanking her for her wonderful help and left before Esther arrived. Frankly, I never looked back . . . I was finally out of there!

But I was not going to let Esther get away with her despicable behavior. During all of this, I was in constant touch with my friend and colleague Joanne Kozberg. Joanne, a fellow Blue Ribbon member as well as a board member who used her professional qualifications to deal with the Music Center Board of Supervisors, was also a target of Esther's denigration and jealousy. I told her that I was going to request a meeting with Joe Pinola, the chairman of the Music Center board, and demand a management review that would include interviews of every staff member and, most importantly, an interview with me. Joanne suggested that Joe and Esther together pick three board members to conduct the interviews. As she pointed out, a management review is standard procedure for all profit and nonprofit organizations.

It occurred to me that Joe would simply turn me down, so I had to have a strategy to make the review happen. I said to Joanne that I would threaten to write an open letter to the *Los Angeles Times* describing all that I had experienced and observed as a volunteer in charge of the twenty-fifth anniversary celebration. Joanne said to please tell Joe that she would join me in signing the letter as well.

I will never forget going to Joe's office on that Wednesday morning at eleven o'clock. He was the chairman of the First Interstate Bank of California and had an elaborate office, with many staff members surrounding him.

When I walked in his office, he was standing behind his desk and started to shout at me in the most hostile manner, "If you're here to criticize Esther Wachtell, one of the best fund-raisers in this country, you may please leave my office now! I am unwilling to listen. By the way, Nancy, I would like to know why *my* picture with *my* wife is not in the back of your book!"

Nothing prepared me for this moment, and I started to cry. I shouted back, "I am not leaving! And don't you know why your picture isn't in the back of the book? Didn't you read the foreword to the pictures? Didn't Esther tell you that they were to honor those donors who gave $10,000 or $25,000 to the twenty-fifth? Joe, *you* donated $5,000!"

He sat down, and so did I. *No more tears,* I thought, *just say your piece, Nancy, and leave.*

I listed my demands to Joe. He looked at me and slowly shook his head. "Nancy, Esther will never agree to this."

I looked him straight in the eye and said, "If you and Esther don't agree to a management review, I will write an open letter to the *Los Angeles Times* detailing my experiences—and Otis will print it. Joanne Kozberg will cosign this letter." I stood up and said, "I won't take any more of your time. Please let me hear from you about yours and Esther's decision." I walked out. Boy, was I ever looking forward to my martini with Alan that night!

Joe and Esther carefully chose three board members, each of whom had the typical problem that I have observed in most men—a delicate ego. Esther had a technique of finding and appealing to this exact weakness; it was not a flirtation on any sexual level but a glowing admiration and wonderment at how incredible these "special" men were. This technique became increasingly evident as she was being challenged, especially by me and Joanne. Men in her camp were knights in armor protecting her against "unfair criticism."

I will never forget my interview with the three board members. They had already made up their minds that the issue was a "female vanity fight." They listened to me quietly and patiently, gently patted me on the back as I left, and told me, "There, there, you are a wonderful lady, and you will get over it."

In the meantime, Esther did an interview for *Los Angeles* magazine, again stating that the twenty-fifth anniversary unfortunately lost money. I was amazed when I received a letter from the Music Center board asking me to stay for another term. Even though the members had been dismissive of me, they were worried enough to be sure that I stay close because I seemed to be a loose cannon. Of course, I sent a letter expressing again my criticism of the running of the Music Center and stated that it would be inappropriate for me to continue as a board member.

The *Los Angeles Times*, bless it, stayed with the story of something not smelling right at the Music Center. Its reporters kept probing for more than a year until finally, to my amazement, it was announced that Esther and Jim Black were leaving the Music Center.

It was only later that I was told that they had been fired. Each was given a year's salary with the understanding that they would not talk to the press. I also heard that Jim Black took the hard drive from his office computer. One year from the day they were dismissed, Joanne Kozberg called me at 6:30 a.m. and exclaimed, "Nancy, get out of bed and go outside and get your *LA Times!*" I whimpered, "Joanne, I'm not awake yet." She was now shouting, "I don't care! Get the paper and call me!"

I unwrapped the paper as fast as I could, and there it was on the front page: Jim Black had gone to the *Times* to tell his story and get his revenge. There was a picture of a check that Esther had written for $10,000 as her gift to the twenty-fifth anniversary; it was very important for her to be a $10,000 donor and have her picture with her husband in the back of the book. Attached to the check, however, was a note that said, "Dear Jim, Return to my account ASAP."

Slowly, I began to put together the pieces to this bizarre puzzle. It amazes me that it took me a number of years to understand what was really going on.

According to many people I spoke with, Esther was conducting something often described to me as a "Ponzi scheme." She announced proudly at the end of each fiscal year that she had made her fund-raising goal, but according to the board members I spoke to years later, this was not the case. I was told that she had coaxed Jim Black into supporting her by cooking the books. If this were the case, of course she had to say that I was losing money— she was using my money to pay the bills for the previous two years! She was desperate to make it clear that I was a failure and that she had to make up for the losses I created.

87

Another Twenty-Fifth Anniversary with Jack Lemmon, Gregory Peck, and Michael Feinstein

Believe it or not, a year and a half after I was through with the Music Center's twenty-fifth anniversary, Gordon Davidson was persuaded by my
champions at Blue Ribbon to appoint me as his chairman for the twenty-fifth
anniversary of the Center Theatre Group at the Music Center. I knew it was an
opportunity for me not only to do a wonderful job for my first love, the theater,
but also for my friend Gordon. It was also an opportunity to prove to myself
that I was capable of succeeding in putting together a major event without
Esther haunting me. It was no surprise to learn that Esther tried to persuade
Gordon not to hire me, but after talking with me about some of my ideas, Gordon gave me the green light anyway. I immediately went to Lew Wasserman
(the original chairman of the Center Theatre Group board) to be my honorary
cochair and selected Debbie Telefson to be my operating chairman again.

As usual, I sat down and asked myself, "What can I create that is unique
and special for the Center Theatre Group?" I wanted to establish something
that could continue to raise money year after year. I remembered going to the
Ninety-Second Street YMCA in New York to attend its special program
called "Lyrics/Lyricists," dedicated to exploring the lyrics of the great American songs of the twentieth century, and thinking it was an incredible evening.
I wanted to re-create it in the Mark Taper Forum and thought of Michael
Feinstein as the perfect host.

Michael had been Ira Gershwin's assistant and possessed an amazing
knowledge of the history of songwriting. He also was a gifted pianist who
captured every nuance of every key change, and I liked the way he sang as
well. I didn't know Michael personally but somehow had the audacity to sit

down and write him a letter asking him to take part once a year on the stage of the Mark Taper Forum in something I had already titled the "Salon Evening." I described an intimate setting with a grand piano and occasionally a small instrumental group, Michael introducing and singing some of the most prominent songs, assisted by local talent, and outlining the history of the lyricist we would honor each year. I suggested our first lyricist should be Ira Gershwin and put together a script for telling Ira's story, which would be interspersed with his songs.

I thank Gordon to this day for allowing me to send that letter and was happy when Michael's agent called me about a week later to tell me that Michael would like to do it.

The good fortune didn't stop there. Nick Vanoff, who had been a prominent member of the Center Theatre Group board, had recently died, and Gordon wanted to give him a special tribute. I suggested that the Salon Evenings should be dedicated to the memory of Nick Vanoff and that a group of his closest friends, who happened to be some of the most powerful members of the entertainment community, be on the permanent Salon Evening committee. Nick's wife, Felisa, was delighted and offered her home for a special private dinner for our largest contributors.

Things were falling into place, but I needed to create a "kick-off event" that would elicit the focus and excitement I needed for this celebration. I decided the ideal would be to give a cocktail reception at the new Peninsula Hotel in Beverly Hills. Of course, I always start with every star I can get to put on the invitation and participate. For the host of the evening, I decided to approach Jack Lemmon, who had performed several times at the Taper, which gave his presence a legitimacy.

I remember sitting in his office and making my usual enthusiastic pitch— including his being there not only to welcome our guests but also to introduce the evening and Gordon, who would then thank everyone in the room who had a special association with the Center Theatre Group. After a half a minute of silence, he looked at me and said, "Nancy, I don't think I can do this. First of all, I don't know what to say when I welcome everyone and introduce Gordon. It should be something a little provocative, and I can't imagine what that something might be."

I refused to accept his turning me down and said, "Please, Jack, let me send you a written introduction that might interest you, and you can make your final decision after that." He walked me to the door, kissed me on the cheek, and reluctantly said, "OK."

I only wish I had kept a copy of the script I wrote. It started with a gracious introduction to the evening and was followed by a joke that I thought only Jack could pull off. I got a call from his secretary the day after he received my script to tell me he would participate.

I will never forget that evening at the Peninsula Hotel. I wore a pale-beige gabardine suit with my topaz-and-diamond earrings, a clip, and cocktail ring. My shoes, of course, matched my jewelry and hair! There was only one frightening moment. I was at the microphone welcoming everyone and introducing Jack Lemmon to this distinguished audience when suddenly the lights went out, and we all stood in total darkness. Thank God the darkness lasted only about twenty seconds, during which time I said, "I want these lights turned on immediately." The lights suddenly illuminated the room, and I said, "I'm more powerful than I thought I was!" The audience laughed, and I gave a lavish introduction to Jack Lemmon, especially highlighting his history of performances at the Mark Taper Forum. Jack got up with his script in his hand and read every single word, including my joke, which provoked an eruption of laughter and appreciation. Jack read my remarks so spontaneously and so "Jack Lemmony" that I'm sure everyone in the audience thought the words were completely his. He seemed pleased to be there, too.

My next target for engaging a superstar was Gregory Peck. Greg not only had been one of the original chairs of the committee working to open the Music Center but also remained the chairman of the Center Theatre Group board for many years after.

I called Greg's house and made an appointment to see him at six o'clock on an evening the following week. I had been there a few years earlier and was amazed again at how huge the house and his property were. It always struck me that people reveal their egos by the size of their homes and the opulence by which they surround themselves. Perhaps that is somewhat unfair to Greg; I think his home was more a reflection of his French wife, Veronique, who always reminded me of someone who needed to be regarded importantly.

When I arrived, it was Greg himself who opened the door and escorted me into the living room. I made my pitch as thoughtfully and appealingly as I could and was surprised by his unenthusiastic response. He didn't want to have to make a speech at any of my scheduled events, and he would show up only at the final gala event. I accepted his terms and said that I wanted him to be an honorary chair for the evening. He responded that he would like to meet with me again after he thought about it. The terms of this request would apparently be negotiated over time.

Our next meeting was the following week, and he wanted to talk about other things, not the twenty-fifth anniversary of the Center Theatre Group. He wanted to talk about me, with a faint touch of flirtation attached to his inquiries. I was surprised and alarmed and to this day do not understand it. Again, he said he would like to meet me the following week.

I went again, rang the doorbell, and this time a maid opened the door and said that Mr. Peck was not yet home, but Mrs. Peck would like to see me in her sitting room. This small, dimly lit room was strangely next to the large living room and looked more like a bedroom than a sitting room. Veronique was reclining on the bed and asked me to sit on the chair facing her. She said to please excuse her; she wasn't feeling well but didn't want me to be alone in the living room—I remember this moment as being lonely, foreboding, and sad. In fact, I was completely baffled in this very quiet, strange place.

Soon, to my relief, the maid came and announced that Mr. Peck had arrived. I excused myself to Veronique and sat with Greg again, who finally said that he and Veronique would attend the gala and that I could use his name as an honorary chair.

These encounters with this giant icon of the twentieth century remain in my memory as among the most mysterious meetings I have ever had. I do know that Greg was married for a long time before he met Veronique. Sometime after they were married, one of his sons with his first wife came to the house in Brentwood Park where Greg and Veronique lived at the time. He stood on the front lawn with a gun threatening suicide. He later killed himself in his room.

After the cocktail party at the Peninsula, there were several performances dedicated to the anniversary, and the most important of all was the debut of the Salon Evening dedicated to the work of Ira Gershwin, starring Michael Feinstein and a group of very special artists.

Lew Wasserman and I walked on stage (I wore a white grosgrain suit with my black-and-white Verdura enamel pin, gold-and-diamond earrings, and black high-heeled, patent-leather pumps). I introduced Lew first as my very special honorary cochair. I then introduced the chairs for the evening seated in the audience and described the beginning of our new series, the "Salon Evening."

To my astonishment, when I turned to Lew for his remarks, he looked at me and turned to the audience and said, "Isn't she beautiful?" I accepted his compliment with as much modesty and grace as I could muster, but it was a moment I will never forget. The event was a tremendous success, which was the most important part of the evening for me.

The last event of the twenty-fifth anniversary celebration, which everything else led up to, was the black-tie gala in the main dining room of the Hilton Hotel on Wilshire Boulevard. I planned it for Friday, May 1, and sent out the invitations, which received a tremendous response, including from Veronique and Gregory Peck, Anne and Kirk Douglas, and, of course, Gordon and Judy Davidson.

But something unforeseen and dreadful happened. Rodney King had been attacked and abused by a group of police officers a year earlier, in March 1991, and their brutality had been caught on video. On April 29, 1992, after the officers involved were acquitted of all charges, a series of riots beginning in South Central Los Angeles began creeping toward us all with violence, fire, and mass destruction. We immediately canceled our event for a future date several weeks later. It was a terrible time for Los Angeles, and everyone still remembers Rodney King's voice pleading, "Can't we all just get along?"

Eventually, the event did take place and was very successful.

In the months that followed, it became clear to me that I had to remove the Music Center from the intense focus of my life that it had become. The Music Center board asked me to remain for another three-year term, and I declined; however, I stayed on the executive committee of Blue Ribbon as a former president and remained a devoted member of that board for many years.

It's interesting that I never gave up contributing ideas to solve some of the challenges this group faced. I wanted to continue making as creative a contribution as I could. That was what was fun for me!

I think the major contributions I've made to Blue Ribbon are bringing the Children's Festival into the theaters and creating a new program that I named the "Sampler Series." This series was designed to give those Blue Ribbon members who rarely attended a performance a chance to come to hand-picked performances of the symphony, opera, and theater. It was not a fund-raiser; in fact, we received a group rate from each performing company. All members and their guests were invited to dinner before the performance, and the Sampler Series has now become part of the fabric of Blue Ribbon today. I asked my good friend Lennie Greenberg to be my cochair as she was on the symphony board, and her husband, Bernie, was on the opera board. I remained on the board of the theaters.

After fifteen years of success, Lenny and I finally turned the series over to two new cochairs, Ames Cushing and Judy Beckmen. I don't let go of things easily! Not one of my better traits.

88

Billy Wilder Tribute

People have asked me over the years if I remained friendly with Billy Wilder. Audrey Wilder, Billy's wife, was a remarkable woman but as completely alien to me as I probably was to her, which made a close relationship between Billy and me impossible. However, they came to occasional dinner parties at my house, and Alan and I were sometimes included at large parties they hosted. Billy and I had an indelible connection; I was a part of his history, as he was a part of mine. But I always wondered what he really thought of me.

Then something happened that surprised both of us. The Directors Guild of America was putting together a tribute to Billy. A lineup of prominent people in the industry were going to discuss his work and success, after which there would be a screening of a new print of *Sunset Boulevard*. When the Directors Guild called me and explained that it would like me to speak before the film, my usual confidence was invaded by insecurity.

I started writing about Billy, remembering that my most successful speeches at the Music Center rarely included the word *I*. This was about him, not me. I asked Alan to help me, and he was incredible. Every time I wandered into my own views, he put me back on the right path, and he offered some brilliant suggestions as well.

It was the hardest speech I ever wrote or had to give. I knew Billy would be there, not only with Audrey but also with his closest buddies, who had never regarded me as anything but a pretty face with the good luck of being in one of Billy's monumental films. I remember carefully choosing to wear a beige pants suit with a string of pearls and gold earrings.

With my heart pounding, I started my speech, with the audience holding their breath, wondering if I could possibly live up to this moment. Actually, excerpts from what I said have been repeated when people write about *Sunset Boulevard*. The applause was loud and mixed with a few "bravos." I saw Billy and his entourage jump up from their seats the moment I was finished and begin exiting the theater. Alan and I left soon after that.

But it was the next night's encounter with Billy that I will never forget as long as I live. Barbara and Marvin Davis (the one-time owner of 20th Century-Fox) were giving their annual extraordinary black-tie Christmas party. Everyone you knew in Hollywood was there, and the excess of champagne and caviar in the dining room is something I have never experienced before or since. I remember walking through the entryway of the large tent behind the house and discovering on each side of it two ice-skating rinks with skaters twirling and jumping. I believe there were around three to four hundred guests, all surrounding a large orchestra. Alan and I were invited each year to this party from the first one to the last—the Christmas before Marvin died.

That night I remember wearing a black-velvet, strapless gown with a diamond-and-emerald necklace, matching earrings, and a beautiful bracelet. The jewelry had been made in the 1930s for women to wear while traveling when they didn't dare take their real gems; however, it was difficult to tell the difference between the real and the copy. Alan and I walked in the door to the receiving line, embracing Barbara first and shaking hands with Marvin next. Barbara kept looking at my necklace and treated me with more respect from that moment on. It was a few moments later that I felt a tap on my shoulder. I turned around, and there was Billy Wilder with a big smile on his face. He said, "Nancy, you were a big hit last night. In fact, you were fantastic. Audrey and the rest of my group couldn't stop talking about you!" I mumbled something like, "Thank you, Billy. I'm so glad you were pleased." Thank God, I was immediately interrupted by another guest, who said, "Nancy, that is the most incredible necklace I have ever seen." What a relief! I headed for the caviar and the champagne as quickly as I could.

Looking back, I am so grateful to have been given the opportunity to let Billy know how much regard I had for him and how well I could express it.

89

Andrew Lloyd Webber

In the early 1990s, Andrew Lloyd Webber, creator of the musical *Phantom of the Opera* and the most successful composer for the musical theater at that time, decided that his next project would be a musical theater version of *Sunset Boulevard*.

Alan and I were invited to all the openings in New York, Los Angeles, and London. Andrew sent Alan and me as well as Billy and Audrey airline tickets to London (first class of course) and provided us with suites at the Connaught Hotel. Unfortunately, on the way to London, Billy and Audrey had the seats behind us on the plane—the one row reserved for smokers. Audrey was a nonstop smoker, and I coughed all the way across the Atlantic Ocean.

I remember meeting Billy and Audrey in the lobby on opening night. It was spring, and I wore a long peach-colored Bill Blass gown with coral earrings and bracelet. I also had a pale-peach ruffled cashmere cape to protect me from the foggy, damp London night. Audrey Wilder was known for her very special and chic way of dressing, so I felt particularly rewarded when she commented on how lovely my outfit was! The production was beautifully executed, and the after-party a very glamorous affair.

The next morning we were picked up and taken to a small hotel in a countryside village just outside of the Webber estate. We all were invited to a lavish dinner party for about four hundred people. Of course, it was again black tie, and I remember wearing a deep-green silk evening gown with a lace top and sleeves in the same color.

Alan and I were seated next to the Webber table, Billy and Audrey of course at Andrew's table. Everyone in the music business from every corner of the world was there, and to my absolute shock and, I must admit, delight, when the word got out that Alan Livingston was in the room, Billy Wilder and every other celebrity there, including me, was forgotten. All of these executives from the music world headed toward our table. They wanted to meet the legendary Alan Livingston.

Before I close this chapter, I have to quote again what Billy had to say about the musical *Sunset Boulevard*: "It's my movie in a permanent long shot." It reminded me again of what Alan Lerner said: no one goes to a bookstore to buy a screenplay. The camera tells the story, and the close-up of a tear on the leading lady's or man's cheek tells you what you need to know; it doesn't have to be written to be understood.

Billy's aging over the next years was, like that of all people, hampered by the inability to function without help. Audrey took magnificent care of him. I remember seeing his wheelchair being lifted into their SUV, with Audrey at the wheel as they drove through the city. I also remember Audrey telling me that he never lost his delightful sense of humor. One morning she walked into his bedroom, looked at him, and asked, "Do you still love me?" He paused and answered, "I have to think about that."

Of course, I was invited to Billy's memorial in 2002 and sat near the front of the Academy Theater with his closest friends. Isn't it amazing how this man, caught in the tragedy of Germany in World War II—both mother and sister murdered at Auschwitz—and having to escape to America, ended his life as one of the most celebrated filmmakers of the twentieth century?

Audrey Wilder finally met her destiny as a compulsive smoker. She lost not only a lung but also one of her legs. She was bedridden for the last year and a half of her life, but I'm sure with special memories that sustained her.

90

An Unforgettable Moment

One morning I opened the mail and found an invitation from Harriet and Ardie Deutsch to attend a dinner party in honor of Frank Sinatra. I showed it to Alan, and his immediate reaction was to call Ardie and explain that Alan and Frank had a very confrontational history, so we didn't want to upset Ardie's relationship with Frank or have any uncomfortable incident take place at his party. I was so surprised that Ardie's reaction was to insist that Alan and I attend: whatever Frank's problem, it was his!

I remember wearing a very pale, beige silk dress, all my pearls circling my shoulders and dripping from my ears. I also remember walking into the foyer with my heart pounding as Alan and I signed the guest book. When we entered the living room, Frank was greeting all the guests, Ardie and Harriet at his side. When Alan approached Frank, Frank looked at him and then slowly held out his hand to grasp Alan's. He seemed deep in thoughtful memory and finally said, "Alan—it's been a long time." Alan answered, "Yes, it has."

91

China

A lan's history with China actually began in the late 1980s. Alan always wanted his classical musical children's record *Sparky's Magic Piano* to be an animated film. Of course, Disney, Warner Bros., Hanna-Barbera—in fact, all of the successful animation studios—were not the least bit interested in re-creating a record that had been made at the end of the 1940s. But, as usual, Alan was determined to make it happen. His research landed him in Shanghai, China, at a small struggling animation company looking for new material. This search introduced Alan not only to another continent and culture but to a possible new career.

Somehow, Alan made *Sparky's Magic Piano* happen. He put together an impressive cast of actors to vocalize the characters: Tony Curtis, Vincent Price, Mel Blanc, Cloris Leachman, William Schallert, and me. Alan also managed to get Lalo Schifrin to conduct the Paris Symphony Orchestra and our friend Leonard Pennario to play all the classical piano solos, giving this project the most glorious musical score that any animation movie has ever had.

I will never forget traveling to France and sitting in the studio listening to the magical music that Lalo and Leonard and that incredible orchestra created. Believe it or not, Alan managed to find producers, in particular a gentleman named Guy Beatty, to finance the entire operation.

Guy was so fascinated with the project and the introduction to China that he and Alan decided to start their own animation company and found the perfect spot in Shenzhen, a free economic zone in China at that time and located only twenty-four miles from Hong Kong.

The Chinese government was eager to welcome Alan and Guy, but it insisted that it be a 50 percent partner in the company. Alan was determined to solely own the company with Guy and so managed to outsmart the Chinese government (or so he thought) and have complete ownership. He found a factory and sent the most sophisticated animation equipment available to Shenzhen. He hired a prominent animator to hire a group of animation teachers to go to China and teach the eager, young, talented Chinese how to use these machines. In the process, he found the most gifted and enthusiastic people to join the company and work on its projects. Alan named the company Pacific Rim Productions Inc. It was the first privately owned American company in China.

Disney hired Pacific Rim Productions to supply additional animation production and painting services, including special-effects animation, for *The Little Mermaid* and many of its other projects. Alan also had Pacific Rim do its own productions, including an animated adaptation of the classic children's book *Little Toot* (Alan hired our son, Chris, and his partner, Frank Piazza, to write an absolutely delightful score), which he had also recorded as a children's record in the late 1940s. In addition, he created and produced the animated series *Cliff Hanger*, a story about a bumbling adventurer who is a cross between Indiana Jones and Inspector Clouseau.

Alan's and my life now included his trips to Hong Kong every two or three months, which kept Alan busy, fulfilled, excited, and challenged. I will never forget the 2:00 a.m. phone calls that cost us a fortune, but it didn't matter. They were so exciting and interesting. Of course, I had to go to China, too.

We picked a date for the two of us to go to Hong Kong and then China on a United Airlines 747. I remember taking the long flight across the Pacific Ocean, landing in Tokyo for refueling, and at sunset starting to descend slowly into Hong Kong.

I will never forget the sensation of flying through a narrow passage between brightly lit apartment buildings. We were so close I could see the laundry flying in the wind on terraces, the colors and designs of the shirts and dresses. As I prayed for a safe landing, we finally touched down on the runway—I was in Asia for the first time.

Our large hotel room had a small terrace facing the bay. As exhausted as I was, I couldn't keep myself from standing on the edge of the balcony, holding the railing, and looking at a different world.

Alan spent three days showing me Hong Kong; we ate and drank cuisine with tastes and textures that I had never experienced before. Every night we met one of the chief animators in a salon that overlooked the bay with windows literally three stories high. I went with Alan to a tailor that made three suits for him to be sent home, and he took me to a jewelry store in which you paid no attention to the price because there was always a negotiation. Alan bought me the most beautiful jade-and-diamond ring and earrings set in gold. They are among my most cherished and treasured pieces of jewelry.

On the fourth day, we got on a train headed to Shanghai. We started in the morning and traveled across mainland China. The sights of life there were fascinating. The Communist government was still in charge, and the landscape and farms looked the same as they had in my high school and college history books. There were women with bars of wood across their shoulders, a pail of water or vegetables hanging on either side. Men plowed the fields with a buffalo pulling an archaic wooden rig.

We did see one indication of an awareness of the new world. On the tops of the huts and the small farm buildings were large satellite dishes that looked more like large megaphones, all pointing toward Hong Kong, obviously anticipating the news from the rest of the world.

When we arrived in Shanghai, we took a very old taxi to a hotel that served foreign visitors. It was sparse but neat and clean and certainly had everything we needed. In the morning, I looked out the window and saw hundreds of bicycles on the road in front of the hotel, an occasional car or taxi interspersed among them. I somehow managed to get to the private home of someone who wanted to sell some of their ancient Chinese porcelain. I bought a bowl with a large red flower hand-painted in the center and a small bottle and vase in the same pattern. They are now on my bedroom mantle under my daughter Liza's portrait. When I wake up in the morning, Liza and these beautiful pieces are the first things I see.

When we came home, Alan talked to Guy Beatty and said that the company's momentum was slowing. He wasn't quite sure what was happening, but what eventually became evident was that the Chinese government had let Alan's company teach the young, talented Chinese how to create the best animation in the world and then slowly took them away to another company that it fully owned. Alan realized that the worst mistake he ever made in his entire career was not to allow the Chinese government to become his partner because it began to steal his equipment as well as his talented workers, and he knew he had to sell the company before it was completely destroyed.

Alan and Guy never lost money, but they didn't make a fortune, either. The new business venture, though, allowed Alan and me to have another journey in our lives that we never forgot.

92

Another Challenge for Alan

As I slowly read these stories of Alan's and my life, I realize that I have been avoiding one of the most challenging issues we had to face. Alan was six feet one, a strong, beautiful man who had dealt with growing up during the Depression, facing anti-Semitism before World War II, joining the army, and starting an amazing career from scratch. He also experienced the death of his first child, a marriage that didn't reward him or succeed, the heartbreak of watching his son struggle with hemophilia and bipolar disease, a second marriage that didn't work, and finally the death of his beloved Peter from AIDS.

Facing adversity in a competitive and a nasty business, having the loving strength to embrace a new life with me, two stepdaughters, and a new son: Alan did it all. Dealing with his own health problems could have been one straw too many, but I honestly think that our love for each other and the happy environment we had created together more than compensated and gave us both a sense of triumph and strength.

One of Alan's saving qualities was his discipline, especially maintaining his body and health. Every morning before I got up, I watched him walk out of his dressing room in his pajamas, kneel to the floor and do thirty push-ups. I begged him to do only ten! I couldn't bear the guilt I felt and told him so. Next came the sit-ups, the jumping jacks, and the running in place. The jumping jacks were the last straw as far as I was concerned!

One morning, though, he suddenly stopped the push-ups and whispered, "I can't catch my breath. Something is wrong." It was apparent to me that he had to call his office to tell them that he wasn't coming in until later that day or the next morning. I asked him to lie down and called his doctor immediately. That afternoon I drove him to Dr. Katz's office, who recognized right away from the EKG and the sound of Alan's heart that he was in trouble.

I took him to Cedars-Sinai Hospital, where we were met by a heart surgeon, who conducted a series of tests. I waited with my own heart pounding, knowing that something was terribly wrong. Finally, the doctor returned and told me that Alan had major blockage in four arteries leading to the heart and that he was implanting a stent to open up the passages. This treatment helped for only about a week before it was obvious open-heart surgery was the only option.

I will never forget sitting in the waiting room waiting to find out whether the surgery had been successful (which it turned out to be) and then being escorted to the intensive-care room where Alan was recuperating. He was awake but couldn't speak because of the oxygen mask covering the bottom half of his face, but his eyes lit up, and he waved and blew kisses to me as I walked in the room. It was clear to me that Alan had already put this serious threat to his life behind him—the problem was solved, and he was ready to move on with our life together. And guess what! Only a few months later he was taking long walks and eventually doing those damn push-ups and jumping jacks at 7:30 every morning.

A few years after his heart surgery, I felt Alan's body changing position one night while in bed. He turned on his side and suddenly woke up screaming in pain. I quickly turned on the light and begged him to tell me what was happening. He whispered through his agony that something had broken in his back. The next day the doctor said he had severe osteoporosis and actually had a small fracture in one of his vertebrae. This was the beginning of an agonizing period of struggle to stop the disintegration of his bone structure.

Alan's health continued to be a challenge. At one routine, yearly check-up, he found out he had the beginning of prostate cancer. Although he was assured that the cancer was under control and not accelerating, he was determined to erase it. He read everything about all of his ailments and thoroughly researched medications that might help him. He did everything in his power to control what was happening to his body. I think we could have filled part of the garage with all the bottles of medication that kept arriving. Part of Alan's personality was his determination to solve problems, erase the negative aspects of them, and stay in control. This characteristic had served him in his career, and although I'm not sure all those pills helped in any way, they made him feel that he was doing everything he could to stay on this planet with me and to continue to enjoy our life together.

93

Completion

There is one memory that seems so symmetrically perfect that it makes me wonder if things never happen by accident. Although Alan was physically weaker, we continued to live as vital a life as we could. We continued our social life as well as having our evening drinks together in our little library and faced each day with pleasure at being together.

Because we had been donors to the Jules Stein Institute at UCLA for many years, we received an invitation from Lew and Edie Wasserman to attend a dinner in the institute's garden. It was a beautiful summer night; Alan was seated across the table from me, and we were surrounded by the establishment of Los Angeles and the distinguished doctors in the community.

I was seated next to a doctor who seemed so interested in me that I felt a little uncomfortable. He was not flirtatious, just extremely probing and examining. At dessert, he turned to me and said, "I knew Alan many years ago. He came to me for a physical, and although he certainly is a very shy man, he revealed that he was suffering from a deep depression. It was obvious that this very beautiful man was special, and because I had majored in psychology before becoming an internist, I had the audacity to suggest that he come to my office every morning at 8:00 a.m., and we could talk for forty-five minutes. For six months he arrived at 8:00 a.m. on the dot. He talked about his failed marriages and his deep concern for his children. Eventually, he stopped coming, and I haven't seen him since."

With tears in my eyes, I turned to the doctor and said that Alan had told me about him and had always regretted not letting him know that we had met and had a beautiful son and a wonderful, fulfilling marriage. When I looked at Alan across the table, he was smiling at both of us.

94

Expanding Our Family Again

In 2002, Chris fell in love and married Carrie Perkins. She was a beautiful, gifted, and special young woman, and they have two fantastic and gorgeous children. Madeline Rose Livingston was born December 6, 2004, and arrived with the most incredible sapphire-blue eyes and blond hair, which surprised all of us because both Chris and Carrie have dark hair, and Chris's brown eyes are dominant in a union. I felt honored that she looked so much like me. Two years later, Graham Christopher Livingston arrived with dark hair and brown eyes, but his profile was definitely inherited from me. It was evident that Graham was a very unique and special child but somewhat perplexing. He was diagnosed with mild-spectrum autism before he was two, with the blessing of possibly being the smartest little boy I have ever encountered. Graham taught himself how to read at age four.

Both children have a loving spirit and an inner structure that is kind and generous and profoundly special. They are Alan's grandchildren and mine. I have to write about Madeline's gift for poetry and music, which she has brilliantly combined in writing songs since she was ten years old. Her first song was "Facing the World," which has the profound line "There's good times and bad times, but even in the good times, you still gotta face the world!" How true! Her second song is titled "Left or Right." My favorite lines are: "Should I go left or right, should I go up or down—if I only go up I'll leave the world behind, if I only go down, I'll never learn to fly. I'm standing in the middle of nowhere. And I don't know what to do. I'm scared and alone, afraid to come home and my heart hasn't got a clue." Wow!

If you want to hear Madeline's incredible voice and songs, stop reading, go to YouTube, and look up "Madeline Rose Livingston." You're in for a treat.

95

Goodbye

It was around the time that Madeline was four and Graham was two that we hired a caretaker for Alan, Augustine, who arrived each morning at nine to help him get up, get dressed, and get into the breakfast room, where he had a glorious brunch. We sat together reading the newspapers and arguing about politics and what was happening in the world. Augustine took Alan back to his room at one o'clock, where he lay down and took a long nap, and Augustine left us until five in the afternoon. I was busy as usual keeping the house going, participating in the world with all my obligations, and keeping track of children, grandchildren, and the stock market.

At five, Augustine returned and got Alan up. He brought him into our little library to read *Time* magazine and the *New Yorker*. At six o'clock, I joined him for our usual cocktail hour; only now I made our drinks. They were small, but we couldn't give up our six o'clock date. Nothing would ever change that. The children were now gone, but our routine never changed.

After our drink, we went to the dining room together, where the candles were lit, and had our usual fabulous homemade dinner. At about 8:30, Augustine took Alan back to the bedroom and helped him undress and get into bed. I joined him a little later, where we watched the news and some of our favorite television shows, kissed each other goodnight, and slept holding hands.

In the last week of Alan's life, I think it was a Tuesday, Chris and Carrie brought Madeline and Graham over, and the six of us had dinner in the dining room. Chris had mentioned for several days that Alan's breathing seemed abnormal. He would breathe regularly and then periodically have to catch his breath. Dr. Nissenbaum told me that he was having heart failure. He discussed with Alan the possibility of putting him in the hospital, but Alan said absolutely not.

That night Madeline was in a chair at the dining-room table, and Graham was in a highchair. After dessert, Chris said, "Madeline, say goodnight to

Goodbye

Grandpa." She ran over, climbed on his lap, and said, "Goodnight, Grandpa!" He smiled at her a long time and said gently, "Goodbye, Madeline."

That Wednesday night was the first night in our decades-long marriage that even though both of us were home, he was unable to join me in the library for our drink. I took a watered-down martini with a lot of ice into the bedroom, and we watched the news together.

Thursday morning Alan insisted on getting completely dressed but accepted a breakfast tray on the bed. I had many errands that morning and realized that both cars were almost totally out of gas. I took each one to the station and came back at about two o'clock. I went into the bedroom, and Alan looked at me and said, "Nancy, where have you been?" I answered, "I lead such an exciting life. I had to take both cars to be gassed." He smiled, and I looked at him and realized how much I loved him and how much I owed him for saving my life, for giving me a beautiful son—for loving my two daughters, for literally making life in this world a joy. I said, "I love you, Alan." He shook his head no and said, "No, I love *you*." I went over and kissed his forehead and whispered, "Alan, go to sleep. I'll see you later." He closed his eyes.

By Thursday night, I became alarmed and scared. I called Dr. Nissenbaum, who was at Cedars seeing patients but said he would come to the house on his way home. He arrived at about eight o'clock and went into Alan's room while I waited at the dining-room table alone. After about a half hour, he came in and sat with me and said that Alan was dying, and he called a hospice to send someone that night. He also said that he had given Alan a large shot of morphine and asked the hospice nurse to stay with him until midnight. She arrived and took charge. She gave Alan another dose of morphine at about midnight and left, saying she would return at 7:30 in the morning.

Alan was now sleeping, and I quietly lay beside him. I dozed off and on, checking to see that he was still with me, but at about five o'clock he woke me with intense breathing and white foam coming out of his nose and mouth. I said, "Oh darling," and ran into my bathroom and got a clean towel to wipe his face. I went to the phone and called the nurse, who said she would be there as soon as she could. She arrived at about seven. I called Chris, and he came right over. Jenny had arrived the day before for a work assignment in Los Angeles and of course joined us with incredible loving anxiety. The nurse gave Alan another large injection of morphine, and his breathing and body suddenly became relaxed. She quietly said, "He's dying."

Ruth, our housekeeper of thirty years, stood with Jenny at the end of the bed. I lay beside him holding his hand. Chris was on his knees next to the bed holding Alan's other hand and talking to him in the most loving way. It took about twenty minutes for Alan to give up life. The color started to leave him at the top of his forehead, the whiteness slowly moving down his beautiful face. His hand gently let go of mine, and soon there was total silence. The nurse came over and listened to his heart with her stethoscope and said, "He's gone."

She called the Westwood Mortuary and asked them to pick up his body. Of course, Alan had long ago arranged for a crypt at the Westwood Mortuary for both of us to reside in for our journey into eternity; it was paid for, and even the inscriptions were paid for. I lay by his side for the next hour until the doorbell rang, and two men asked to see me privately in the library. They were obviously trained well, making the transition of taking Alan away forever in the most gentle and reassuring manner.

I finally understood that when one dies, the body has no significance or value any longer. In fact, we could have put his body out on the street for the garbage to collect—it was no longer needed. Alan was in our home with me, slowly dissolving and joining every atom in the universe. It is a wondrous mystery—both being born and dying. Alan was physically a beautiful man, but the essence he has left in this world is even more magnificent. What an unusual, special human being. What a gift he gave me when he asked me to spend the rest of his life with him. What did I ever do to deserve his stepping in my life and saving it?

96

La Dolce Vita

It has always amazed me that Alan's personal decisions made so many years ago still surround us. Shortly after Alan died, I was persuaded to dine with a few friends at one of our neighborhood restaurants, La Dolce Vita. I was seated next to Whitey Keller, who knew Alan and me socially but was not that familiar with Alan's career. The restaurant is dark and cozy, with deep leather booths, and everyone knows almost everyone else who is there. To enhance the atmosphere, there is a soft sound of music playing most of the standards that we all can hum. I was surprised to find Whitey so interested in Alan's past and was only too happy to tell him. I repeated the story about how Alan signed Frank Sinatra after Columbia Records had let Frank go.

Whitey was amazed to hear that at that time Columbia Records and all the other record labels considered Frank's career over. It was only Alan who recognized that Frank needed a fresh repertoire and a new arranger-conductor. I told him how reluctant Frank was to work with anybody except the people he was used to, but Alan managed to trick him with an incredible new song and a reservation in a studio with arranger-conductor Nelson Riddle. Of course, Alan knew this song was destined to be a hit and a turning point for Frank.

When we finished dinner, we started to leave our booth when Whitey turned to me and said, "Nancy, do you hear what they're playing?" I sat down and listened . . . it was Frank Sinatra singing "Young at Heart," recorded on that Sunday afternoon so long ago.

I think that among the secret ingredients of Alan's incredible success were not only his own integrity but also his understanding of the value of authentic talent and the intuitive depth of a true artist. And perhaps he was one of the last executives in the entire entertainment industry who recognized the difference between gimmicks, phony imitations, publicity campaigns, and especially zealous agents selling second-rate talent. There was never any question in Alan's mind about who had it and who didn't. That was all he searched for because he knew that what he presented then would live on to this day. Our son, Christopher, has pointed out to me many times that Dad follows us everywhere we go—in elevators, restaurants, television, radio, the internet, you name it—at some point during the day, Alan will remind us of what he created.

It is fitting to share that several years later, in 2013, the Recording Academy voted to give Alan Wendell Livingston its Trustee Award, a lifetime Grammy given to those individuals who have made a significant contribution to the field of recording. I attended the Grammy ceremony with Christopher and Alan's daughter, Laura. The three of us got up on stage and graciously accepted the Grammy on Alan's behalf, our only wish being that Alan could have been there to receive the well-deserved accolade for himself.

97

Laura

Looking back, I realize that when one lives many years, one is bound to experience every emotion, from the most blissful, successful ego-fulfilling recognition by the world, loved by one's partner and children and grandchildren, to the most heartbreaking events, episodes of failure, having to learn the hardest lessons to survive, and, most of all, the loss of our loved ones. When Alan left this world, he had experienced it all, but thank the good Lord, he did not also have to witness the tragedy of his beautiful daughter Laura's passing.

All the struggles that Laura faced growing up made her one of the most resourceful and determined human beings I have ever known. She simply would not—could not—accept failure. It was part of her DNA and resulted in making a challenging marriage successful anyway; raising two lovely daughters, Kate and Jenna Gibson, who became responsible and charming human beings; and finally using her creative talents to start a career that blossomed into rainbows of success.

Laura had a friend who taught her how to use beads to make necklaces, bracelets, earrings—everything a woman loves to possess and wear. She discovered (not to my surprise) how talented and original she was in putting these magnificent colored stones and beads together. She was also a shrewd businesswoman and became one of the most successful private jewelry designers in the country with her company Laura Gibson Designs.

It was shortly after her younger daughter, Jenna, married a very successful and ambitious young lawyer, Oramel Skinner (we call him OH), that Laura had a seizure in the middle of the night, which alarmed everybody, particularly her doctor. As it turned out, Laura had a large cancerous tumor on the right side of her brain that could never be removed by surgery because it was too entangled in the vital parts of her temporal lobe.

The news was an enormous emotional blow for us all, but Laura was determined to beat the odds and so (like her dad) proceeded to investigate and utilize every available cure. She was able to shrink that tumor so that it was barely visible by X-ray, when suddenly the process went into reverse, and she was given three months to live. Of course, Laura would never leave us on any ordinary day of the year. She died Christmas morning, December 25, 2015. Thank God, Alan was not here—the loss would have been too devastating.

98

Family Updates

I have written that Liza married Porter Bibb and had an adorable baby girl, Zoe. However, after a number of years together, Liza and Porter divorced, but they remain close friends and devoted parents. I'm happy to report that Zoe recently found love with and married her longtime beau, Jim Bright, and I recently became a great-grandmother, welcoming Zoe's beautiful baby boy, James Porter Bright, into the world! Liza is a very successful interior designer, remodeling every other Manhattan apartment and country getaway in New York State, and she has produced plays for Broadway, including her father's musical *On a Clear Day You Can See Forever*, starring Harry Connick Jr. Liza was always extremely artistic, and it isn't surprising she found a career utilizing her many talents. Her beautiful watercolors adorn my home—particularly my bedroom, where I wake up to her pastel-hued flowers. It's amazing how the creative streak continues in the genes and finds different outlets for self-expression.

I have written about Jenny and her marriage to Carlyle Fraser. Soon after their nuptials, Jenny and Carlyle moved into a lovely apartment in New York City and had beautiful twin girls (not identical), Lily and Kate, my granddaughters. When Lily and Kate were about four years old, Jenny and Carlyle also went their separate ways. The girls have blossomed into the loveliest young women—it didn't hurt that Jenny is an amazing parent, having gently but firmly put both her daughters on a path of education and successful careers. Jenny is a very highly regarded publicist in New York City and has found her ideal partner, Joe Del Maestro, to spend the rest of her happy life with. One additional note, my granddaughter Lily is engaged to her longtime love, Mathew Siegfried, and my granddaughter Kate, has also recently become engaged to her beau, Douglas Holt.

I have written about Chris and his marriage to Carrie. They have two of the most special and beautiful children, Madeline Rose and Graham Christopher.

335

Their marriage is ending as well, but Chris and Carrie remain committed parents and have done all they can to raise Madeline and Graham with love and care. On the career front, Chris is a talented songwriter who has written songs for movies and television (he just so happens to be one of the most gifted lyricists I know—and I've known a lot of them!). He recently released his first album, *Chris Livingston Thirty Years Unplugged.* Chris has also written a number of screenplays and has directed several independent feature films, most notably the award-winning comedy *Hit and Runway,* which was released theatrically all over the country in 2001 to wonderful reviews. Chris also just finished writing his first novel, *Supernova,* which will be available soon.

Laura's and Peter's children have also been making their way in the world. Kate Gibson, Laura's eldest daughter, just recently found love and married a wonderful man, Anthony Bull, in a beautiful ceremony in northern California, and they have just had a beautiful baby girl, Bailey Livingston Bull. Jenna Skinner, Laura's younger daughter, has with her husband OH two beautiful and healthy daughters, Alora and Eden. Alora was named after her mother, Laura, and after her grandfather, Alan (Livingston), by combining their two names together. Finally, Peter's son, Alex, has had some recent career success as a professional poker player. He managed to make it to thirteenth place in the World Series of Poker, and just recently he reached third place in that event, raking in a small fortune.

99

Ending This Book

I am ninety-three and will turn ninety-four this summer on Bastille Day, July 14, 2022. I have to stop writing—telling stories—sharing memories—but how do I end this book?

In the twenty-first century, you can send your saliva to a company called 23andMe, and it will send you your genetic ancestry. I know that I am mostly Scandinavian—it turns out something like 67 percent. I know that I have a little English and Scottish in me, but what I was most curious about was finding out if I have French-German ancestry in my DNA, somewhere in the vicinity of 6 percent. Let me explain.

A long time ago, my mother told me the story of visiting Stockholm to spend time with some of her cousins, one of them a genealogist. She told my mother that in a small village in northern Sweden in the early nineteenth century a young woman had an illegitimate son. It was the custom at that time for whoever impregnated a woman out of marriage to step forward in the community, identify himself as the father, and take full responsibility of the child. In this case however, no male member of the town stepped forward, and the young woman did not identify anyone.

The little boy had uncharacteristically dark, wavy hair and an unusual aptitude. In fact, he was given credit for changing the direction of the well in the center of town to increase the water supply. But it was not until his mother was on her deathbed that she whispered to her sister that the father of her son was the king of Sweden and Norway, who was of French and German descent, not Scandinavian.

Her son married and had six sons of his own, and my mother's cousin claimed that my mother's father, Victor Bergstrom, was a son of one of those sons. She took my mother to a museum to show her a portrait of the king. My mother told me that she gasped when she looked at the painting and exclaimed, "That's my father!"

Is it possible that I am a direct descendent of a king of Sweden? How bizarre. How strange. How interesting.

When my DNA report came back from 23andMe, there it was, 5¾ percent French-German. The timetable of when these genes were introduced matched perfectly. There is no other French ancestor in my family.

I have to share a secret. All my life, people have treated me differently, beginning with my beloved father, who always made me feel treasured. Does it surprise me that I might actually be a princess? I refuse to answer that.

However, I will tell you this. When I told this story to my granddaughter Madeline, she said, "Granny, I'm not surprised. You've always had a certain elegance about you." That is the most satisfying, delectable compliment I have ever had. I said to Madeline, "It must be in our genes because you have the same quality."

100

Stories I Hesitate to Tell

If you live long enough, you will hear stories about parts of your life that you never knew. Some of them can fill you with a great joy and pleasure, but the ones that remain with me the most are the saddest.

Many years after Alan Lerner divorced Micheline, a friend of mine told me about a relationship he had with Jean Kennedy Smith soon after his marriage with Micheline ended. I know that Alan was desperately trying to rectify his damaged reputation; Micheline was an outrageous person, which everybody seemed to understand. Alan was at the peak of his celebrity at the time and was eagerly included in New York society; however, women were a little hesitant to get too involved with him. Believe it or not, I think he used me to try to untarnish his reputation. He told me that he had become great friends with Jean Kennedy, Jack's sister, and I remember him saying, "Nancy, you should be very pleased to hear me tell stories about you." I didn't pay much attention to what he was saying at that time.

However, a friend of mine told me he was not only a friend to Mrs. Smith but enormously seductive with her, and even though she felt a relationship with him would be dangerous, she couldn't stop herself from responding compulsively. One of Alan's great problems was living up to the uncomfortable truth. He was enjoying captivating her and couldn't be honest that he was having another, much more serious romance with someone else.

It's hard for me to understand where Alan was at this time of his life, but it was clear that he was losing all of his personal integrity. He actually let Jean fly to Paris, telling her he would meet her there so they could discuss their future. He also cautioned her not to mention anything to her husband before they worked out their own plans. He knew all along he was never going to meet her in Paris, but, as amazing as it may seem, he let her go there with expectations of a new life and romance.

My friend who told me this story was very close to Pat Kennedy Lawford, Jean's sister. Pat got a call from Jean, who was at the Plaza Athenee Hotel in Paris. Jean was hysterical after receiving a call from Alan, saying he was not coming to Paris but was on his way to Miami to marry his fifth wife, Karen Gundersen (a doctor's daughter, by the way). Pat took the next plane from Los Angeles to Paris, arrived there forty-eight hours later, and when she entered Jean Kennedy Smith's bedroom, she found her sister sitting on the windowsill about to jump.

There are many more stories that have become hazy in my memory or that I have chosen to tuck away forever. A recent story I heard fills me with such sadness, however, that I feel compelled to write about it.

About six months ago, my friend the writer Cari Beauchamp asked me to join a group of performers to read excerpts from her recent book depicting the stars of old Hollywood. There were four of us, and I was designated to tell the story of Colleen Moore.

I arrived early and was escorted to the back of the small stage, where I could relax and talk to some of my fellow performers. There were about ten people roaming about, one of them the publisher, who was known for publishing books on the beginning of Hollywood. He came over to me, introduced himself, and asked, "Nancy, were you married to Alan Lerner when he wrote *Paint Your Wagon*?" I answered, "Yes, I was." "Well," he said, "I was a great friend of Olga San Juan and her husband, Edmond O'Brien. Did you know that Alan had an affair with Olga, that she became pregnant, and that Alan insisted and arranged for her to have an abortion? She was Hispanic with a Catholic upbringing and never recovered. She spent most of the rest of her life in and out of institutions with regular shock treatments. Edmond never forgave her."

I felt such a deep sadness for Olga and in a strange way for Alan as well. He hurt so many women for his own survival. How could he ever be truly forgiven or forgive himself?

A few minutes later, a young man came up to me and asked, "Do you know Michael Lerner?" I answered, "Yes, of course. He's the half-brother of my two daughters, Liza and Jenny, and we all are quite close; as a matter of fact, he and his family join ours every Christmas Eve at my house!" The young man went on and asked if I had known Micheline, and did I realize that she was a true narcissist with deep psychological issues that hurt every-one around her? I wondered how many more people backstage were going to tell me more stories I did not want to hear. But this story also made me think about Alan's relationship with Micheline. It was different from any other rela-tionship he ever had. All of the women he left were his victims, but in the case of Micheline *he* was the victim. He wrote *Camelot* when he was married to her, and you might remember that Guinevere left the king, not the other way around.

I didn't want to think about this anymore. Thank God, the stage manager came and said it was time to go on stage and be introduced.

Two other stories reflect perfectly what our world is dealing with today.

My friends Lennie and Bernie Greenberg had their fiftieth wedding anniversary celebration at a well-known restaurant in Los Angeles, which they took over for the whole evening. They filled it with their friends and gra-ciously included me.

I was seated next to a gentleman who came from the original corporate and wealthy leaders of Los Angeles. He was particularly close to all of the Chandlers. Somehow our discussion turned to Otis and how I discovered that the Chandler clan had wanted to get rid of him because he was turning the *Los Angeles Times* into a "liberal" newspaper.

He looked at me and started to laugh. He said, "That's not why they wanted to get rid of him—they wanted to get rid of him because he was expanding their newspaper with bureaus all around the world and was hiring famous editors! He was spending too much of their money!!!" I was stunned. It seems I am reminded every day that it's always "all about money!"

It is amazing to me that in 2017 there was an earthquake of revelations about men in positions of power or even the smallest authority abusing women. All women have experienced some domination by men and their primitive needs, but part of our culture over the years has been for women to accept this quietly and do their best to stay out of a man's way. I still don't completely understand this sudden burst of anger and mounting outrage and its total acceptance at this particular time, but I am thankful it is finally happening.

Every day we are bombarded with new descriptions of abuse. I remember being outraged when I heard about President Bill Clinton (whom I voted for twice) actually unzipping his fly and having oral sex in the Oval Office with a young girl who didn't have the maturity to understand how her seduction would affect our nation. In fact, I think it changed the course of our presidential history and our place in the world.

Al Gore would most likely have been president in 2000 if not for Clinton's unbelievably improper behavior. The scandal made Clinton a liability to Gore's campaign in 1999, and Gore was unable to utilize Clinton's genius to assist him in his effort to become president. As a result, the vote was so close in Florida, it demanded a recount, which unfortunately, even though Gore had won the popular vote, the Supreme Court stopped.

As much as sexual predatory behavior can be damaging to the person being exploited, in the case of Clinton its damage was far reaching. It resulted in the tragedy that Mr. Bush and Mr. Cheney came into power and unlawfully took us into a war in Iraq (which spiraled into a hornet's nest of other problems in the Middle East), and it sparked an era of division in politics the likes of which have never been seen before in this country. Karl Rove's singling out and exploiting of a disenfranchised faction of far-right voters became a formula for success and is now responsible for many of the problems we are facing today. Also, because of Gore's focus on green energy, Clinton's choice to prey on a young intern lost us an opportunity to address the environmental crisis affecting the globe today, where it seems that half the world is literally on fire.

It's good that the American people were outraged by the Clinton scandal; however, even after something so reprehensible, the suppression of women's voices has remained in place—until recently, when Harvey Weinstein was exposed, and the revelations of his abuses opened the floodgates for other women to share their stories of being victimized. The revolution has begun. Women are waking up with memories of humiliation and debasement, and they can no longer suppress their feelings and their voices. The door has opened and will never be closed again.

Interestingly, with all the recent outpouring of outrage, several weeks ago I woke up with a memory that has haunted and enflamed me ever since I acknowledged that it actually happened. I have never shared it with anyone until now.

In 1993, Alan and I were invited to a small dinner party by two longtime friends to meet and donate to their friend Tom Lantos, who was running for

Congress in northern California. He was running as a Democrat, and although Alan was highly suspicious of most Democrats, he said Lantos sounded moderate enough, and he didn't want to disappoint our friends. I don't remember what I wore except that it was a dress, not a pantsuit.

The hostess had removed her dining-room table and replaced it with a long narrow table that extended from her dining room into her den. There were approximately ten to twelve guests on both sides, with our host and hostess at either end. I was seated to the right of Mr. Lantos, almost directly across the table from Mrs. Lantos.

After the first course was served, and we started our main course, I felt Mr. Lantos's trembling hand reach over and clutch my left thigh, pushing its way under my skirt toward my crotch. I was startled, shocked, and instinctively grabbed his hand to pull it away. This maneuver did not work—he grabbed *my* hand and pulled it over to *his* thigh and *his* crotch!!

With my background in Hollywood, it seems unusual to say that nothing like this had ever happened to me before. Jack Kennedy had pulled me into an embrace, but when I pushed him away, he accepted my rejection. Howard Hughes summoned me to his office but didn't stand up and unzip his fly when I walked in. Nothing from my past or upbringing prepared me for this moment.

When I think about this incident today, I have a fantasy of standing up and shouting, "Stop it!," in front of his wife and all the guests. However, I just did my best to move as far to my right as I could, pushing my elbow into his side as a warning not to touch me again. It didn't work, and as I struggled, I talked incessantly to my guest on the right. At dessert, I looked at Mrs. Lantos to see if she had been aware of what had happened. She seemed clueless.

I cannot believe that I finished the evening, went home with Alan, let him write the check, and never ever told him this story. In fact, I completely buried it until last week.

After this memory surfaced, I called my good friend Cari Beauchamp, who had worked for Governor Jerry Brown in the 1990s. Of course, she knew who Tom Lantos was and said she would do a little investigating.

She called me back a few days later and said that her research came up with a comment from the present congresswoman Jackie Speier, who said it was well known that "no woman should ever be in the cloakroom alone with Tom Lantos!"

Then I talked to my friend Joanne Kozberg, who had worked for Governor Pete Wilson in the 1990s as secretary of state and head of consumer affairs. We were discussing the front-page story about Steve Wynn and his sexual assaults. I asked Joanne if she had experienced any predatory sexual behavior while she was working in the state government.

She said that Bob Packwood from Oregon had trapped her in a garage and that she had narrowly escaped by pushing him off her and running away as fast as she could. She also told me about one other experience she would never forget.

Joanne wanted to take her two teenage children, Anthony and Lindsey, to Washington, DC, to give them a tour of our nation's government. She contacted Tom Lantos's office and asked if she could visit him with the children and if he could perhaps take them all through the congressional building.

He immediately said that he and Mrs. Lantos would be honored to greet them, give them a tour, and take them to lunch. The outing was all very successful until they sat down at their table to eat. Barely a minute and a half went by before his hands were all over her under the table. She struggled as I did, insisted the children have only one course, and made an exit as fast as possible.

There is a footnote to the earlier observation regarding Clinton:

I was recently at a small dinner party at Lennie and Bernie Greenberg's. One of their guests was the former head of the Supreme Court of California, Ron George. Somehow, the conversation turned to Bill Clinton and the subsequent election of Bush and Cheney. I turned to Ron and asked if he ever discussed with Sandra Day O'Connor (who was appointed by the Republican Ronald Reagan as the first female Supreme Court justice) about her crucial "yes" vote to stop the Florida recount between Al Gore and George Bush in the 2000 election. He slowly turned toward me and said, "Sandra is a very close friend of mine, and she has reminded me many times that the biggest mistake she ever made on the court was to stop the recount vote in Florida."

A final story that haunts me:

I have described the summers following my divorce from Alan Lerner and how I would bring Liza and Jenny to Los Angeles in August to be with my parents. We always looked forward to staying at the Oceana and looking every day at the beautiful Pacific Ocean in all its glory.

Years later, Bill Holden bought a building and kept a small, one-bedroom apartment for himself. He could no longer control his addiction to alcohol, and one evening he tripped on the bedroom rug, hit his head on the bedside table, and died ten minutes later on the bedroom floor.

His great friend and love, Stephanie Powers, had not heard from Bill in several days. She had a key, went to his apartment, opened the door, and found Bill gone.

The building was the Oceana.

IOI

Ending This Book Again

I MUST END THIS BOOK!! But how?

First and foremost, I want to say to Liza, Jenny, and Chris how much you mean to me, how special you are, how much I think the world is graced by your presence, and how humbled I am by being your mother.

I want to say to Zoe, Kate, and Lily that you astound me with your inner beauty and sweetness and that I am dazzled by your being three of the most attractive young women in the world. Zoe, I know you will pass on all of your unique gifts to my new great grandson, James. Kate and Lily, I know you will do the same with your future children!

I want to say to Kate, Jenna, and Alex, Alan's beautiful grandchildren (three of the best-looking young people in the world), that each one of you has an inner standard filled with the highest level of integrity that guides you in your relationship with the world and everyone in it. (Jenna, I know you will pass this on to your toddlers, Alora and Eden, and Kate, I know you will do the same with your beautiful new daughter, Bailey!)

With tears in my eyes, I want to say to Madeline and Graham that I feel like the most rewarded grandmother in the world by your *being* in this world. How is it possible that I produced such special and beautiful grandchildren?

What last observation do I want to share with you all about what I know and what I have learned in my life?

Let me describe it this way . . .

I think of everyone's life as a grand painting.

Each of us starts with an empty canvas with a specific palette of colors. The colors represent our DNA, our temperament, IQ, the color of our eyes, even the shape of our nose. Slowly, we begin to form a picture. As we interact with others, the colors of their palettes mix with ours.

What has always fascinated me is how each person's canvas is so completely different. My painting at this point in my life is almost finished, its colors and forms quite indelible and vivid; they reflect who I am, where I have been, and where I am ending my life today—the shapes have evolved into something that one can easily recognize as my unique journey.

Your paintings are still works in progress. What you have done so far is very beautiful. If I had two words of advice to give each of you, it would simply be these:

"Keep painting."

TO BE CONTINUED . . .

Index

Index

Greenberg, Lennie and Bernie, 315, 341, 344
Gregson, Richard, 246, 263
Griffith, Andy, 197–98

Hammerstein, Oscar, 97–98
Handleman, David, 260–61
Harbach, Billy, 285
Harburg, Yip, 61
Harriman, Pamela, 273
Harrison, George, 216, 224, 226
Harrison, Rex, 98, 102, 105–6
Hart, Kitty Carlisle, 106, 271–73
Hart, Moss, 103, 105–6, 271–73
Harvard University, 12, 40, 56, 73, 90–91, 156, 182
Hasty Pudding Club, 56, 90, 182
Hawks, Howard, 46
Head, Edith, 41, 58, 67
Hepburn, Audrey, 58
Holden, William, 6, 34, 38–45, 75–76, 132, 295, 344–45
Holliday, Judy, 109
Holt, Douglas, 335
Hope, Bob, 34
Hopper, Hedda, 54, 218–19
Huckleberry Finn, 95
Huffington, Arianna, 151
Hughes, Emmet, 36–37, 123–30, 133–35, 138, 140, 149–50, 157
Hughes, Howard, 36–37, 343
Hutton, Betty, 58, 158, 206

"I Tawt I Taw a Puddy Tat," 194
"I've Grown Accustomed to Her Face," 103–5

Jacobson, Max, 188
James, Harry, 197
Javits, Jack, 124, 269
Javits, Marion, 124
John, Elton, 256
Johnson, Lars, 13
Johnson, Nancy Anne, 13–15
Jones, Jennifer (Simon), 238–41
Jourdan, Louis, 109

Kazan, Elia, 66
Keithley, Dutch, 23–24, 26, 30, 55, 67, 161

Keithley, Ethel, 10, 12, 23–24, 26, 30, 55, 67, 161
Keller, Whitey, 331
Kelly, Cynthia, 161
Kelly, Gene, 223–25, 236
Kelly, Princess Grace, 259–62
Kemeny, Diana, 138–40, 144, 149–50, 161–62, 187, 249
Kennedy, Jackie, 119–20, 212
Kennedy, John F., 48–51, 95, 120, 135–37, 188, 343
Kennedy, Ted, 135, 212
Kennedy Center Honors, 287–88, 298
Kennedy Smith, Jean, 339–40
Kenton, Stan, 197
Kerr, Jean, 154–55
Kerr, Walter, 155
King Cole Trio, 195
Kintner, Bob, 201–2
Kozberg, Joanne, 291–92, 302, 307–9, 343–44

Ladd, Alan, 34
Ladd, Alan, Jr., 257
Lambs Club, 73
Lane, Burton, 61–62, 95–96
Lantos, Tom, 342–44
Laurents, Arthur, 260–62
Leachman, Cloris, 32, 321
Leigh, Janet, 233
Lemmon, Jack, 40, 310–12
Lennon, John, 215–16, 224–25
Lerner, Alan Jay: courtship and marriage to Nancy, 54–72, 161; death of, 3–7, 284–85; divorce of, 112–20; Fredrick Loewe, 72–74; *Gigi*, 108–11; married life of, 44, 75–77, 80–87, 92–111, 141, 271, 298, 319; *My Fair Lady*, 97–99, 102–7; postdivorce, 128–30, 132, 134, 145–47, 156, 171, 187–89, 242–43, 288, 339–41, 344; upbringing, 88–91
Lerner, Bobby, 89–91
Lerner, Jennifer: adult life of, 10, 167, 269–70, 275, 283–85, 288, 329, 335, 340, 346; birth of, 94–95; early childhood of, 97, 117–18, 128, 133, 143, 145–47, 150, 152–53, 155–57; later childhood of, 161, 172–75, 184, 186–89,

Index

343; relationship with Kitty Carlisle
Hart, 106, 271–73; relationship with
Natalie Wood, 263–64; relationship
with Sydney Chaplin, 109–10, 119,
121–22; relationship with William
Holden, 6, 34, 38–45, 75–76, 132, 295,
344–45; spending an evening with
Grace Kelly in Monaco, 259–62;
spending an evening with Nelson
Rockefeller, 125–27, 271–72; spending
an evening with William Faulkner,
141–44, 163; taking EST training and
meeting Werner Erhard, 248–51;
therapy with Diana Kemeny, 138–40,
144, 149–50, 161–62, 187, 249;
working with Blue Ribbon, 254–55,
274–82, 287–95, 301, 305, 307, 310,
314–15; working with the Music
Center, 242, 252–55, 274, 276, 279–81,
289, 294–316; working on the twenty-
fifth anniversary for the Center Theatre
Group, 310–15; working on the
twenty-fifth anniversary for the Music
Center, 294–309; working with Walt
Disney and Disney Studios, 130–34,
158, 194, 321–22
O'Malley, Walter, 183–84
On a Clear Day You Can See Forever, 4, 335
Oswald, Lee Harvey, 212
Ovitz, Michael, 297

Pacific Rim Productions, Inc., 321–23
Paint Your Wagon, 3, 6, 73, 75, 80–82, 113,
340
Pakula, Alan and Hannah, 271
Palmer, Lilli, 106
Paper Dolls, 281–82
Paramount Pictures, 6, 31–32, 34–43, 54,
59, 246, 259
Peck, Gregory, 238, 253–54, 312–14
Piazza, Frank, 322
Pinola, Joe, 304–5, 307–8
Pollyanna, 130–32
Poor, Anne, 70
Poor, Henry, 66, 70
Porter, Cole, 33, 51, 112–13, 204
Powell, Jane, 95
Previn, Andre, 246

Previn, Dory, 246
Price, Vincent, 321
Pride and Prejudice, 29
Prince, Hal, 297, 305

Radziwill, Lee, 119
Rainier, Prince, 259–62
"rain in Spain," 98–99, 106
Ray, Aldo, 100–101
RCA Records, 201–2, 214, 227, 246
Reagan, Nancy, 3, 175, 286–93
Reagan, Patti, 175
Reagan, Ronald, 286–93, 344
Redford, Robert, 246
Reeves, George, 31
Reiner, Carl, 210
Reston, James, 124
Riddle, Nelson, 168, 199–200, 331
Rockefeller, Happy, 125–27, 271–72
Rockefeller, Nelson and Mary, 125–27
Rodgers and Hammerstein, 97–98
Rodgers, Richard, 74, 97–98
Royal Wedding, 95
Rush, Barbara, 219–20, 233

San Juan, Olga, 80–82, 94, 340
Sarnoff, General David, 201–2
Schlesinger, Arthur, Jr., 135–36, 285
Schwartz, Arthur, 61, 95–96
Scott, Randolph, 34–35
Send Me No Flowers, 129–30
Share, 232–37
Shaw, Artie, 197
Siegfried, Mathew, 335
Sills, Beverly, 276–78
Simon, Norton, 238–40, 296
Sinatra, Frank: Capitol years, 167, 168,
199–200, 203–4, 208, 214, 245; post
Capitol, 233, 290, 320, 331
Skinner, Alora, 336, 346
Skinner, Eden, 336, 346
Skinner, Jenna Gibson, 333, 336, 346
Skinner, OH, 336
Slack, Freddie, 197
Son of Flubber, 158, 233
Sparky's Magic Piano, 194, 321
Speier, Jackie, 343
Stafford, Jo, 197, 232

Index

Screen Classics

Screen Classics is a series of critical biographies, film histories, and analytical studies focusing on neglected filmmakers and important screen artists and subjects, from the era of silent cinema through the golden age of Hollywood to the international generation of today. Books in the Screen Classics series are intended for scholars and general readers alike. The contributing authors are established figures in their respective fields. This series also serves the purpose of advancing scholarship on film personalities and themes with ties to Kentucky.

Series Editor
Patrick McGilligan

Books in the Series

Olivia de Havilland: Lady Triumphant
    Victoria Amador
Mae Murray: The Girl with the Bee-Stung Lips
    Michael G. Ankerich
Harry Dean Stanton: Hollywood's Zen Rebel
    Joseph B. Atkins
Hedy Lamarr: The Most Beautiful Woman in Film
    Ruth Barton
Rex Ingram: Visionary Director of the Silent Screen
    Ruth Barton
Conversations with Classic Film Stars: Interviews from Hollywood's Golden Era
    James Bawden and Ron Miller
Conversations with Legendary Television Stars: Interviews from the First Fifty Years
    James Bawden and Ron Miller
You Ain't Heard Nothin' Yet: Interviews with Stars from Hollywood's Golden Era
    James Bawden and Ron Miller
Charles Boyer: The French Lover
    John Baxter
Von Sternberg
    John Baxter
Hitchcock's Partner in Suspense: The Life of Screenwriter Charles Bennett
    Charles Bennett, edited by John Charles Bennett
Hitchcock and the Censors
    John Billheimer
A Uniquely American Epic: Intimacy and Action, Tenderness and Violence in Sam Peckinpah's The Wild Bunch
    Edited by Michael Bliss

My Life in Focus: A Photographer's Journey with Elizabeth Taylor and the Hollywood Jet Set
Gianni Bozzacchi with Joey Tayler

Hollywood Divided: The 1950 Screen Directors Guild Meeting and the Impact of the Blacklist
Kevin Brianton

He's Got Rhythm: The Life and Career of Gene Kelly
Cynthia Brideson and Sara Brideson

Ziegfeld and His Follies: A Biography of Broadway's Greatest Producer
Cynthia Brideson and Sara Brideson

The Marxist and the Movies: A Biography of Paul Jarrico
Larry Ceplair

Dalton Trumbo: Blacklisted Hollywood Radical
Larry Ceplair and Christopher Trumbo

Warren Oates: A Wild Life
Susan Compo

Improvising Out Loud: My Life Teaching Hollywood How to Act
Jeff Corey with Emily Corey

Crane: Sex, Celebrity, and My Father's Unsolved Murder
Robert Crane and Christopher Fryer

Jack Nicholson: The Early Years
Robert Crane and Christopher Fryer

Anne Bancroft: A Life
Douglass K. Daniel

Being Hal Ashby: Life of a Hollywood Rebel
Nick Dawson

Bruce Dern: A Memoir
Bruce Dern with Christopher Fryer and Robert Crane

Intrepid Laughter: Preston Sturges and the Movies
Andrew Dickos

Miriam Hopkins: Life and Films of a Hollywood Rebel
Allan R. Ellenberger

Vitagraph: America's First Great Motion Picture Studio
Andrew A. Erish

Jayne Mansfield: The Girl Couldn't Help It
Eve Golden

John Gilbert: The Last of the Silent Film Stars
Eve Golden

Stuntwomen: The Untold Hollywood Story
Mollie Gregory

Jean Gabin: The Actor Who Was France
Joseph Harriss

Otto Preminger: The Man Who Would Be King, updated edition
Foster Hirsch

Saul Bass: Anatomy of Film Design
Jan-Christopher Horak

Lawrence Tierney: Hollywood's Real-Life Tough Guy
Burt Kearns

Hitchcock Lost and Found: The Forgotten Films
Alain Kerzoncuf and Charles Barr

Pola Negri: Hollywood's First Femme Fatale
Mariusz Kotowski

Ernest Lehman: The Sweet Smell of Success
Jon Krampner

Victor Fleming: An American Movie Master
  Michael Sragow
Aline MacMahon: Hollywood, the Blacklist, and the Birth of Method Acting
  John Stangeland
My Place in the Sun: Life in the Golden Age of Hollywood and Washington
  George Stevens, Jr.
Hollywood Presents Jules Verne: The Father of Science Fiction on Screen
  Brian Taves
Thomas Ince: Hollywood's Independent Pioneer
  Brian Taves
Picturing Peter Bogdanovich: My Conversations with the New Hollywood Director
  Peter Tonguette
Carl Theodor Dreyer and Ordet: *My Summer with the Danish Filmmaker*
  Jan Wahl
Wild Bill Wellman: Hollywood Rebel
  William Wellman Jr.
Clarence Brown: Hollywood's Forgotten Master
  Gwenda Young
The Queen of Technicolor: Maria Montez in Hollywood
  Tom Zimmerman